… ON COMPROMISE

On Compromise

with 'Mr. Swinburne's New Poems'

John Morley

Edited by John Powell

KEELEUNIVERSITY**PRESS**

This edition first published in 1997 by
Keele University Press
22 George Square, Edinburgh

© Introductory material and notes, John Powell

Typeset by Carnegie Publishing Ltd
18 Maynard St, Preston
Printed and bound in Great Britain

ISBN 1 85331 117 0

For Grady
'The search for Truth is its own reward.'

Contents

Acknowledgements	ix
Introduction	1
Notes	27
Bibliography	35
A Note on the Text	40
ON COMPROMISE	43
Chapter I Introductory	52
Chapter II Of the Possible Utility of Error	70
Chapter III Intellectual Responsibility and the Political Spirit	88
Chapter IV Religious Conformity	112
Chapter V The Realisation of Opinion	137
Note to Page 154 The Doctrine of Liberty	165
Editor's Notes	175
'MR. SWINBURNE'S NEW POEMS'	182
Appendices	192
I. Anonymous Review from *The Athenaeum*, 17 October 1874	192
II. Review by W. H. Mallock from the *Quarterly Review*, January–April 1889	198
III. Chrisopher Kent from *Brains and Numbers*, 1978	210
IV. Maurice Cowling from *Religion and Public Doctrine in Modern England*, 1985	221
V. Peter C. Erb, 'Adaptation and *Compromise*: An Examination of Ludwig Haller's *Ueberzeugungstreue*'	228
VI. Morley's Epigrams	235
Index	239

Acknowledgements

The value of Morley's *On Compromise* alone suggested the need for this edition. I am grateful to many people who have assisted in its production: to the administration of Penn State Erie, the Behrend College, for generous financial support; to Wendy Eidenmuller for technical assistance; to Andrew Croker for a good ear and ever-ready resources. I wish to thank Maurice Cowling and Christopher Kent for allowing me to reprint indispensable assessments of *On Compromise*, previously published in larger works. It has been a great pleasure to work with Peter Erb, who undertook the daunting task of evaluating Dr Ludwig Haller's German adaptation of Morley's little classic. A. F. Thompson and John Bicknell have graciously helped in clarifying particular points. Nicola Pike has been an exceptional editor, and has played no small part in the pleasure of this project. Finally, I reserve the last word of honour, richly deserved, for Janice, Grady, Tessa and Ellen.

Introduction

'It makes all the difference in the world whether we put Truth in the first place or in the second place.' Thus John Morley began his examination of 'the limits that are set by sound reason to the practice of the various arts of accommodation, economy, management, conformity, or compromise'. And it was Truth with a capital 'T', above all else, that dictated the philosophy of the journalist who got himself into trouble by spelling God with a lower-case 'g'. It is a great irony that the prevailing image of John Morley is as staunch defender of the British cultural establishment, when we consider that at the age of thirty he could not get a parliamentary candidature because of his radicalism.[1] It is similarly ironic that Morley's most philosophic work, *On Compromise*, still bears the characterization of early wits who proclaimed that the only compromise was in the title.[2] Though false, the epigram has overwhelmed the truth, and few scholars recently have cared to go beyond this easy characterization of Morley's aggressive polemic.

In an age steeped in relativism, a fresh look at this much-known but little-read minor classic is in order. Morley's urgent call for all individuals to judge their circumstances, search their souls, know their minds and always to show the courage of their convictions will not convince romantics or theorists of any stripe, for it leaves no room for hazy half-truths or systematic short cuts to the truth. As one critic observed, 'there is nothing hazy or misty about Mr. Morley. He knows what he means to say, and he says it.'[3] For many today *On Compromise* fails as an intellectual prescription, for its assumptions are unfashionable, and its requirements hard. To take Morley seriously, one must accept the existence of moral truth, the ability to know it, and the absolute duty of each person to make moral judgments. How ironic, then, that the personal philosophy of the rigid agnostic of the 1870s should appeal in the late twentieth century to people of the deepest religious sensibilities. Truth, however, is now enjoying a certain vogue. And for those unconcerned about it, there is still something to be gained in better understanding the mysterious man who put it above all else, and the complex factors that are always at work in cases of literary influence. Fortunately too, even for those who disagree with the author, *On Compromise* 'bristles with epigrams', and is freely laced with the caustic wit that does so much to ennoble the discourse of disagreement.[4] Of course, Morley was earnest. He was also young, ambitious, insecure, talented, clever, on the make, and devoted to his wife of four years with whom he had lived for seven – give or take a year.

Morley as journalist

Morley first made his reputation as a journalist. While at Lincoln College, Oxford (1856–9) he declared his spiritual doubts, refused to take holy orders, as his father wished, and had his allowance cut off. It has been presumed that this was done 'wrathfully', and taken for granted that it produced a 'preoccupation thereafter with finding some way of relieving the pain and grief and of remedying the psychological disturbance'.[5]

This is a plausible frame in which to cast Morley's writing, but by no means the necessary one. Even before the rift with his father, Morley had displayed the bent towards philosophy and rationalism that would characterize much of his later writing, and which gave him so much pleasure throughout life. In the absence of clear evidence to support the notion that Morley was preoccupied with the rift, it seems more reasonable to assume that he was troubled, got over it and carried on with his life, writing about subjects that had long interested him, in a style that was being self-consciously fashioned for the press.

With no money and few prospects, Morley left Oxford with a pass degree, and in 1860 migrated to London where he survived by 'penny-a-lining' for a variety of journals and newspapers. Within two years, however, his anonymous articles in the *Literary Gazette* had attracted the attention of John Douglas Cook, editor of the *Saturday Review*, who was looking for 'writers of complete freshness and first-rate ability'.[6] Though Morley's social and literary criticism for the *Saturday Review* was sometimes diffuse and unpolished, his youthful articles were full of bracing epigrams and hallmark vignettes of the ongoing intellectual war between ideas and received tradition. His 'New Ideas' (October 1865) attracted John Stuart Mill's attention, and produced an invitation to meet. As Francis Hirst observed, 'it was a proud moment for an obscure journalist who had only just struggled to his feet to have won such approval as this from the world-famous author of Liberty'.[7]

Morley went on to prove that Cook's approbation in 1863, and Mill's in 1865, were the result of a marked and peculiar literary talent, rather than simply a matter of luck. Whether reviewing literary or historical works, interpreting the Enlightenment for English readers, or tracing the growth of progress through the lives of prominent Englishmen, Morley demonstrated a vitalizing sense of purpose and a unique literary style which commanded attention. He eventually wrote more than one hundred articles for influential journals of opinion, including the *Saturday Review*, *Fortnightly Review*, *Macmillan's Magazine* and the *Nineteenth Century*, as well as some two dozen books. A natural zeal for press combat, combined with a strong work ethic and a wide knowledge of European and English literature, enabled him to produce penetrating essays which cast long shadows and were widely discussed by the cultural élite.[8] Morley's chief aim, however, was to write books and articles that would sell, for he had no other income.[9]

Morley's own interest in the intersection of culture, religion and politics coincided with a general public interest, enabling him to be financially successful in pursuing his radical agenda. Material success, however, made him appear more at home among the establishment than he actually was.[10] To later critics, his insistence on the personal ethics, individualism and élitism so often identified with high Victorian culture marked him as representative of a set of values quite distinct from their own, and hence identified as 'Victorian'.[11] This is misleading on two counts. First, as a young author in the 1860s and 1870s, Morley was most often viewed as a dangerous prophet of rationalistic modernism. J. A. Spender's recollection here is telling, of an evangelical relative who, upon finding a copy of the *Fortnightly Review*, took it with a pair of tongs, 'marched downstairs and placed it on the kitchen fire', while an astonished household looked on.[12] Morley earned his moniker as a Saint of Rationalism long before society generally believed the rationalist to be worthy of sainthood.[13]

Yet even if one concedes that Morley later in life represented an important segment of the cultural establishment that he had himself helped to create, it should be remembered that his writings did more than simply represent. They also played a significant part in extending the currency of individualism, rationalism, 'manliness' and duty into the 1950s and beyond, by which time George Kitson-Clark had undertaken the historiographical rehabilitation of the Victorian age. It is this kind of influence that contemporary reviewers, even clever ones like W. H. Mallock, could not have foreseen. Nor is it now possible exactly to quantify it – as Morley said, 'so complex, subtle, and impenetrable, are the filaments that secretly bind men's thoughts and moods together'.[14] It is certain, however, that his view of the world affected the behaviour of his contemporaries, and that his conception of the late Victorian age continues to affect the way we think about it.[15]

One example here will suffice to suggest how Morley's gift for propagating a culture of ethical earnestness, which he himself helped to fashion with studies like *On Compromise*, influenced future generations. He undertook his three-volume *Life of Gladstone* in 1898, at a time when he considered the moral atmosphere of England 'really hellish'.[16] Gladstone's example of high morality, commitment to the public good and personal discipline was the perfect antidote to the inroads of modernism. Morley's remarkable biography, produced after five years of steady labour, was utterly traditional in form, yet quickly sold 30,000 sets at 42s. (£2.10) when it was published in 1903, and became the standard by which Macmillan employees gauged their workload. Two years later it was issued in a two-volume cheap edition at 5s. (25p), and the following year in fifteen 6d. (2½p) parts. In 1908 there was still enough demand to require a new printing of 50,000 copies at 5s. By 1911 Macmillan offered Morley's biography of the 'Grand Old Man' in three volumes at 1s. (5p) each. Within ten years, 130,000 copies of the *Life of Gladstone* had found their way into the hands of all classes of British society.[17]

In some cases, this might signify nothing more than a public mood or a moral fashion. Yet Gladstone had not been an untarnished idol, even to Liberals, when he resigned in 1894. And 'Gladstonian' ideals in 1903 carried with them the distinct mustiness of a worn-out political consciousness. The truth is that Morley's particular portrayal of the Grand Old Man played a substantial role in the biography's success. It was a multi-faceted gem, crafted in defence of a broad but decaying political sensibility. It was, of course, biography also. But while Morley was for the first time coherently tracing Gladstone's long and varied public career, he was also appealing to the public's nostalgia for a bygone age, in which honour, clarity of purpose and a weighty sense of responsibility were necessary for the purchase of public respectability.

Fifteen years later, Lytton Strachey's *Eminent Victorians* (1918) was supposed to have so cleverly undermined this 'Victorian' cult of respectability that neither the Victorian worthies themselves nor the official lives by which they were known could any longer be respected, encouraging the cynical mood of the Bloomsbury élite. Yet Strachey's devastating critique made virtually no impact upon the practice of political biography, or on the sale of the double-decker tomes that he criticized, and it was unable to shake the reputation of Morley's *Life of Gladstone*, which had consciously been designed in 1898 to stave off the degenerating effects of the literary modernism of that decade, which Strachey was later to crystallize so brilliantly in *Eminent Victorians*.

For three generations Morley's biography continued to be the principal guide to the multitudinous genius of Gladstone, who was presented as a monument to Liberal progress and the individualistic spirit.[18] As biography, it reinforced traditional standards for writing and interpreting political lives, standards that were barely touched by the methods of Strachey and Freud until after the Second World War.[19] Even today, with the field of biographical writing having been so widely infiltrated by theory and subjectivism, Morley's architectonic masterpiece remains the normative model for representing the lives of British statesmen – long, detailed, chronological and rooted in the kinds of evidence that can be rationally used. This approach to biographical writing has its weaknesses; it also has proven strengths in dealing with the lives of public figures whose careers have been bound up in the flow of debates, legislation, commissions of enquiry and elections.

Of course, Morley's biography has suffered somewhat in the century since it was written, but this stems mostly from the routine enlargement of historical perception rather than from any fundamental weakness in Morley's method or use of materials. With the publication of the *Gladstone Diaries*, one may now see the extent of the difficulties that he faced – and which every biographer faces – in representing the complexities of a lifetime of unique conjunctive experiences and sensibilities. Professor Matthew observed aptly: 'how often the modern scholar thinks he has found a startling quotation or a new idea, only to have to admit it is already "in Morley"!'[20] No one has yet superseded Morley, and, given both his relationship to Gladstone and his skill in crafting the factual parts, one can never be quite sure that he does not offer an insight that must altogether have escaped the latter-day biographer.

As an author alone, Morley's distinctive voice of 'responsible radicalism' would have assured his place in the history of British culture.[21] If he did not occupy the seat of a prophet, his place was nonetheless substantial. Evolution, collectivism, 'Freudianism' and the historic method eventually enjoyed their day as models for interpreting British culture, but not without a stubborn opposition that owed as much to the positive exposition of doctrines of rationalism and individual responsibility by authors such as Morley, as to the habitual passive resistance to change which is common to people generally.[22] The diversity of today's world of letters owes much to Morley's clear voice of common sense, which combines to resonate quietly in readers who have tired of theoretical determinism and refined intellectual ambiguities.

Had Morley never written a book or article, however, his wide-ranging editorial influence would have made him an important figure in the Victorian cultural landscape. Cotter Morison's judgment was questioned when, in 1867, he recommended a young man, not yet thirty and suspect for his doctrinaire positivism, as George Henry Lewes's successor as editor of the *Fortnightly Review*. But Morley did not disappoint his masters. While editing the *Fortnightly Review* (1867–82), *Pall Mall Gazette* (1880–3) and *Macmillan's Magazine* (1883–5), he sought both to refine the public's ethical sensibilities, and to bring his radically progressive views to bear directly in political matters. In fifteen years at the *Fortnightly Review*, he turned it into the premier journal of opinion, setting the tone in his own editorial articles, and inviting the often controversial work of authorities such as Matthew Arnold, Leslie Stephen, George Meredith, Walter Pater, Joseph Chamberlain, Mark Pattison and Edmund Gosse. In a sense, Morley was clearly borrowing glory.[23] He was also promoting a radical agenda whose goals of undermining militarism, extending secular education and securing a more liberal administration of Ireland were foremost in his mind. How better to do this than to trade in the authority of political figures and the genius of the cultural élite, whose voices might otherwise be scattered and diffused?

A second and equally important result of Morley's editorships was less directly tied to the intellect of others. As editor, he had the power to elevate the discussion of a wide range of social and cultural issues in a way that no single author could. He refused to publish simplistic solutions to difficult problems, and saw to it that important issues were addressed by people of real insight. Thus, at a time when many perceived the newspaper press as a 'great engine for keeping discussion on a low level', Morley consistently used his influence to promote a serious and responsible attitude toward the treatment of public issues (65). He did not, of course, do this alone, but then neither did anyone else, and it might be argued that no one did more than Morley during the 1870s and 1880s to elevate the quality of public discourse that passed through the periodical literature of the day.

Morley's opportunities for influencing both politics and the exchange of ideas were surprisingly diverse. While editing the *Fortnightly Review*, he continued as a reader for Macmillan, a position seldom noticed in the estimation of cultural influence, but of considerable importance when a publisher trusted a reader as Macmillan trusted Morley.[24] If one believes that the 1880s and 1890s was a pivotal period in the transformation of British culture, as is often averred, it should be remembered that the 'modernists' of that period enjoyed only limited success in defining cultural values. It is easy to undermine the positive contribution of those in positions of power, imagining instead that they were only fighting rearguard actions against inevitable change. Following this logic, it would be equally valid to argue that, since social change inevitably occurs, those who bring it forward bear little responsibility or deserve small credit for their accomplishments. Both propositions are preposterous. Men like George Bernard Shaw, Oscar Wilde, Havelock Ellis, Aubrey Beardsley and David Lloyd George did have a large hand in creating a range of new sensibilities which significantly informed British culture during the first half of the twentieth century. But, in evaluating the nature of cultural changes, one must always consider, in addition to the changes themselves, the speed with which they are brought forward and the particular forms they take. One must ask what the dominant characteristics of British culture might have been had Morley and others not so vigorously defended and promoted conservative attitudes.[25]

In some cases, Morley's editorial chair afforded him intimate access to the political process. He became a confidant of Joseph Chamberlain just as the latter burst onto the national political scene, and it was Morley who published in the *Fortnightly Review* his seminal 'The Liberal Party and its leaders', insisting upon 'a free church in a free state' and suggesting a motto for a new party – 'Free Church, Free Land, Free Schools, and Free Labour'.[26] Recognizing the potential of the press in an increasingly democratized society, Morley met regularly with Chamberlain and Charles Dilke between 1873 and 1882 to receive and pass on political information, and to publicize a radical political policy. Though it is always risky to claim too much for press influence, it would be equally foolish to ignore it, especially as the politicians themselves could not. Journalism was playing an increasing role in both politics and culture more generally – a role 'hardly inferior to parliament itself', according to Matthew Arnold.[27] Morley helped to make Chamberlain a national political figure by providing him with a public platform at the *Fortnightly Review*, and together they helped to forge a new radical consciousness. This involved more than a simple exchange of ideas. Morley's demands for Irish justice in the *Pall Mall Gazette* during the spring of 1882, for instance, finally 'created a situation' in the midst of which Irish Secretary William Forster resigned. The skill of Morley's judgement may be questioned, and the weight of his public onslaught debated, but his journalism did have political consequences.[28]

Morley's work as editor and author also brought him to notice among other Liberals, including Gladstone. The same fervour and insight that attracted the attention of Cook, Mill and Morison in the 1860s were evident to the political and cultural élite twenty years later, and helped secure for him the candidature for Newcastle in 1883. According to Arnold, Morley was unique in having 'all the ideas of a man of the best insight', as well as 'the skill for making these ideas pass into journalism'.[29] With both style and substance, in print and in the back-room, Morley was a significant figure in plotting a new radicalism which directly influenced the future of the Liberal Party, and indirectly the course of party politics more generally. He did not always have his way, but he spoke clearly and often, and many of his observations grew in the public mind.

Morley's conception and execution of the highly successful 'English Men of Letters' series of brief biographies for Macmillan helped to transform both the practice of biography and the accessibility of critical biographical insights. His idea of publishing a series of 'biographical and critical' essays, written by men and women of distinction, 'about twice as long as a *Quarterly* article, in a little volume to sell at about half-a-crown', was both a good business proposition and a means of propagating healthy values.[30] While it is an exaggeration to say that readers of the series discovered a 'bulwark against disruptive forces that seemed to threaten society', it is clear that Morley's selection of Leslie Stephen, J. A. Symonds, Goldwin Smith, James Anthony Froude, Frederic Harrison and Henry James, among others, to interpret the English cultural canon for a general English-speaking readership played an important role in the continuing justification of an élite-driven culture.[31] And in an age addicted to biography, the series was more influential than it might now seem.[32]

By the early 1880s, Morley's influence extended in many directions. He was an entertaining reviewer and master of the savage epigram; the aggressive cohort of Chamberlain and Dilke in promoting the new radicalism; the respected interpreter of the French Enlightenment; a man of judgement and innovation in the publishing industry; and the patriarch of 'young Oxford men' seeking to make their mark in London journalism.[33] As a journalist, then, Morley had made the most of opportunities. He had something to say, said it well and convinced many people who mattered that it made sense to have Morley on their side.

Morley as politician

It is Morley's second career, as politician, that tends to obscure the weight of his influence, for he never found the distinctive niche in politics that he enjoyed in the world of letters. He had early entertained the hope, almost impossible for a young man without connections, of entering politics. He failed to obtain candidatures at Preston and Blackburn in 1868, and was defeated for Blackburn the following year. Though he devoted more of his writing in the 1870s to political subjects, he made a virtue of necessity and consoled himself with the thought that he might best serve the political process outside its institutions. He was, nevertheless, clearly disappointed.

Professor Hamer's suggestion that Morley at this stage was strongly influenced by Matthew Arnold's recommendation to young intellectuals to stand aloof from the political battleground, from 'the rougher and coarser movements going on round us', is worth examining in relation to both Morley's career and the nature of intellectual history.[34] As a young man he had been much impressed with Arnold's criticism. In old age he was comforted by Arnold's verse, and reflected on his 'incomparable' influence at a time when social criticism was especially needed.[35] Yet none of this warrants Hamer's implication that in 1868 a disappointed Morley was heeding Arnold's advice from *Culture and Anarchy* (1867). Morley would have given up his exalted intellectual aloofness in an instant had he been able to command the votes, just as he relinquished the influential editorship of the *Pall Mall Gazette* in 1883 after being elected to Parliament for Newcastle. He justified his attitude in a letter to Frederic Harrison in 1874, suggesting that 'writing about dead Frenchmen' – his principal claim to distinction as an author – seemed 'rather a piece of ignavia' while other men were 'fighting the political battle'.[36]

There were, however, personal as well as public grounds that attracted Morley to politics. He had come a long way from his modest Blackburn beginnings, but intended to go farther, and, as he observed in *On Compromise*, anyone in England with any real ambition sought to enter Parliament. Emotionally, Morley longed for the concrete achievements of legislation and the immediate gratification of public applause. 'Are we not apt to make too much of [literature]', he wondered, as only a successful author could. 'Of course literature inspires and stimulates actions, but how many books have had any profound influence on the world?'[37] He had written successfully on serious subjects, but was still unsatisfied, and had learned painfully that intellectual activities – like lecturing on positivism – were not likely to elicit the fervour of a crowd.[38] What he later acknowledged, and what one senses was always just below the public façade, was his longing for the adulation of the crowd – all the more keenly felt because he had so strenuously maintained throughout his career the duty of conscience at the expense of popularity. 'I think I would sooner "sit down amid loud cheers"', he confessed in 1907, 'than stop an expedition against the Zakka Khels in my Cabinet!'[39] Morley was not born to politics, but his deepest sensibilities were those of the politician rather than the scholar.[40]

Finally elected as member for Newcastle in 1883, Morley proved to be an effective Irish Secretary (1886, 1892–5), and a trusted adviser to Gladstone on Irish Home Rule. After Gladstone's death in 1898, Morley stood back from politics, principally devoting himself to opposing the Boer War and to writing Gladstone's biography. When the Liberals returned to power in 1905 Campbell-Bannerman appointed him Secretary of State for India (1905–10), an unusual position of autocratic authority, many thought, for a man who had so often preached on the virtues of liberty and individualism. Though Morley was less active in general policy development than he had been under Gladstone, the India Office at that moment afforded considerable opportunity for a conscientious Liberal, and Morley made the most of it, initiating and overseeing a series of reforms which expanded provincial councils to include elected Indians. In 1908 Morley was elevated to the House of Lords as Viscount Morley of Blackburn. Two years later he resigned the India Office to become Lord President of the Council, and once more emerged as a factor in the central councils of the party. In 1914, after more than a score of threats, he resigned from the government over British entry into the Great War, thus ending his political career.

Morley was not ideally suited to parliamentary politics. Before the age of forty, he had no money and thus little time for an avocation. He had few connections within the political establishment, and could make little use of his literary ones – politicians were more useful to the editor than were men of letters to the minister. He was thin-skinned and deeply imbued with the kind of élitism that recognizes the rights of the masses, while at the same time wishing them more deserving of those rights. He was never as nimble in compromise or debate as he had been in critical phrase-making, and he was more than a little prone to waver in decision-making. Yet many politicians have been effective despite such faults. Morley might have been perceived as a more successful politician – and hence might have been better at it – had he not suffered the constant stigma of the amateur, lately come to the field of action.[41]

But government is full of business that transcends public perception, and Morley's colleagues found many admirable qualities to balance the weaknesses. For almost a decade he was Gladstone's primary lieutenant, assisting in the development of the party's foremost policy objective – Irish Home Rule – which was still in a fluid state and open to almost unlimited modification. Goldwin Smith perceptively observed the nature of their relationship: that 'Gladstone, though little open to argument, was very open to infusion', and 'Morley had a great hand in infusing into him Home Rule'.[42] By 1892, six years after the defeat of the first Government of Ireland Bill, as Gladstone geared up for a second try, he reckoned Morley to be his 'best stay'.[43] Morley was a good speaker and a competent departmental minister. He also had clear principles and was not afraid to speak them, a quality that appealed to many late Victorians. In a suggestive tribute following Gladstone's death, Canon MacColl wrote to Lord Salisbury that Morley, despite his agnosticism, had 'more influence in the country than any Liberal leader, because of his moral earnestness and conscientious fidelity to his convictions'.[44] Though MacColl may have exaggerated the breadth of Morley's influence, his encomium reminds us how prominent the issue of 'character' stood in the public's assessment of their leaders around the turn of the century.

Morley's personality

E. T. Raymond, in his acute little portrait of Morley, observed that the pride of the upper classes was relatively simple when compared to the pride of the middle classes, which was 'as nicely compounded as the melancholy of Jacques'.[45] And Morley had more than his share of compounding factors. As we have already mentioned, his convictions did not lead to a good start for a young man of ambition. A political career seemed out of the question for a writer of middle articles, no matter how highly he had been praised by famous men. With little concern for a public reputation, then, around 1867 he began living with Rose Mary Ayling, who already had several children and who may or may not have been married when she met Morley.[46] John and Rose Mary married in 1870, and all evidence suggests that they lived together happily until Morley's death in 1923.

'All the evidence', however, is not much, and the nature of the

Morleys' relationship remains ambiguous, as does the rest of his private life. Lady Morley seldom went out in public, perhaps because of private temperament, but also, one might surmise, because the 'cloud' over her past was well known.[47] She and Morley had no children of their own. This, in conjunction with his effeminate frame and 'womanly' characteristics, led gossips to guess that he was homosexual or bisexual – an attribution for which, it should be stressed, there is no evidence whatsoever.[48]

Nor did Morley do much in his own lifetime to provide anyone with the details of his domestic life or private thoughts. We have no records to suggest that he had emotional confidants; we have many, on the other hand, which point to the rich variety of his intellectual ones. As a revered elder statesman, he refused to believe that fame had enhanced the worthiness of his ordinary actions, or had transformed his private thoughts into prophetic observations of the human condition. For a man of his eminence, he seems to have been unusually content in putting his public life squarely before the public, and in keeping his private joys and pains to himself. In considering a man of Morley's public stature, it is incredible that so little is known of his life before the age of thirty, or of any of his private life. This may be explained in part by his reticence, in part by his relative obscurity prior to the mid-1860s, and in part by his deliberate destruction of letters and papers which might have told us a great deal.

As a result of these factors, the texture of Morley's personality has always appeared smoother than it actually was, a perception based upon a public persona and published writings. Modern scholars have extended the life of this caricature by taking his rhetorical austerity at face value, as if he actually lived according to the dogmas of a religion of high rationalism, which critics found represented throughout his writings. There is scarcely a page in Hamer's admirable work, for instance, that does not paint his subject as a slave to principle, disconsolate and brooding over the weight of intellectual and ethical responsibilities, and most recent writers have in some measure taken their cue from him. Intellectual history of the sort that Hamer practises, however, presumes a mental consistency which must be present, however deeply buried. It is not designed to illuminate personality, nor is it sufficient to suggest the range of factors – many non-intellectual in nature – contributing to the spread of ideas.[49] Instead, it has led to a thumbnail impression of Morley, which can be clearly seen, for instance, in the most recent work on the Macmillan publishing house. Although Alexander Macmillan described him in 1869 as 'the bravest, clearest headed fellow I know', Richard Davenport-Hines is sure that Morley was really 'a vain and fretful nag', who scorched contemporaries with 'the white heat of his gloomy earnestness'.[50]

Given the high seriousness of Morley's language, it is not surprising that contemporary critics without personal knowledge of him would imagine that his rhetorical tone corresponded with his mental state. It would be hard to think otherwise of an author who appeared so certain of himself, conjuring up images of philosophical cribbed decks on which men were 'doomed to tread', and 'vast spaces of an eternal sea' which 'oppressed' the soul; and characterizing self-deception as the Gospels' 'sin against the Holy Ghost', no more 'shocking to the most devout believer' than it was to 'people who doubt whether there be any Holy Ghost or not' (88–91).[51] Morley's interest in large and weighty matters – like a national ethical revival – and his regular use of words and phrases such as 'doom', 'sin' and the 'abomination of desolation', might, understandably, suggest a secular Jeremiah who ought not to be trifled with, particularly if one accepts his words at face value and as the full expression of his beliefs.[52]

In properly estimating Morley as a man, however, one must temper the 'savage appeal[s] to sincerity' that characterize his formal writing with the clever banter and ordinary daily discourse that often prevailed in conversation and private letters.[53] In relative frequency of use, and thus perhaps in habit of mind, the latter were far more numerous than the former, and define with greater accuracy the mood in which he transacted business, pursued his goals and met the necessities of politics, personalities and circumstances beyond his control. Just as Morley could covet political office while making the intellectual case for staying out, he could think in loose and ordinary terms while writing in a more strident, philosophical language. He could think of the Holy Ghost and sin and compromise in casual, even light-hearted ways, as well as oppressive ones. His friendship with Joseph Chamberlain was built by dealing with serious political matters in an amusing, tragicomic style not employed with intellectual friends like Frederic Harrison. Morley, for instance, recounted for Chamberlain the dinner in 1880 at which Gladstone 'took me to a corner and reavealed his Coercion [scheme] much as a man might say (in confidence) that he found himself under the painful necessity of slaying his mother'; and he listened gleefully as Chamberlain in 1873 boasted of giving the '"Beer and Bible" Tories a most smashing defeat ... One person declared at a public meeting that the Holy Ghost was on their side – on which "Three cheers for the Holy Ghost" were called for and I believe given ...'[54]

Morley was not an intellectual prig. As he had written in *Burke*, he 'valued words at their proper rate', knowing that 'some of the greatest facts in the life and character of man' could 'find no description and no measurement in words'.[55] Nor was he above tailoring message to audience. When he informed Chamberlain of his intention to write on contemporary affairs for the *Fortnightly Review*, he realized that his public tone would not correspond with that of his private confidences. 'Don't be surprised', he wrote, 'if the thing comes out rather more literary, general, semi-meditative, critico-philosophical, than you have bn. expecting.'[56] Morley's rhetorical strategies are only notable because the fervour and consistency of his intellectual 'line' has been given far too much weight in defining the quality and character of his life.

Nor was Morley above contradiction in pursuing the ideals of which he wrote with such force and clarity. In 1874 he was advising readers of the absolute necessity, for both self-respect and the good of society, of refraining from 'false professions', or even profession by implication, as when one might 'attend services, public or private, which are to him the symbol of superstition and mere spiritual phantasmagoria' (183). It was a view he never renounced; indeed, he affirmed it again and again as he reviewed his text and brought out successive editions of *On Compromise* between 1874 and 1921. At least from the 1880s, however, Morley on occasion beseeched the deity whose cultural influence he had so stridently deplored in print, parting with a 'God bless you' when deeply touched, or requesting prayer in troubled moments.[57] In trying to explain what really are the last phrases one would expect to hear coming from Morley's mouth, given the general outlines of the portrait that has been painted of him, one might say that he was speaking symbolically or ironically, but the evidence suggests otherwise. In either of these cases, his traditional appeal to God would amount to exactly the kind of unthinking, cowardly, or casual approach to the use of words with regard to truth which he had found to be such a bane in English society.

In one of the most acute studies of Morley, Professor Cockshut argues that his 'habitual quasi-religious feeling about the unknowable and unfathomable' was a tool rather than a mirror, always used 'as a foil to definite practical certainties about secular knowledge'.[58] This is true with regard to his formal writing, but has little bearing on the passing use of such religious phrases. Morgan suggests that this element of contradiction owes to the 'plaintive importunities of childhood's memories', which were 'sometimes very strong'.[59] Another possible explanation is that Morley might occasionally have doubted his secular faith, might have imagined that some unfathomable God with a capital 'G' still looked upon the earth, and then been brave enough to be true in the moment to the 'phantasmagoria' which ever so briefly clouded his head. After all, Morley professed – and I think genuinely – to be interested in Truth above all things, and certainly above any pedantic consistency that small minds might imagine his writings to have imposed.[60] Only a latter-day disciple could really imagine that Morley's early work, written in the austere 'style of a man who has himself under perfect control', fully represented the inner life of a man who had experienced a full share of public and private tribulations.[61]

If any single thing about Morley's personality can be known, it is that he seldom allowed intellectual 'cribbed decks' to interfere with his enjoyment of life. Virtually every person who knew him well scoffed at the notion that his personality could be measured by the tone of his literature. St Loe Strachey echoed a common feeling in observing how wrong most people had been in thinking of Morley only as 'a stern, unbending, intellectual Radical'. He continued: 'No doubt a good deal can be quoted from Morley's writings and speeches which to hurried and anxious minds might seem to support this view. Yet, as a matter of fact, it gave an utterly false impression of his personality.'[62]

This is not to minimize Morley's austerity, but rather to recognize, as we do in thinking about individuals whom we know personally, that the first impression is not necessarily representative of their character. As J. A. Spender recalled, after once enduring what he believed to be an unwarranted reproach, Morley remained 'a charmer' who did not let his frankly expressed opinions, austere as they seemed, interfere with his friendships.[63]

In the end, Morley managed to find purpose without system, leaning towards the use of theological language which did not, and could not, express the breadth of either his perplexity or his ultimate means of sidestepping what were purely technical difficulties of a philosophical or theological nature. Despite the sound of Morley's strident rhetorical voice, the evidence gives every impression that he was psychologically secure and intellectually self-confident, not without his weaknesses and doubts, but quite able to overcome them 360 days in the year.

On Compromise

On Compromise has enjoyed unusual success for a study so narrowly tailored to the intellectual temper of a small class of rational agnostics of the 1870s. From its publication in 1874, it was in print for more than seventy years. It was translated into many languages and sold in bookstalls from San Francisco to Bombay, from Berlin to Volgograd.[64] It was revered as a moral guide by a generation of serious young liberals, who opposed the wave of collectivism and cultural degeneracy which they saw beginning to sweep across Europe during the final years of the nineteenth century.[65] Without claiming too much for what necessarily must have been one intellectual and moral influence among many, it is not difficult to see how two prominent themes – the pre-eminence of individual conscience as the intellectual standard, coupled with the practical loophole of compromise in social application – played to the needs of those who praised it, among them Asquith, Churchill and Harold Wilson. *On Compromise* became a handbook for the high-minded and the well-educated, who wished to be reassured that the exercise of their individual judgement was nothing less than the fulfilment of a moral obligation.

On Compromise was not, however, designed as a handbook. Nor did Morley intend it as a manifesto for alienated Victorians who had lost faith and were desperately searching for a secular creed to replace it. Stefan Collini elegantly characterizes it as a 'case for systematic and clear-sighted reasoning – essentially agnosticism and radical Liberalism in parade uniform'.[66] According to Hamer, 'intellectuals, like Morley, thought in terms of system and synthesis' because they 'wanted a substitute for the Christian religion'.[67] While there are clearly signs of both system and religion in Morley's work, discovering these evidences and fashioning them into an explication of his intent is primarily the work of a specific kind of intellectual history, which may or may not represent Morley's own perceptions and experience.

Taking *On Compromise* as a piece of intellectual history of this sort, it would be hard to improve upon the explications of Professors Christopher Kent and Maurice Cowling, and for that reason I have appended their analyses.[68] Their examinations naturally follow the logic of Morley's arguments, and the degree to which he was a disciple of Comte, of Burke, or of Mill. In the introduction to this edition, however, I am examining the work as a piece of contemporary journalism, emanating more from the circumstances of a particular six-month period than the eternal condition of man. In launching his vigorous attack as part of the culture wars of the late Victorian era, Morley was undoubtedly displaying his intellectual pedigree. He was not, however, speaking timelessly, or crusading in the traditional sense of the term. He was most immediately trying to enlarge his reputation, enhance the influence of the *Fortnightly Review*, and make inroads with politicians – the movers and shakers of the 1870s.⁶⁹ Only secondarily was he thinking of immutable principle.

The composition of *On Compromise* was anything but systematic, and had little to do with creedalism of any sort. Couched in the heated religious rhetoric of the 1870s, it was primarily a call to rational individualism, rigorously applied, rather than to any form of secular religion. Moreover, it was an amalgamation of several clever pieces of journalism, which coalesced almost accidentally in the wake of Mill's death in May 1873.

On Compromise began in the editorial room of the *Fortnightly Review*. Morley had been agitated by James Fitzjames Stephen's critique of Mill's doctrine of liberty, which had been published as 'Liberty, Equality, Fraternity' in the pages of the *Pall Mall Gazette* from November 1872 until January 1873, and issued in book form by Smith, Elder and Co. in April. Mill himself did not 'rate the book highly'.⁷⁰ Morley, however, recognized the powerful attraction of Stephen's philistine appeal to the English love of common sense, and pulled out his biggest gun in order to deal with the 'insufferable' man. Writing to Frederic Harrison in April, he urged him to undertake the review of *Liberty, Equality, Fraternity*, as Harrison could 'make him ridiculous in a different way from that in which he makes himself ridiculous'. When Harrison's critique was completed and subsequently published as 'The Religion of Inhumanity' in the June *Fortnightly Review*, Morley professed himself thoroughly pleased with a 'most masterly' review.

The controversy might have ended there had it not been for the convergence of Mill's death, Morley's creeping discontent with positivism and the natural combativeness of both Morley and Stephen. Morley did not have time on his hands. He was full of editorial business, deeply involved in writing a series of articles on educational reform, and just beginning to recover from the 'profound upset' of taking a new house at Tunbridge Wells in June as a result of his wife's ill health. Mill's death in May had been a personal shock which continued to prompt reflection. And though outwardly pleased with 'The Religion of Inhumanity', Morley had a gnawing sense that Harrison had not adequately met all of Stephen's criticisms. This sent him back to Mill's *On Liberty*, which he read concurrently with *Liberty, Equality, Fraternity*. At the end of June, he raised with Harrison the possibility of a 'close step-by-step refutation' of Stephen's treatment of Mill's doctrine of liberty, suggesting a genuine difference of purpose between the two radical friends. Morley, however, had a larger, strategic purpose for making time to answer Stephen, who was, he knew, contemplating a second edition in which he would respond to his significant critics. Morley rapidly produced 'Mr. Mill's Doctrine of Liberty', which was published in the *Fortnightly Review* in August 1873.

Morley knew his antagonist. Stephen's second edition of *Liberty, Equality, Fraternity*, published early in 1874, included a preface of 8,500 words aimed squarely at 'the most important' of his critics, 'Mr. John Morley and Mr. Frederic Harrison', with Morley the first and principal target.[71] Though Morley was satisfied that he had defended the essence of Mill's doctrine of liberty, he did not believe that Stephen's 'noble common sense' could be answered in a point-by-point examination of philosophical principles. As he had written to Harrison in April of the previous year, Stephen's work was really a 'long-winded and pompous Amen to a number of propositions which Englishmen have accepted for hundreds of years'.[72] What was needed was to prove that radicals were 'as fond of order and good government, and as firm for it, as Stephen is ... that we recognise as clearly as he does the hard facts of the world, and know as well as he, that they cannot be evaded by fine phrases and soft sawder ...' Though both Harrison and Morley had met a number of Stephen's intellectual arguments, neither had substantially undermined the cumulative weight of the English cultural prejudices to which he appealed. Unlike Mill, Morley sensed that Stephen's work was important because it crystallized the intuitive biases that often operated independently of the intellect, even in the minds of sensible and well-educated Englishmen.

By March 1874, Morley was working on 'a fierce jeremiad' over 'things in general'. He had become disillusioned with the philosophical system of Comte, and even with some of the pronouncements of his intellectual master, Mill. His appeal to the supremacy of individual conscience was thus undertaken at a time when systems of thought, and the power of ideas, both religious and secular, had been called into question, and when some new rationale was being sought as a basis for a life of action rather than thought. But Morley did not attempt to construct a new religion or philosophic system, or to fashion an original exposition of his principles. Instead he plainly urged a handful of intellectual foundations for the modern age, upon which each individual should build – 'the right of thinking freely and acting independently, of using our minds without excessive awe of authority, and shaping our lives without unquestioning obedience to custom'. Appropriating his adversary's best weapons, Morley transported his principles on the back of concrete examples and common sense, drawing upon a wide range of contemporary circumstances and classic literature, especially from his recent studies of Voltaire, Rousseau and Mill. In so doing, he wished to demonstrate that individualism, rationality and a vigorous search for truth were consistent with the fundamental English love of liberty and cautious common sense. In April he published the first of four *Fortnightly Review* articles entitled 'On Compromise', Chapter 1. In June he was still writing the fourth chapter, and did not publish the conclusion until August.

While reading the articles as they appeared, George Meredith was struck by the unusual combination of characteristics which made 'On Compromise' such an unusual piece of literature. 'Are the instances a trifle over-familiar for the dignity of the Essay?', he wondered to his friend. 'Still, they at least give your meaning clearly and bring them home.' After reading the final instalment in August, Meredith refined his criticisms, recognizing that in a 'desire for directly applying' his meaning, Morley might have deliberately avoided the 'philosophical altitudes' in order to say 'what no one else dares or can say'.[73]

By September Morley had 'carefully revised' his articles, added about one third of his 'Mr. Mill's Doctrine of Liberty' as a 'footnote', and brought them out together in the first book edition of *On Compromise*, published by Chapman and Hall in Britain, and by Macmillan in the United States. Morley's indication in the 'Note to the First Edition' that he had 'carefully revised' the original articles is misleading. In fact, he had done little more than amplify transitions, add a few footnotes and divide sentences, in an attempt to meet objections raised by both Meredith and Harrison.[74]

The 1874 revision of his *Fortnightly Review* articles had been undertaken hastily, in the midst of a dozen editorial duties and writing projects. Yet Morley's personal sensibilities had been so deeply threatened by the intellectual temper of the times that his hurried response emerged as a model of clarity. Despite finding the 'intolerance of the school of philosophy' to which he belonged in every sentence, the reviewer for the *Athenaeum* confessed that Morley knew exactly what he wanted to say, and said it clearly.[75] This is not the gift of genius which characterizes the work of cultural prophets like Thomas Carlyle and Matthew Arnold, but such clarity in conception and exposition is rare, and remains one of the chief reasons for reading Morley today.[76]

Morley himself was surprised at how seriously the critics regarded *On Compromise*. He had, after all, produced it in pieces, like a basketful of literary pastries served up on demand. When its financial success afforded the opportunity for a 'second revised edition' late in 1877, as a part of a uniform edition of his works, Morley could have taken his critics as seriously as they had taken him, and argued his points more rigorously. In fact, he had no inclination to do so, for his time was completely swallowed up with other duties, not the least of which involved maintaining a finger on the imperial pulse in the wake of Disraeli's aggressive foreign policy in the Near East and India. As he wrote to his sister early in 1878:

> At this moment I am simply overwhelmed. (1.) All my books are going through the press for a new and cheap editon, and I have to revise the proofs – sets coming in by every post. (2.) The Series is beginning – MSS., proofs, etc. [English Men of Letters Series, which had been launched] (3.) Completion of Diderot. (4.) F. R. which is doing well. (5.) MSS. for Macmillan. (6.) Refusing invitations to dinner ... I forget if I told you that last week I dined with Chamberlain one night and Dilke the next.[77]

Morley had penned *On Compromise* as one of a dozen duties, in the heated tone of periodical press warfare. He never intended to compose a philosophic rule for young liberals, and declined to do so when he had the chance.

The 1877 revision, which serves as the copytext for this edition, begins with the disclaimer that 'the present little volume' made 'no pretensions to be anything more than an Essay [45]. To judge such a performance as if it professed to be an exhaustive Treatise in casuistry, is to subject it to tests which it was never designed to bear.' Morley added a few fresh lines, including reference to Bagehot's death earlier in the year, and some further discussion of his objection to the notion that 'religion may be morally useful without being intellectually sustainable', which he had dealt with more extensively in 'Mr. Mill's Three Essays on Religion', published in the *Fortnightly Review* in January 1875. Beyond this kind of minor tinkering, however, Morley simply sharpened his caustic wit in a handful of places and presented the world with the little classic that would be reprinted at least thirteen times without revision between 1877 and 1921.

In June 1920, Macmillan contacted Morley about bringing out a new edition of his collected works, which offered an opportunity for re-evaluating a philosophy of life that scholars have inextricably linked with the spiritual tumult of the 1870s. Morley was glad to cooperate, in part because it would not amount to much work, the copy having been so thoroughly revised in previous years. Again, in writing, Morley's instincts were always those of the journalist, rather than the scholar. Once he had moved on to a new topic, he was not inclined to go back. And when he did, he appealed to 'the old Greek principle that a man may once say a thing as he would have it said, δις δε συκ ευδεχεται – he cannot say it twice'.[78] He was nevertheless unsettled when he actually thought about John Morgan reviewing the new Edition deLuxe for the *Times Literary Supplement*. He was glad for Morgan to have the old Eversley editions of *Cromwell*, *Burke*, *Walpole*, and the *Miscellanies*, but was 'rather anxious' that he should have the new revisions of *On Compromise*, which included substantial 'modifications'.[79]

For all Morley's expressed concern, however, and given the enormous material, cultural and philosophical changes that had occurred in British society across forty-six years, he altered very little. He tacitly agreed with both admirers and critics that *On Compromise* was, in its common way, 'unanswerable'.[80] He took notice of few of the criticisms that had appeared in the press, though he did occasionally nod in their direction. He had been roundly criticized, for instance, for suggesting that 'principle is only another name for a proposition stating the terms of one of these larger expediencies' (53–4, 163). As a philosophical proposition, it was suspect. But Morley had never intended it as such, and probably omitted it from the Edition deLuxe, not because he considered it intellectually inadequate, but rather because the deleted four-paragraph block of which it was a part had been designed in 1874 to speak specifically to 'the time and the circumstances which we know best, or at least whose deficiencies and requirements are most pressingly visible to us'. He had had opportunities to excise the sentence in 1874 and in 1877, but did not. Clearly, by 1920, however, this sequence would not represent 'time and the circumstances' which anyone knew well, much less best.

The argument which probably drew widest notice was his assertion that history was 'a *pis-aller*', which he could easily imagine 'improved in certain respects' (85–6). If so, a critic for the *Contemporary Review* argued, 'where is the storehouse in which he looks for our sanctions or our encouragements?' W. H. Mallock considered the whole notion that history could be other than it was as 'mere midsummer madness'.[81] In face of such criticisms, Morley persisted in the controversial statement, his only concession to the critics being the addition of a phrase, 'whether it be true or not that history is a *pis aller*, it has assuredly not moved without the relation of cause and effect'.

Morley also omitted an important section in which he had argued that women were 'at present far less likely than men to possess a sound intelligence and a habit of correct judgment' (126). This simply reflected a change in the times rather than in Morley's philosophy, for the assertion had always been conditional. In 1874 he had explained clearly why he believed it to be true – because women had 'less ready access than men to the best kinds of literary and scientific training' and had been socially excluded 'from all those kinds of public activity, which are such powerful agents both in fitting men to judge soundly, and in forming in them the sense of responsibility for their judgments being sound'. These social conditions having been altered, Morley naturally recognized that more and more women were in a position to develop and use their intellectual powers.

The most significant change in the revisions of 1920 was one of tone. In dozens of instances he softened the rhetoric of his firebrand years. He omitted reference to the 'profound immorality of the priestly profession' (133). Instead of referring to a passage in the life of Hume as 'the coarsest and most revolting shape which the doctrine of conformity can assume', he alluded simply to 'the boldest shape' (89). He omitted the final, and really superb, clause when arguing that:

> all of us know men who deliberately reject the entire Christian system, and still think it compatible with uprightness to summon their whole establishments round them at morning and evening, and on their knees to offer up elaborately formulated prayers, which have just as much meaning to them as the entrails of the sacrificial victim had to an infidel haruspex. (123)

In the more mellow spirit which befitted a man of long experience, he was willing to delete some of his best epigrams, including one especially deserving of attention today: opposing a culture in which 'one is conjured to respect the beliefs of others, but forbidden to claim the same respect for one's own' (59). None of these changes, however, altered his essential arguments. Instead of spreading the gospel of agnosticism with the hell-fire of the Protestant evangelist in his veins, Morley now plied his message in a calmer spirit of reflection.

This change in tone had little to do with the critics of 1874 who had noted the intolerance, arrogance and vulgarity of Morley's caustic diatribe. Instead it spoke to the experience of a man who had grown to be eighty-three years old, who had seen the power of organized religion decline dramatically, who had witnessed the failure of Comtism and the inability of any secular religion to take the place of the old. In half a century Morley had gone from being a radical critic of religion and culture to a spiritual guardian of what many critics perceived to be an inexplicable faith in reason, progress and the dignity of the individual. He may have lost faith in God, and in the power of any new religious synthesis, but he could never quite shake his belief in morality and the potential of progress.

Examining the changes of 1920 also suggests which parts of *On Compromise* were fundamental to his philosophy of life, and which were incidental. Morley's rhetoric of 1874 did suggest the vision of a young man who imagined that he might facilitate the development of a new religion of ethics. But much of this language disappeared in the Edition deLuxe. In 1874, for instance, Morley argued that neither women nor men could be happy without a religion – clearly a secular religion in Morley's case (126). This he omitted in 1920, as he did the following: 'If the religious spirit leads to a worthy and beautiful life ... such a spirit is on the whole a good thing' (127). The militantly religious language in which he often couched his strident arguments was also softened. Note the tone of 1874: 'To the indifferent person one can say nothing. We can only acquiesce in that deep and terrible scripture, "He that is filthy, let him be filthy still." To those who despair of human improvement or the spread of light in the face of the huge mass of brute prejudice, we can only urge ...' (135). Compare this with that of 1920: 'To the indifferent one can say nothing. To those who despair of human improvement or the spread of light in the face of the huge mass of rough prejudice, we can only urge that ...' The lesson is the same, but Morley is clearly less willing to play the Jeremiah of an agnostic faith. What was consistently most important to him was that each person should examine affairs in light of reason, and to affirm that all individuals were responsible for living their own lives according to the best light available to them.

So many critics who have fastened upon Morley's religious rhetoric have failed to see that its use was, in large measure, a habit of the mid-Victorian mind. Lytton Strachey had cleverly (and incidentally) alluded to this religiosity in reviewing Morley's *Recollections*, when he observed that even the atheists of the Victorian Age, '(Lord Morley was one of them)', were religious.[82] Yet because Morley often thought in religious categories and wrote accordingly, it does not follow that he was seeking to formulate a secular religious rule.

Instead, his rhetoric reflected the deep-seated and individual spiritual sensibility which no organized religion adequately represents, even for its adherents. H. W. Massingham caught the spirit of this distinction when he argued that Morley was 'so little at war' with the 'humanities of the Christian faith', that 'he may be claimed, with Tolstoy, as of the spirit of Jesus, if not of his visible household'.[83] This, of course, may be taken as a platitude. But the evidence in Morley's case suggests an approach to the truth. W. T. Stead, ardent Christian and Morley's intimate subordinate for three years at the *Pall Mall Gazette*, wondered if Morley, the atheist, were not 'much more deeply religious than I, the Christian':

> There is a depth of reverence about him and a fine sympathy of soul to which I can lay no claim. Would it were otherwise! I, on the other hand, am so impatient, so vehement, so anxious ever to jog the elbow of the Almighty, that I fancy Mr. Morley's mood of mind harmonizes much more with the truly religious ideal, which perhaps is more devotional, more meditative, more resigned than mine could ever be.[84]

One need not ignore traditional definitions to say that Morley set his own ethical standards higher than most professing Christians, and that his sense of life's seriousness and high purpose were so great that he was praised by orthodox Christian leaders despite his agnosticism.

These characteristics say much about Morley. They become more meaningful when placed in the context of the unusual intimacy between two friends whose religious beliefs have been habitually caricatured: Morley, as arch-agnostic; and Gladstone, as last of the great Christian statesmen. In terms of intellectual statements of faith, which they both shared freely with the world in letters, books and articles, they were poles apart. I would suggest that in more deeply-rooted, sometimes subconscious ways, they shared similar religious impulses based upon a reverence for the design of life which made small and narrow attitudes contemptible. Nowhere have these complex and mysterious wells of action been more succinctly stated than in Morley's speech at the unveiling of the Gladstone statue in Manchester in October 1901:

> No man that I have ever known was so slow to pronounce verdicts on his fellow-creatures. In no man that I have ever known was the broad and rational spirit of charity so vigorously alive. Few men can have been so true to their conception of duty as a power, as he himself described it, co-extensive with the action of our intelligence, that goes with us where we will, and only leaves us with the light of life. No man so hated and despised moral cowardice and the faint heart. No life was ever less left to the shaping of haphazard. In small

affairs or great, in public affairs or private, he acted from pre-meditated reasons and trusted nothing to chance, luck, and the casual stars. In every sense of the word, and within the whole range of the spirit of the word, he abhorred a gambler. Again, is there a single example in our history of such vigorous progress in mental life? His beginnings, as he has left on record, were exceedingly narrow. They were, as he said, concentrated – they were concentrated (these are his own words) in the Church, understood in the narrowest fashion ... The thought with which he rose in the morning and went to rest at night was of the universe as a sublime moral theatre, in which an omnipotent Dramaturgist uses kingdoms and rulers, laws and policies, to exhibit sovereign purposes for good ... He, at all events, in face of the exigent demands of practical politics, did his best to bring truth and justice into the minds and hearts of his countrymen.[85]

Here are found all the essential themes of *On Compromise* – rationality, duty, diligence, moral courage, love of truth, optimism – but shorn of much of the polemic that had characterized Morley's exposition of them in 1874. For Gladstone, these qualities emerged from a narrow Christian past; for Morley, from a sterile Comtean heritage. This striving for ethical living in the midst of public service led to an essential convergence of minds under the star of Burke, who had 'the sacred gift of inspiring men to use a grave diligence in caring for high things, and in making their lives at once rich and austere'.[86] Morley and Gladstone together cared for 'high things', which served as a firm basis for the last great friendship of Gladstone's life.

And what of compromise? Morley was all for it, except in the expression of one's opinion, where there were no excuses for timidity. Had he written the same essay a dozen years later, he probably would not have changed his argument. His actions as a politician suggest, however, that he would have elaborated on the 'excellent reasons why a statesman immersed in the actual conduct of affairs, should confine his attention to the work with which his hands find to do' (93). Being an intellectual journalist in 1874, Morley shifted the burden of thought and principle to the writers and intellectuals who helped to shape the public opinion, which in turn informed the politician. As a result, his thesis reflected a seldom articulated, but widely practised pattern among Liberals, that 'in the positive endeavour to realise an opinion, to convert a theory into a practice, it may be, and very often is, highly expedient to defer to the prejudices of the majority, to move very slowly, to bow to the conditions of the status quo, to practise the very utmost sobriety, self-restraint, and conciliatoriness' (95). It thus makes sense that Morley would admire Gladstone for the 'tact and compromise' with which he managed his business.[87]

Conclusion

In an age of relativism, *On Compromise* forces readers to face the proposition that Truth matters to the well-being of individuals and their society. Morley's élitism will remain suspect, many will condemn his secular morality on both philosophical and religious grounds, and most will regard his concern for character as typically Victorian. Yet no one reading this essay is likely to turn the final page without asking themselves if they are guilty of 'a shrinking deference to the *status quo*'; or, through 'indolence and timidity', of 'flaccid latitudinarianism, which thinks itself a benign tolerance for the opinions of others'. 'It is in truth', he argued, 'only a pretentious form of being without settled opinions of our own, and without any desire to settle them' (105). Morley urged that we ennoble ourselves by confronting the issues that divide society, by thinking deeply about them, and then by courageously expressing the opinion that reason has suggested, so as to aid in the progress that must follow.

This does sound austere. But one must remember that before becoming a caricature of the dour representative of the Victorian cultural establishment, Morley was a 'dashing journalist, ardent rationalist, impetuous radical' and 'critic of church and throne'.[88] The vital, varied and prolific early career, which earned him the right to be a petulant elder in the twentieth century, is nowhere better captured than in this clever and suggestive bit of doggerel written by the First Earl of Lytton less than a year after the publication of *On Compromise*:[89]

> What are you doing, John Morley, John Morley?
> What are you doing in town?
> Are you sorely, John Morley, assaulting the Tory
> Lawgivers, and smiting them down?
> While you list to the chatter of ... the satyr,
> For your sake does he dish up to breakfast a bishop,
> Or parso, grown fatter by railing at matter,
> With a sinner or two, such as Maxse and you,
> And, to garnish the platter, a Turk or a Jew,
> Between Moody and Sankey and Swinburne – who'll flavour

> The whole with an aphrodisiacal savour
> Lascivious and Grecian? Does Lowe the logician,
> Whose head is as white as our insular rocks and stern,
> By the light of pure reason? Or do you talk treason
> With the Fortnightly chiefs of the Radical garrison,
> Implacable Beesly and high-minded Harrison?
> Whose manners are mild as his pen is audacious,
> And whose spouse is so pretty, so clever, so gracious,
> That were I in his place ('tis a figure of speech, Sir)
> I'd wish things to remain as they are. But whatever
> Your Editorship is about, I beseech, Sir,
> Send me news, send me news of John Morley. For never
> Can this 'present writer,' though now out of reach, Sir,
> Be tamely resigned to be quite out of mind.
> So deliver – you bold anti-clerical Tamerlane!
> Are you still, in unholy alliance with Chamberlain,
> Riding fiercely atilt at the rickety steeple
> Of that church where Will Gladstone (sublimest of curates!)
> Is now shaking hands with all sorts of odd People?
> Are you settling the school rates, 'reforming' the poor rates?
> Or flirting with muggism, never excessive,
> Like Kimberley's priggism, mildly progressive?
> Or best of all, painting some portrait, perchance,
> Of the last of last century's worthies in France?
> Well, whate'er you be doing, John Morley, remember
> That you owe now a letter (and the sooner 'tis written
> The better, the better, John Morley!) to Lytton.

And in this personal note – far removed from the artificial academic rhetoric of analysis – one may glimpse the frenetic diversity of Morley's cultural influence, and the happy earnestness that characterized it: 'Looking back I only know that men vastly my superiors, alike in letters and the field of politics, have held me in kind regard and care for my friendship. I do not try to analyse or explain. Such golden boons in life are self-sufficing.'[90]

Notes

1. Morley as establishment figure is well portrayed in W. L. and Janet Courtney's obituary notice indicating that he 'never failed to command respect,

and as the years went on, and one by one the great Victorians passed into silence, John Morley came to symbolize for his countrymen that tradition of honesty, uprightness and uncompromising devotion to the truth as he saw it'. 'John Morley: 1838–1923', *North American Review* 218 (1923), p. 765.
2. Courtney, 'John Morley', pp. 770–1; J. W. Robertson Scott, *The Life and Death of a Newspaper: An Account of the Temperaments, Perturbations and Achievements of John Morley, W. T. Stead, E. T. Cook, Harry Cust, J. L. Garvin and three other Editors of the* Pall Mall Gazette (Methuen, London: 1952), p. 31; F. W. Knickerbocker, *Free Minds: John Morley and His Friends* (Harvard University Press, Cambridge, Mass.: 1943), p. 175.
3. *Athenaeum*, 17 October 1874, p. 505. See below, Appendix I, p. 193.
4. Ibid; see Appendix VI, below, for a selection of Morley's epigrams.
5. D. A. Hamer, *John Morley: Liberal Intellectual in Politics* (Clarendon Press, Oxford: 1968), pp. 1–2.
6. T. H. S. Escott, 'John Morley', *Fortnightly Review* 114 (July–December 1923), pp. 705–6.
7. F. W. Hirst, *Early Life and Letters of John Morley*, 2 vols (Macmillan, London: 1927), 1: 52. Distinguishing oneself with the pen was not easy in a culture burgeoning with publications and publishing houses. The rector/scholar Augustus Jessop observed that among all his acquaintances 'above the lower middle class', he knew 'no man of forty – except he be a country parson – who has not written a book', *Random Roaming, and Other Papers* (G. P. Putnam's, New York: 1893), p. 84.
8. An intellectual antagonist, Albert Venn Dicey, admitted that Morley 'had studied letters' in a way he suspected to be 'rare with either politicians or reviewers'. Letter to Lady Farrer, 1 December 1917, in R. Rait (ed.), *Memorials of Albert Venn Dicey: Being Chiefly Letters and Diaries* (Macmillan, London: 1925), p. 258. Among many examples of Morley's contemporary influence, see Albert Mordell, *Notorious Literary Attacks* (Boni and Liveright, New York: 1926), pp. xxxvii, 171–84; Gladstone quoting from *Burke* in the Irish debate of 16 March 1868, in M. R. D. Foot and H. C. G. Matthew (eds), *Gladstone Diaries, with Cabinet Minutes and Prime-Ministerial Correspondence*, 14 vols (Clarendon Press, Oxford: 1968–94), 6: 579; and George Meredith recommending *On Compromise* to Frederick Maxse as 'bold work that cannot but be beneficial', in C. L. Cline (ed.), *The Letters of George Meredith*, 3 vols (Clarendon Press, Oxford: 1970), 1: 490. Among examples in unexpected places, see the surprise of J. B. Atkins at the 'deep respect' afforded Morley's views by the Conservative Hooligans, in *Incidents and Reflections* (Christophers, London: 1947), p. 135; also Amy Strachey, *St. Loe Strachey: His Life and His Paper* (Victor Gollancz, London: 1930), p. 161. In terms of ongoing perceptions of influence, see Morley anthologized herein, pp. 4–8; H. Steeves and F. Ristine (eds), *Representative Essays in Modern Thought* (American Book Company, New York: 1913), pp. iii–iv, 141; W. Taylor, *Essays of the Past and Present* (Harper and Brothers, New York: 1927), pp. 394–401.
9. Upon receiving a long-awaited biography by Goschen of his grandfather, Morley reflected upon the contradictory imperatives of writing: 'You see I am an old hand in the authors' trade, and know all the temptations and

solicitations that beset it, unless the necessities of larder, cellar, wardrobe, and the rest drive one to resist fastidiousness.' Letter to Goschen of 8 February 1903, in A. Elliot, *The Life of George Joachim Goschen, First Viscount Goschen, 1831–1907*, 2 vols (Longmans, Green and Co., London: 1911) 2: 229.
10. The perception that Morley had risen above his class, though subtly expressed, was common. After a visit to Morley's house, Viscount Esher wrote to Maurice Brett of Morley's reminiscing on 'some Lancashire village in which he was born ... What then is the secret? Why has power been given by his fellow-countrymen to this man, who has inherited neither position nor wealth? ... I do not pretend to explain – but it is certainly not that he remained content with half-knowledge or low standards.' Letter of 31 December 1906, cited in J. Lees-Milne, *The Enigmatic Edwardian: The Life of Reginald, 2nd Viscount Esher* (Sidgwick and Jackson, London: 1986), p. 166. See, too, Rait, *Memorials of Dicey*, p. 257; S. Koss, *The Rise and Fall of the Political Press in Britain* (Fontana, London: 1990), p. 13.
11. L. Strachey, 'A statesman: Lord Morley', in *Characters and Commentaries* (Chatto and Windus, London: 1933), pp. 227–31.
12. J. A. Spender, 'John Morley', *Fortnightly Review* (December 1938), cited in Knickerbocker, *Free Minds*, p. 111.
13. Robertson Scott, *Life and Death of a Newspaper*, p. 48.
14. J. Morley, *Notes on Politics and History: A University Address* (Macmillan, London: 1914), p. 36.
15. One example here will suffice to suggest the sometimes unexpected course which literature may take. In 1888, Mrs. Humphry Ward published *Robert Elsmere*, the best-selling novel about an earnest young clergyman who lost his Christian faith to a higher secular Truth. Scholars have traditionally traced Ward's characters and attitudes to the Oxford of her youth, and to the influence of her famous family, she being the granddaughter of Dr Thomas Arnold, and the niece of Matthew Arnold. All of these undoubtedly played a part in the development of story and character. But the tone of the work reeks of what Ward called Morley's 'savage appeal to sincerity', and could never be mistaken for Arnoldian prose. Consider Elsmere's argument that miracles were to his time what the law had been to the early Christians. 'We must make up our minds about it one way or the other', he preached from his deathbed. 'And if we decide to throw it over as Paul threw over the law, then we must fight as he did. There is no help in subterfuge, no help in anything but a perfect sincerity. We must come out of it. The ground must be cleared; then may come the rebuilding': *Robert Elsmere* (John B. Alden, New York: n. d.), p. 655. Dozens of similar passages attest to the impress of *On Compromise* upon Robert Elsmere, and suggest the share that it had in the novel's controversial success. Cited in W. Staebler, *The Liberal Mind of John Morley* (Princeton University Press, Princeton: 1943), p. 182.
16. Cited in A. O. J. Cockshut, *Truth to Life: The Art of Biography in the Nineteenth Century* (Collins, London: 1974), p. 179.
17. J. H. Morgan, *John, Viscount Morley: An Appreciation and Some Reminiscences* (Houghton Mifflin, Boston: 1924), p. 191; J. Morley, *Recollections*, 2 vols (Macmillan, London: 1917), 2: 90–3.

18. See D. M. Schreuder, 'The making of Mr. Gladstone's posthumous career; the role of Morley and Knaplund as "monumental masons", 1903–27', in B. Kinzer (ed.), *The Gladstonian Turn of Mind: Essays Presented to J. B. Conacher* (University of Toronto Press, Toronto: 1985), pp. 197–214.
19. On the limits of Strachey's influence on the practice of political biography, see J. Powell, 'Official lives: Lytton Strachey, the queen's cabinet and the eminence of aesthetics', *Nineteenth-Century Prose* 22 (Fall 1995), pp. 129–52.
20. H. C. G. Matthew, *Gladstone, 1809–1874* (Clarendon Press, Oxford: 1986), p. 256.
21. M. Cowling, *Religion and Public Doctrine in Modern England*, 2 vols (Cambridge University Press, Cambridge: 1985), see below, Appendix IV, p. 224.
22. Knickerbocker, *Free Minds*, p. 171.
23. This can be readily seen in Morley's attitude toward Gladstone. At a time in 1877 when he was writing to Alexander Macmillan that Gladstone had 'nothing to say to men like you and me', Morley was not above urbanely begging Gladstone to contribute to his lists: 'If someday it occurs that there are any crumbs from your table after those older guests are satisfied, I will hope that the *Fortnightly Review* may have the benefit of them.' In the following year he complained to Chamberlain that 'the F. R. is the only magazine in which he does not write – the voluminous animal. Still, he's a famous mortal.' S. Nowell-Smith (ed.), *Letters to Macmillan* (Macmillan, London: 1967), p. 165; Hirst, *Early Life of Morley*, 2: 60; S. Koss, *John Morley at the India Office, 1905–1910* (Yale University Press, New Haven: 1969), p. 15n.
24. Morley as reader, for instance, is only mentioned once in passing in Hamer. Morley's influence is suggested, but only that, in 'John Morley's influence' in C. Morgan, *The House of Macmillan (1843–1943)* (Macmillan, New York: 1944), pp. 101–18. See, too, I. Nadel, *Biography: Fiction, Fact and Form* (St Martin's, New York: 1984), p. 32.
25. How different might the 1890s have been, for instance, had Morley not blasted Swinburne's *Poems and Ballads* in 1865 (182–91), or fourteen years later blocked Shaw's career as novelist and thus channelled it in other directions. This does not, however, imply that Morley alone was responsible for shaping careers, or that he always saw himself as a cultural guardian. Shaw recognized that in 1879 he was 'too young and raw to be possible'. M. Holroyd, *Bernard Shaw*, vol. I: *1856–1898: The Search for Love* (Knopf, New York: 1988), pp. 80, 204; J. W. Robertson Scott, *The Story of the Pall Mall Gazette, of its First Editor Frederick Greenwood, and of its Founder George Murray Smith* (Oxford University Press, London: 1950), p. 154.
26. J. Chamberlain, 'The Liberal Party and its leaders', *Fortnightly Review* 81, new series (1 September 1873), pp. 294–5. On the development of their relationship, see J. L. Garvin and L. S. Amery, *The Life of Joseph Chamberlain*, 6 vols (Macmillan, London: 1932–68), 1: 156–407; P. Marsh, 'Tearing the bonds: Chamberlain's separation from the Gladstonian liberals, 1885–6', in Kinzer (ed.), *Gladstonian Turn of Mind*, pp. 123–6. Hirst is inadequate on their friendship, as he focuses almost exclusively upon Morley's intellectual work.
27. M. Arnold, 'A word more about America' (February 1885), in *The Complete*

Prose Works of Matthew Arnold, 10 vols (University of Michigan Press, Ann Arbor, MI: 1974), 10: 215–16.
28. Garvin and Amery, *Life of Chamberlain*, 1: 361; Koss, *Rise and Fall of the Political Press*, pp. 240–1. Morley himself did not exaggerate his role, but it was widely recognized. Morley, *Recollections*, 1: 175–7.
29. Arnold, 'A word more about America', p. 216.
30. Cited in Nadel, *Biography*, pp. 30–8.
31. J. Kijinski, 'John Morley's "English men of letters series" and the politics of reading', *Victorian Studies* 34 (1991), p. 223.
32. See W. Dunn, *English Biography* (J. M. Dent, London: 1916), pp. 157–9; Nadel, *Biography*, p. 13.
33. J. A. Spender, *Life, Journalism and Politics*, 2 vols (Frederick A. Stokes, New York: 1927), 1: 29–30.
34. Hamer, *John Morley*, p. 72.
35. Morley, *Recollections*, 1: 125–32.
36. Hirst, *Early Life of Morley*, 1: 269. See, too, his later assurance to Austen Chamberlain, that 'not for untold publishers' royalties would he exchange the satisfaction of saying "yea" or "Nay" in great affairs of State for the solitude, the nervous exhaustion, the introspection of the life of letters'. Cited in Koss, *John Morley at the India Office*, p. 3.
37. Cited in Robertson Scott, *Life and Death of a Newspaper*, p. 30. Conversely, Gladstone, as man of action, tended to elevate the power of ideas: 'It seems to me that what we must do in the world of action, we at least may do in the world of thought ... Take any branch of mental effort, be it what it may, educative, creative, inquisitive, or materially productive, none should be pursued without a purpose, and all real purpose, though it may be atomic, is permanent and indestructible': W. Gladstone, 'Universitas hominum, or the unity of history', *North American Review* 373 (December 1887), p. 602. This mutual respect for their differing spheres of achievement played a significant part in the friendship between Morley and Gladstone.
38. Hirst, *Early Life of Morley*, 1: 248–9.
39. Cited in A. Chamberlain, *Politics from Inside: An Epistolary Chronicle, 1906–1914* (Cassell, London: 1936), p. 69. See, too, Spender, *Life, Journalism and Politics*, 2: 150.
40. By way of contrast, see the true intellectual's defence of his craft in ideas, culminating in the wish that 'Mr. Disraeli could have stuck to his novels instead of rising to be prime minister of England ... Persons who think the creation of a majority in the House of Commons a worthy reward for the labours of a lifetime will, of course, differ from this conclusion.' Leslie Stephen, 'Mr. Disraeli's novels', *Fortnightly Review* 16 (July–December 1874), p. 430. Morley would have agreed in wishing that Disraeli 'had stuck to his novels', but only because it would have saved the country so much political trouble.
41. Koss, *John Morley at the India Office*, pp. 10–11.
42. Goldwin Smith to G. W. Prothero, 23 February 1903, in Arnold Haultain (ed.), *A Selection from Goldwin Smith's Correspondence* (London: n. d.), pp. 393–4. See, too, Hutchinson, *Portraits of the Eighties* (T. Fisher Unwin, London: 1920), p. 65.

43. H. C. G. Matthew, *Gladstone, 1875–1898* (Clarendon Press, Oxford: 1995), p. 331.
44. Cited in Robertson Scott, *Life and Death of a Newspaper*, p. 49.
45. E. T. Raymond, 'John Morley', in *Portraits of the Nineties* (Charles Scribner's Sons, New York: n. d.), p. 167.
46. The question of Lady Morley's origins is thoroughly covered in J. W. Bicknell and C. L. Cline, 'Who was Lady Morley?', *Victorian Newsletter* 44 (Fall 1973), pp. 28–31.
47. Robert Rhodes James, *Rosebery: A Biography of Archibald Philip, Fifth Earl of Rosebery* (Weidenfeld and Nicolson, London: 1963), p. 310.
48. Speculation that Morley was homosexual or bisexual is common, though published implications are subtle, and perhaps subconscious. See, for instance, Edward Alexander's estimation of Morley's use of the words 'manly' and 'wholesome' in describing favoured writers, the frequent use of which 'twentieth-century readers (perhaps wrongly) find suspicious'. E. Alexander, *John Morley* (Twayne, New York: 1972), p. 142.
49. These limitations have led to a fresh approach to intellectual history, which seeks 'a balance between human familiarity and cultural remoteness'. S. Collini, *Public Moralists: Political Thought and Intellectual Life in Britain, 1850–1930* (Clarendon Press, Oxford: 1991), p. 1.
50. R. Davenport-Hines, *The Macmillans* (Mandarin, London: 1993), p. 82.
51. Courtney, 'John Morley', p. 772.
52. One imagines a sniggering typesetter congratulating himself on his cleverness in secretively upstaging a pious Morley by omitting a hyphen in the following sentence:

    ... The currency of the notion that earnest sin
    cerity about one's opinions and ideals of conduct ...

    J. Morley, *On Compromise* (Macmillan, London: 1886), p. 248.
53. Staebler, *Liberal Mind of Morley*, p. 182.
54. Cited in Garvin and Amery, *Life of Chamberlain*, 1: 127, 332.
55. J. Morley, *Burke*, English Men of Letters series (Macmillan, London: 1885), p. 208.
56. Letter to Chamberlain of 9 December 1875, cited in Hamer, *John Morley*, p. 115. Cf. the critics' expectations of 'Mr. Morley's peculiar vein of historico-biographical criticism': 'John Morley's essays', *Contemporary Review* 30 (June–November 1877), p. 516.
57. J. H. Morgan, *John, Viscount Morley*, p. 36; See, too, F. Whyte, *The Life of W. T. Stead*, 2 vols (Jonathan Cape, London: n. d.), 1: 90; Hirst, *Early Life of Morley*, 2: 193.
58. Cockshut, *Truth to Life*, pp. 178–9.
59. J. H. Morgan, *John, Viscount Morley*, p. 36.
60. Note W. T. Stead's surprise at Morley's 'frank humility' in admitting that 'he had changed his mind or had abandoned an untenable position'. In this case, Morley did not renounce his religious views, but he may well have wavered in the strength with which he held them. Whyte, *Life of Stead*, 1: 78–9.
61. J. H. Morgan, 'The works of Lord Morley', *Times Literary Supplement*, 11 February 1921, p. 81; Hirst, *Early Life of Morley*, 1: xii.

62. J. St Loe Strachey, 'Lord Morley: a personal recollection', *Spectator*, 29 September 1923, p. 415. On the same point, see Whyte, *Life of Stead*, 1: 76.
63. Spender, *Life, Journalism and Politics*, 1: 72. See, too, Whyte, *Life of Stead*, 1: 76; Robertson Scott, *Life and Death of a Newspaper*, p. 51; Raymond, 'John Morley', pp. 167–8'; H. W. Massingham, 'Morley the humanist', *Fortnightly Review* 114 (July–December 1923), p. 695; W. L. S. Churchill, 'John Morley', in *Great Contemporaries* (Reprint Society, London: 1941), p. 83.
64. Morley, *Recollections*, 1: 102; Maurice Baring, *The Puppet Show of Memory* (Little, Brown, Boston: 1922), p. 381.
65. Among many references, see Churchill, *Great Contemporaries*, p. 85; Hamer, *John Morley*, pp. 245–7; Robertson Scott, *Life and Death of a Newspaper*, pp. 25, n3, 28; Knickerbocker, *Free Minds*, pp. 175–6; Staebler, *Liberal Mind of Morley*, p. 182; Massingham, 'Morley the humanist', p. 695; P. Ziegler, *Wilson: The Authorised Life of Lord Wilson of Rievaulx* (Weidenfeld and Nicolson, London: 1993), p. 19; M. DeWolfe Howe (ed.), *Holmes–Laski Letters: The Correspondence of Mr. Justice Holmes and Harold J. Laski, 1916– 1935*, 2 vols (Harvard University Press, Cambridge, Mass.: 1953), 1: 593.
66. Collini, *Public Moralists*, p. 103.
67. Hamer, *John Morley*, pp. 2–6.
68. C. A. Kent, *Brains and Numbers: Elitism, Comtism, and Democracy in mid-Victorian England* (University of Toronto Press, Toronto: 1978), pp. 124–33; Cowling, *Religion and Public Doctrine in Modern England*, pp. 171–6. See below, Appendices III and IV, pp. 210–27.
69. As Collini warned, one should not be too ready to mine articles published in the periodical press for views and theories, for they were usually written within the confines of certain preconditions characteristic of the genre. I would add that they were always written within a peculiar set of public and personal circumstances, which affected tone, rhetoric and construction. Collini, *Public Moralists*, pp. 51–2.
70. Unless otherwise indicated, quotations in this and the following seven paragraphs regarding events leading to the publication of *On Compromise* are taken from Hirst, *Early Life of Morley*, 1: 238–53.
71. J. F. Stephen, *Liberty, Equality, Fraternity*, ed. S. Warner (Liberty Fund, Indianapolis: 1993), p. 229.
72. Sixteen years later, Beatrice Webb ironically accused Morley of much the same thing – of being 'a mere moral preacher of old-fashioned commonplaces' – which simply demonstrates how relative to time and temperament are all critical assessments. Norman and Jeanne MacKenzie (eds), *The Diary of Beatrice Webb*, vol. I: *1873–1892, Glitter Around and Darkness Within* (Belknap Press, Cambridge, Mass.: 1982), p. 348.
73. Cline, *Letters of Meredith*, 1: 484–92.
74. Harrison had suggested that he make his style 'simpler'. It has the 'elements of by far the best English now written – bar George Eliot alone' – yet was 'not at its best, by reason of its excessive richness, audacity and complexity'. Hirst, *Early Life of Morley*, 1: 250. Meredith noted 'phrases running with sentences that are cast in a tone too purely argumentative for that proper to the essay: showing as it were the want of absolute compression of your

own thought in awaiting the objections of an opponent.' Cited in Cline, *Letters of Meredith*, 1: 492.
75. *Athenaeum*, 17 October 1874, p. 505. See below, Appendix I, p. 193.
76. One might argue that Arnold followed his own notion of good style: 'to have something to say, and to say it as clearly as you can'. But after reading his criticism, full of the keenest insight into the inherent ambiguities associated with morality and culture, one is often left wondering where Arnold himself stood. His 'theology', for instance, was subtle, and hence unclear. Morley left no one in doubt as to his theology, at least not in his formal writing. See G. W. E. Russell, *Collections and Recollections* (Thomas Nelson, London: n. d.), p. 139; A. Briggs (ed.), *Gladstone's Boswell: Late Victorian Conversations by Lionel A. Tollemache and Other Documents* (Harvester Press, Sussex: 1984), p. 50; S. Lipman, 'Did Arnold believe in God?', *Nineteenth-Century Prose* 21 (Fall 1994), pp. 1–7.
77. Cited in Hirst, *Early Life of Morley*, 2: 56–7.
78. Morley, *Burke*, p. [v]. Morley's journalistic mindset is further evident in his attitude towards the use made by others of his work. See below, pp. 228–9, 233.
79. J. Morley to Frederick Macmillan, 12 October 1920, Macmillan Archives, British Library, Add. MS. 55057, f. 107.
80. J. H. Morgan, 'Works of Lord Morley', p. 82; idem, *John, Viscount Morley*, pp. 38–9; Morley, *Recollections*, 1: 99–102.
81. 'Mr. John Morley's essays', *Contemporary Review* 30 (June–Nov. 1877), p. 517 (herein, pp. 205–6).
82. Strachey, 'A statesman: Lord Morley', p. 231.
83. Massingham, 'Morley the humanist', p. 702.
84. Whyte, *Life of Stead*, 1: 91.
85. J. Morley, *Speech on the Occasion of Unveiling the Gladstone Statue, Manchester, October 23, 1901* (Macmillan, London: 1901), pp. 28–31.
86. Morley, *Burke*, p. 3.
87. Nowell-Smith, *Letters to Macmillan*, p. 165.
88. Hirst, *Early Life of Morley*, 1: xii.
89. B. Balfour (ed.), *Personal and Literary Letters of Robert, First Earl of Lytton*, 2 vols (Longmans, Green, London: 1906), 1: 325.
90. Morley, *Recollections*, 1: 63.

Bibliography

The modern view of Morley has been substantially shaped by twentieth-century admirers who had little or no personal knowledge of his life before the age of forty. Unlike many Cabinet politicians who served apprenticeships in office and thus elicited notice early in their careers, Morley was little written about before entering politics. Though known as an author, he was foremost a journalist and thus did not command the kind of biographical attention paid to systematic philosophers or social critics. The extent of his influence as an editor was hidden behind the scenes and only gradually came to light. As a result, by the time he had become newsworthy, his youthful eccentricities, quirks and inconsistencies were shrouded, as were important facets of his personality.

Nor was Morley an exhibitionist who later revelled in public disclosures of his private life. He kept few letters, neither did many of his early correspondents, and he was not anxious to fill in the blanks. Our best and indispensable guide to his early life remains Francis Hirst, who was not born until Morley was thirty-five and did not know his mentor before the age of sixty. As necessary as is the official *Early Life and Letters of John Morley*, Hirst again and again betrays the fact that he did not know Morley as a young man, and that he received few private confidences. In 1927 Hirst did a good service by showing that Morley had not always been 'cautious', 'responsible' and 'slow to action', but he had an inordinate reverence for Morley's writings and their ability to convey the complexities of his inner life. One can hardly accept at face value the work of a biographer who argues of his subject, that, 'from the day he assumed the editorship of the *Fortnightly*, down to the very last efforts of enfeebled voice and trembling pen, a golden thread of consistent idealism runs unbroken' (Hirst, *Early Life of Morley*, 1: xii; 2: 133).

I. Manuscript Sources

Macmillan Archives, British Library. Contains extensive correspondence relating to Morley's forty-year association with Macmillan, including material on revisions for *On Compromise.*

Morley Papers

India Office Library. Official papers while serving as Secretary of State for India.

A. F. Thompson, Wadham College, Oxford. Morley disliked accumulations of paper, so never developed the extensive archives characteristic of many of his political colleagues. At his death, what had been amassed was left to his sister Grace, who, in accordance with his will, immediately began to destroy letters and other papers containing personal references. Morley's friend and biographer, F. W. Hirst, persuaded her to refrain from further destruction, and it was the remaining papers that Hirst used for his *Early Life and Letters of John Morley.* In 1950 Hirst gave these papers to Edmund Boyle, Conservative MP for the Handsworth division of Birmingham (1950–70), who intended to write on Morley, but did not. In 1962 Boyle handed them to A. F. Thompson, who intends to deposit them eventually in the Bodleian Library.

According to Thompson, the papers contain little on Morley's writings, and nothing, so far as he can find, on the origins and development of *On Compromise.*

Ashburne Hall, University of Manchester. Houses Morley's extensive library, including a proof copy of a book which he wrote but did not publish, and a commonplace book containing quotations and related notes.

II. Secondary Sources

Books

Alexander, E., *John Morley.* New York, 1972. A good introduction to
    Morley's career as man of letters.
Arx, J. von, *Progress and Pessimism: Religion, Politics, and History in Late
    Nineteenth-Century Britain.* Cambridge, Mass., 1985. Contains a

thoughtful chapter on 'John Morley and the politics of destruction', in which the context of the contemporary English scholarship of men like Leslie Stephen and W. H. Lecky is incorporated along with the rarefied philosophy of Comte and Mill.

Bicknell, J., 'The Unbelievers', in Richard deLaura (ed.), *Victorian Prose Writers: A Guide to Research*. New York, 1974.

Churchill, W. L. S., 'John Morley', in *Great Contemporaries*. London, 1941.

Cockshut, A. O. J., *Truth to Life: The Art of Biography in the Nineteenth Century*. London, 1974.

Cowling, M., *Religion and Public Doctrine in Modern England*, vol. 2: *Assaults*. Cambridge, 1985.

Das, M. N., *India under Morley and Minto*. London, 1964.

Davenport-Hines, R., *The Macmillans*. London, 1993.

Gardiner, A. G., 'Lord Morley of Blackburn', in *Prophets, Priests and Kings*. London, 1908.

Gross, J., *The Rise and Fall of the Man of Letters*. New York, 1969.

Hamer, D. A., *John Morley: Liberal Intellectual in Politics*. Oxford, 1968. The essential guide to Morley's intellectual landscape, based upon the whole of his published work. Includes a bibliography of Morley's writings.

Hirst, F. W., *Early Life and Letters of John Morley*, 2 vols. London, 1927. The indispensable starting point for understanding Morley's character and early career, though decidedly partisan.

Kent, C., *Brains and Numbers: Elitism, Comtism, and Democracy in Mid-Victorian England*. Toronto, 1976.

Knickerbocker, F. W., *Free Minds: John Morley and His Friends*. Cambridge, Mass., 1943.

Koss, S., *John Morley at the India Office*. New Haven, 1969. The best extensive treatment of Morley as politician; especially useful for references to evaluations in the Indian press.

—— *The Rise and Fall of the Political Press in Britain*. London, 1990. The definitive encyclopedic treatment of press connections.

Morgan, C., *The House of Macmillan (1843-1943)*. London, 1944.

Morgan, J. H., *John, Viscount Morley: An Appreciation and Some Reminiscences*. London, 1924.

Morley, J., *Burke*, English Men of Letters series. London, 1885.

—— *Nineteenth-Century Essays*, ed. P. Stansky. Chicago, 1970. Reprints fifteen of Morley's essays from the *Fortnightly Review*, along with a brief but perceptive introduction to his periodical writings.

—— *Recollections*, 2 vols. London, 1917.

—— *Speech on the Occasion of Unveiling the Gladstone Statue, Manchester, October 23, 1901*. London, 1901.
Nadel, I., *Biography: Fact, Fiction and Form*. New York, 1984.
Nowell-Smith, S. (ed.), *Letters to Macmillan*. London, 1967.
Powell, J., *Art, Truth and High Politics: A Bibliographic Study of the Official Lives of Queen Victoria's Ministers in Cabinet, 1843–1969*. Metuchen, NJ, 1996.
Robertson Scott, J. W., *The Life and Death of a Newspaper: An Account of the Temperaments, Perturbations and Achievements of John Morley, W. T. Stead, E. T. Cook, Harry Cust, J. L. Garvin and three other Editors of the* Pall Mall Gazette. London, 1952.
—— *The Story of the* Pall Mall Gazette, *of its First Editor Frederick Greenwood, and of its Founder George Murray Smith*. London, 1950.
Schreuder, D. M., 'The making of Mr. Gladstone's posthumous career: the role of Morley and Knaplund as "monumental masons", 1903–27', in B. Kinzer (ed.), *The Gladstonian Turn of Mind: Essays Presented to J. B. Conacher*. Toronto, 1985.
Sirdar, Ali Khan Sayed, *Life of Lord Morley*. London, 1923.
Spender, J. A., *Life, Journalism and Politics*. New York, 1927.
—— *The Public Life*, 2 vols. London, 1925.
Staebler, W., *The Liberal Mind of John Morley*. Princeton, 1943.
Stansky, P., *Ambitions and Strategies: The Struggle for the Leadership of the Liberal Party in the 1890s*. Oxford, 1964.
Strachey, L., 'A statesman: Lord Morley', in *Characters and Commentaries*. London, 1933.
Sullivan, A., *British Literary Magazines: The Victorian and Edwardian Age, 1837–1913*. Westport, CT, 1984.
Wolpert, S., *Morley and India, 1906–1910*. Berkeley, 1967.

Articles

Anon., review of *Critical Miscellenies*, in *Athenaeum*, 21 July 1877, pp. 71–2.
Anon., review of *On Compromise*, in *Athenaeum*, 17 October 1874, pp. 505–6. See below, Appendix I.
Anon., 'Mr. John Morley's essays', *Contemporary Review* 30 (June–November 1877), pp. 515–16.
Bicknell, J. W. and C. L. Cline, 'Who was Lady Morley?', *Victorian Newsletter* 44 (1973), pp. 28–31.
Courtney, W. L. and J. E., 'John Morley: 1838–1923', *North American Review* 218 (1923), pp. 765–75.

Escott, T. H. S., 'John Morley', *Fortnightly Review* 114 (July–December 1923), pp. 703–12.

Foot, M. R. D., 'Morley's Gladstone: a reappraisal', *Bulletin of the John Rylands Library* 51 (1968–9), pp. 368–80.

Hayley, W., 'John Morley', *American Scholar* 51 (Summer 1982), pp. 403–9.

Kijinski, J., 'John Morley's "English men of letters" series and the politics of reading', *Victorian Studies* 34 (1991), pp. 205–25.

Koss, S., 'Morley in the middle', *English Historical Review* 82 (1967), pp. 553–61.

Mallock, W. H., 'Mr. John Morley's collected writings', *Quarterly Review* 168 (January–April 1889), pp. 249–80. See below, Appendix II.

Massingham, H. W., 'Morley the humanist', *Fortnightly Review* 114 (July–December 1923), pp. 695–702.

Morgan, J. H., 'The works of Lord Morley', *Times Literary Supplement*, 11 February 1921, pp. 81–2. Substantially reproduced in his *John, Viscount Morley: An Appreciation and Some Reminiscences* (1924).

Spender, J. A., 'Lord Morley, last of the Victorian liberals', *Living Age* 319 (1923), pp. 207–10.

St Loe Strachey, J., 'Lord Morley: a personal recollection', *Spectator*, 29 September 1923, pp. 415–16.

A Note on the Text

There are four variants of the text of *On Compromise*, though the main lines of Morley's argument did not change. As the manuscript itself has not been located (and probably was not kept), the text of this edition follows the '2nd edition revised', published by Chapman and Hall in 1877. Excepting minor printer's corrections, this edition remained unchanged until Morley significantly revised portions of it for the Edition deLuxe of his collected works, published early in 1921. Substantial differences between the various texts are indicated in the Editor's Notes. Essential characteristics of each variant are noted below:

1. *Fortnightly Review* version

Morley's study was initially published in a series of four articles in the *Fortnightly Review* (April–August 1874). Reference to these articles is abbreviated throughout this edition as *FR*.

2. First book edition

In October 1874, an expanded version was published in book form in Britain by Chapman and Hall, selling for 7s. 6d. (37½ p). Macmillan owned rights in the United States. Responding to criticisms of the *FR* text, Morley selectively revised the work, restating some arguments for clarity, shortening sentences and paring superfluous words.

3. Second edition revised

Three years later Chapman and Hall produced a '2nd edition revised' at 3s. 6d. (17½ p), in which Morley added 'three or four additional illustrations in the footnotes', and heightened the strident tone which became its most characteristic feature. In print continuously for forty-four years (1877–1921), it was in this version that *On Compromise* was most widely read. Macmillan first published the '2nd edition revised' in Great Britain in 1886 at 5s. (25p). It became a staple on their list, being reprinted in 1891, 1893, 1896, 1898, 1901, 1903, 1906, 1908, 1910, 1913, 1917 and 1921.

4. Edition deLuxe

During 1920 Morley significantly revised some portions of *On Compromise*, especially Chapter Five, as part of a general revision of his collected works, published early in 1921 as the 'definitive Edition de Luxe', and selling for 31s. (£3.75). The text in all subsequent editions followed that of the Edition deLuxe.

When Macmillan added *On Compromise* to its inexpensive 'Caravan Library' in 1928, the text of the Edition deLuxe was retained, adding a modified version of Morley's 'A word of epilogue', drawn from his *Recollections* (1917). Using the Caravan Library edition as a model, in 1933 Watts added *On Compromise* to its 'Thrift Library' at 1s. 6d. (7½p). This edition remained in print into the 1950s.

All footnotes are Morley's. Editorial notes, marked with a dagger (†) in the text, will be found on pp. 175–81.

'It makes all the difference in the world whether we put Truth in the first place or in the second place.'

WHATELY

JOHN MORLEY

On Compromise

Note

The writer has availed himself of the opportunity of a new edition, to add three or four additional illustrations in the foot-notes. The criticisms on the first edition call for no remark, excepting this, perhaps, – that the present little volume has no pretensions to be anything more than an Essay. To judge such a performance as if it professed to be an exhaustive Treatise in casuistry, is to subject it to tests which it was never designed to bear. Merely to open questions, to indicate points, to suggest cases, to sketch outlines, – as an Essay does all these things, – may often be a process not without its own modest usefulness and interest.

May 4, 1877.

Note to the First Edition

The chapters which form the present volume have already appeared in the *Fortnightly Review*. They have since been submitted to careful revision; some of the arguments have been re-stated; and considerable additions have been made to the discussion, with a view to meeting various criticisms that were offered upon some parts of the essay in their original shape.

September 25, 1874.

Contents

CHAPTER I

Introductory

Design of this Essay	52
The question stated	53
Suggested by some existing tendencies in England	53
Comparison with other countries	54
Test of this comparison	55
The absent quality specifically defined	55
History and decay of some recent aspirations	56
Illustrations	57
Characteristics of our present mood	58
Analysis of its causes	
(1) Influence of French examples	60
(2) Influence of the Historic Method	63
(3) Influence of the Newspaper Press	65
(4) Increase of material prosperity	65
(5) Transformation of the spiritual basis of thought	66
(6) Influence of a State Church	67

CHAPTER II

Of the Possible Utility of Error

Question of a dual doctrine lies at the outset of our inquiry	70
This doctrine formulated	70
Marks the triumph of *status quo*	72
Psychological vindication of such a doctrine	72
Answered by assertion of the dogmatic character of popular belief	73
And the pernicious social influence of its priests	74
The root idea of the defenders of a dual doctrine	75
Thesis of the present chapter, against that idea	75
Examination of some of the pleas for error	77

I.	That a false opinion may be clothed with good associations	77
II.	That all minds are not open to reason	78
III.	That a false opinion, considered in relation to the general mental attitude, may be less hurtful than its premature demolition	80
IV.	That mere negative truth is not a guide	83
V.	That error has been a stepping-stone to truth	83

We cannot tell how much truth has been missed   85
Inevitableness is not utility   86

CHAPTER III

Intellectual Responsibility and the Political Spirit

The modern *disciplina arcani*   88
Hume's immoral advice   89
Evil intellectual effects of immoral compromise   89
Depravation that follows its grosser forms   91
The three provinces of compromise   92
Radical importance of their separation   93
Effects of their confusion in practical politics   93
Economy or management in the Formation of opinion   94
Its lawfulness turns on the claims of majority and minority over one another   95
Thesis of the present chapter   95
Its importance, owing to the supremacy of the political spirit in England   96
Effects of the predominance of this spirit   97
Contrasted with epochs of intellectual responsibility   100
A modern movement against the political spirit   100
An objection considered   102
Importance to character of rationalised conviction, and of ideals   102
The absence of them attenuates conduct   103
Illustrations in modern politics   103
Modern latitudinarianism   105
Illustration in two supreme issues   105
Pascal's remarks upon a state of Doubt   106
Dr. Newman on the same   107
Three ways of dealing with these issues   108
Another illustration of intellectual improbity   109
The Savoyard Vicar   110

Mischievousness of substituting spiritual self-indulgence for
reason   111

CHAPTER IV

Religious Conformity

Compromise in Expression	112
Touches religion rather than politics	112
Hume on non-resistance	112
Reason why rights of free speech do not exactly coincide with rights of free thought	113
Digression into the matter of free speech	114
Dissent no longer railing and vituperative	114
Tendency of modern free thought to assimilate some elements from the old faith	115
A wide breach still remains	117
Heresy, however, no longer traced to depravity	118
Tolerance not necessarily acquiescence in scepticism	119
Object of the foregoing digression	120
The rarity of plain-speaking a reason why it is painful	121
Conformity in the relationship between child and parent	121
Between husband and wife	123
In the education of children	130
The case of an unbelieving priest	133
The case of one who fears to lose his influence	133
Conformity not harmless nor unimportant	135

CHAPTER V

The Realisation of Opinion

The application of opinion to conduct	137
Tempering considerations	137
Not to be pressed too far	138
Our action in realising our opinions depends on our social theory	139
Legitimate and illegitimate compromise in view of that	140
The distinction equally sound on the evolutional theory	140
Condition of progressive change	141
A plea for compromise examined	142

A second plea	143
The allegation of provisional usefulness examined	144
Illustrated in religious institutions	145
In political institutions	146
Burke's commendation of political compromise	148
The saying that small reforms may be the worst enemies of great ones	149
In what sense true	149
Illustration in the Elementary Education Act	149
Wisdom of social patience	150
The considerations which apply to political practice do not apply to our own lives	151
Nor to the publication of social opinions	151
The amount of conscience in a community	152
Evil of attenuating this element	153
Historic illustration	153
New side of the discussion	153
Is earnestness of conviction fatal to concession of liberty to others?	153
Two propositions at the base of an affirmative answer	154
Earnestness of conviction consistent with sense of liability to error	154
Belief in one's own infallibility does not necessarily lead to intolerance	155
The contrary notion due to juristic analogies in social discussion	156
Connection between the doctrine of liberty and social evolution	157
The timid compromiser's superfluous apprehension	159
Material limits to the effect of moral speculation	159
Illustration from the history of Slavery	159
Illustration from French history	161
Practical influence of a faith in the self-protecting quality of a society	163
Conclusion	163

APPENDIX. *note to page 154*

The Doctrine of Liberty	165

On Compromise†

Chapter I

Introductory

The design of the following essay is to consider, in a short and direct way, some of the limits that are set by sound reason to the practice of the various arts of accommodation, economy, management, conformity, or compromise. The right of thinking freely and acting independently, of using our minds without excessive awe of authority, and shaping our lives without unquestioning obedience to custom, is now a finally accepted principle in some sense or other with every school of thought that has the smallest chance of commanding the future. Under what circumstances does the exercise and vindication of the right, thus conceded in theory, become a positive duty in practice? If the majority are bound to tolerate dissent from the ruling opinions and beliefs, under what conditions and within what limitations is the dissentient imperatively bound to avail himself of this toleration? How far, and in what way, ought respect either for immediate practical convenience, or for current prejudices, to weigh against respect for truth? For how much is it well that the individual should allow the feelings and convictions of the many to count, when he comes to shape, to express, and to act upon, his own feelings and convictions? Are we only to be permitted to defend general principles, on condition that we draw no practical inferences from them? Is every other idea to yield precedence and empire to existing circumstances, and is the immediate and universal workableness of a policy to be the main test of its intrinsic fitness?

To attempt to answer all these questions fully would be nothing less than to attempt a compendium of life and duty in all their details, a Summa of cases of conscience, a guide to doubters at every point of the compass. The aim of the present writer is a comparatively modest one; namely, to seek one or two of the most general principles which ought to regulate the practice of compliance, and to suggest some of the bearings which they may have in their application to certain difficulties in modern matters of conduct.

It is pretty plain that an inquiry of this kind needs to be fixed by reference to a given set of social circumstances tolerably well understood. There are some common rules as to the expediency of compromise and conformity, but their application is a matter of endless variety and the widest elasticity. The interesting and useful thing is to find the relation of these too vague rules to actual conditions; to transform them into practical guides and real interpreters of what is right and best in thought and conduct, in a special and definite kind of emergency. According to the current assumptions of the writer and the preacher, the one commanding law is that men should cling to truth and right, if the very heavens fall. In principle this is universally accepted. To the partisans of authority and tradition it is as much a commonplace as to the partisans of the most absolute and unflinching rationalism. Yet in practice all schools alike are forced to admit the necessity of a measure of accommodation in the very interests of truth itself. Fanatic is a name of such ill repute, exactly because one who deserves to be called by it injures good causes by refusing timely and harmless concession; by irritating prejudices that a wiser way of urging his own opinion might have turned aside; by making no allowances, respecting no motives, and recognising none of those qualifying principles, which are nothing less than necessary to make his own principle true and fitting in a given society. The interesting question in connection with compromise obviously turns upon the placing of the boundary that divides wise suspense in forming opinions, wise reserve in expressing them, and wise tardiness in trying to realise them, from unavowed disingenuousness and self-illusion, from voluntary dissimulation, and from indolence and pusillanimity. These are the three departments or provinces of compromise. Our subject is a question of boundaries.[1] And this question, being mainly one of time and circumstance, may be most satisfactorily discussed in relation to the time and the circumstances which we know best, or at least whose deficiencies and requirements are most pressingly visible to us.[†]

Though England counts her full share of fearless truth-seekers in most departments of inquiry, yet there is on the whole no weakening, but a rather marked confirmation, of what has become an inveterate national characteristic, and has long been recognised as such; a profound distrust, namely, of all general principles; a profound dislike both of much reference to them, and of any disposition to invest them with practical authority; and a silent but most pertinacious measurement of philosophic truths by political tests. 'It is not at all easy, humanly speaking,' says one who has tried the experiment, 'to wind an Englishman up to the level of dogma.' The difficulty has extended further than the dogma of theology. The supposed antagonism between expediency

---

[1] See below, ch. iii.

and principle has been pressed further and further away from the little piece of true meaning that it ever could be rightly allowed to have, until it has now come to signify the paramount wisdom of counting the narrow, immediate, and personal expediency for everything, and the whole, general, ultimate, and completed expediency for nothing. Principle is only another name for a proposition stating the terms of one of these larger expediencies. When principle is held in contempt, or banished to the far dreamland of the philosopher and the student, with an affectation of reverence that in a materialist generation is in truth the most overweening kind of contempt, this only means that men are thinking much of the interests of to-day, and little of the more ample interests of the many days to come. It means that the conditions of the time are unfriendly to the penetration and the breadth of vision which disclose to us the whole range of consequences that follow on certain kinds of action or opinion, and unfriendly to the intrepidity and disinterestedness which make us willing to sacrifice our own present ease or near convenience, in the hope of securing higher advantages for others or for ourselves in the future.

Let us take politics, for example. What is the state of the case with us, if we look at national life in its broadest aspect? A German has his dream of a great fatherland which shall not only be one and consolidated, but shall in due season win freedom for itself, and be as a sacred hearth whence others may borrow the warmth of freedom and order for themselves. A Spaniard has his vision either of militant loyalty to God and the saints and the exiled line of his kings, or else of devotion to the newly won liberty and to the raising up of his fallen nation. An American, in the midst of the political corruption which for the moment obscures the great democratic experiment,† yet has his imagination kindled by the size and resources of his land, and his enthusiasm fired by the high destinies which he believes to await its people in the centuries to come. A Frenchman, republican or royalist, with all his frenzies and 'fool-fury' of red or white, still has his hope and dream and aspiration, with which to enlarge his life and lift him on an ample pinion out from the circle of a poor egoism. What stirs the hope and moves the aspiration of our Englishman? Surely nothing either in the heavens above or on the earth beneath. The English are as a people little susceptible in the region of the imagination. But they have done good work in the world, acquired a splendid historic tradition of stout combat for good causes, founded a mighty and beneficent empire; and they have done all this notwithstanding their deficiencies of imagination. Their lands have been the home of great and forlorn causes, though they could not always follow the transcendental flights of their foreign allies and champions. If Englishmen were not strong in imagination, they were what is better and surer, strong in their hold of the great emancipating principles. What great political cause, her own or another's, is England befriending to-day? To say that no great cause is left, is to tell us that we have reached the final stage of human progress, and turned over the last leaf in the volume of human improvements. The day when this is said and believed, marks the end of a nation's life. Is it possible that, after all, our old protestant spirit, with its rationality, its austerity, its steady political energy, has been struck with something of the mortal fatigue that seizes catholic societies after their fits of revolution?†

We need not forget either the atrocities or the imbecilities which mark the course of modern politics on the Continent. I am as keenly alive as any one to the levity of France, and the ὕβρις of Germany. It may be true that the ordinary Frenchman is in some respects the victim of as poor an egoism as that of the ordinary Englishman; and that the American has no advantage over us in certain kinds of magnanimous sentiment. What is important is the mind and attitude, not of the ordinary man, but of those who should be extraordinary. The decisive sign of the elevation of a nation's life is to be sought among those who lead or ought to lead. The test of the health of a people is to be found in the utterances of those who are its spokesmen, and in the action of those whom it accepts or chooses to be its chiefs. We have to look to the magnitude of the issues and the height of the interests which engage its foremost spirits. What are the best men in a country striving for? And is the struggle pursued intrepidly and with a sense of its size and amplitude, or with creeping foot and blinking eye? The answer to these questions is the answer to the other question, whether the best men in the country are small or great. It is a commonplace that the manner of doing things is often as important as the things done. And it has been pointed out more than once that England's most creditable national action constantly shows itself so poor and mean in expression that the rest of Europe can discern nothing in it but craft and sinister interest. Our public opinion is often rich in wisdom, but we lack the courage of our wisdom. We execute noble achievements, and then are best pleased to find shabby reasons for them.

There is a certain quality attaching alike to thought and expression and action, for which we may borrow the name of grandeur. It has been noticed, for instance, that Bacon strikes and impresses us, not merely by the substantial merit of what he achieved, but still more by a certain greatness of scheme and conception. This quality is not a mere idle decoration. It is not a theatrical artifice of mask or buskin, to impose upon us unreal impressions of height and dignity. The added greatness is real. Height of aim and nobility of expression are true forces. They grow to be an obligation upon us. A lofty sense of personal worth is one of the surest elements of greatness. That the lion should love to masquerade in the ass's skin is not modesty and reserve, but imbecility and degradation. And that England should wrap herself in the robe of small causes and mean reasons is the more deplorable, because there is no nation in the world the substantial elements of whose power are so majestic and imperial as our own. Our language is the most widely spoken of all tongues, its literature is second to none in variety and power. Our people, whether English or American, have long ago superseded the barbarous device of dictator and Cæsar by the manly arts of self-government. We understand that peace and industry are the two most indispensable conditions of modern civilisation, and we draw the lines of our policy in accordance with such a conviction. We have had imposed upon us by the unlucky prowess of our ancestors the task of ruling a vast number of millions of alien dependents. We undertake it with a disinterestedness, and execute it with a skill of administration, to which history supplies no parallel, and which, even if time should show that the conditions of the problem were insoluble, will still remain for ever admirable. All these are elements of true pre-eminence. They are calculated to inspire us with the loftiest consciousness of national life. They ought to clothe our voice with authority, to nerve our action by generous resolution, and to fill our counsels with weightiness and power.

Within the last forty years England has lost one by one each of those enthusiasms which may have been illusions, – some of them undoubtedly were so, – but which at least testified to the existence among us, in a very considerable degree, of a vivid belief in the possibility of certain broad general theories being true and right, as well as in the obligation of making them lights to practical conduct and desire. People a generation ago had eager sympathy with Hungary, with Italy, with Poland, because they were deeply impressed by the doctrine of nationalities. They had again a generous and energetic hatred of such an institution as the negro slavery of America, because justice and humanity and religion were too real and potent forces within their breasts to allow them to listen to those political considerations by which American statesmen used to justify temporising and compromise. They had strong feelings about Parliamentary Reform, because they were penetrated by the principle that the possession of political power by the bulk of a society is the only effective security against sinister government; or else by the principle that participation in public activity, even in the modest form of an exercise of the elective franchise, is an elevating and instructing agency; or perhaps by the principle that justice demands that those who are compelled to obey laws and pay national taxes should have a voice in making the one and imposing the other.

It may be said that the very fate of these aspirations has had a blighting effect on public enthusiasm and the capacity of feeling it. Not only have most of them now been fulfilled, and so passed from aspiration to actuality, but the results of their fulfilment have been so disappointing as to make us wonder whether it is really worth while to pray, when to have our prayers granted carries the world so very slight a way forward. The Austrian is no longer in Italy; the Pope has ceased to be master in Rome; the patriots of Hungary are now in possession of their rights, and have become friends of their old oppressors; the negro slave has been transformed into an American citizen. At home, again, the gods have listened to our vows. Parliament has been reformed, and the long-desired mechanical security provided for the voter's freedom. We no longer aspire after all these things, you may say, because our hopes have been realised and our dreams have come true. It is possible that the comparatively prosaic results before our eyes at the end of all have thrown a chill over our political imagination. What seemed so glorious when it was far off, seems perhaps a little poor now that it is near; and this has damped the wing of political fancy. The old aspirations have vanished, and no new ones have arisen in their place. Be the cause what it may, I should express the change in this way, that the existing order of facts, whatever it may be, now takes a hardly disputed precedence with us over ideas, and that the coarsest political standard is undoubtingly and finally applied over the whole realm of human thought.

The line taken up by the press and the governing classes of England during the American Civil War may serve to illustrate the kind of mood which we conceive to be gaining firmer hold than ever of the national mind. Those who sympathised with the Southern States listened only to political arguments, and very narrow and inefficient political arguments, as it happened, when they ought to have seen that here was an issue which involved not only political ideas, but moral and religious ideas as well. That is to say, the ordinary political tests were not enough to reveal the entire significance of the crisis, nor were the political standards proper for measuring the whole of the expediencies hanging in the balance. The conflict could not be adequately gauged by such questions as whether the Slave States had or had not a constitutional right to establish an independent government; whether the Free States were animated by philanthropy or by love of empire; whether it was to the political advantage of England that the American Union should be divided and consequently weakened. Such questions were not necessarily improper in themselves, and we can imagine circumstances in which they might be not only proper but decisive. But, the circumstances being what they were, the narrower expediencies of ordinary politics were outweighed by one of those supreme and indefeasible expediencies which are classified as moral. These are, in other words, the higher, wider, more binding, and transcendent part of the master art of social wellbeing.

Here was only one illustration of the growing tendency to substitute the narrowest political point of view for all the other ways of regarding the course of human affairs, and to raise the limitations which practical exigencies may happen to set to the application of general principles, into the very place of the principles themselves. Nor is the process of deteriorating conviction confined to the greater or noisier transactions of nations. It is impossible that it should be so. That process is due to causes which affect the mental temper as a whole, and pour round us an atmosphere that enervates our judgment from end to end, not more in politics than in morality, and not more in morality than in philosophy, in art, and in religion. Perhaps this tendency never showed itself more offensively than when the most important newspaper in the country criticised our great naturalist's scientific speculations as to the descent of man, from the point of view of property, intelligence, and a stake in the country, and severely censured him for revealing his particular zoological conclusions to the general public, at a moment when the sky of Paris was red with the incendiary flames of the Commune.[†] It would be hard to reduce the transformation of all truth into a subordinate department of daily politics, to a more gross and unseemly absurdity.

The consequences of such a transformation, of putting immediate social convenience in the first place, and respect for truth in the second, are seen, as we have said, in a distinct and unmistakable lowering of the level of national life; a slack and lethargic quality about public opinion; a growing predominance of material, temporary, and selfish aims, over those which are generous, far-reaching, and spiritual; a deadly weakening of intellectual conclusiveness, and clear-shining moral illumination, and, lastly, of a certain stoutness of self-respect for which England was once especially famous. A plain categorical proposition is becoming less and less credible to average minds. Or at least the slovenly willingness to hold two directly contradictory propositions at one and the same time is becoming more and more common. In religion, morals, and politics, the suppression of your true opinion, if not the positive profession of what you hold to be a false opinion, is hardly ever counted a vice, and not seldom even goes for virtue and solid wisdom. One is conjured to respect the beliefs of others, but forbidden to claim the same respect for one's own.[†]

This dread of the categorical proposition might be creditable, if it sprang from attachment to a very high standard of evidence, or from a deep sense of the relative and provisional quality of truth. There might even be a plausible defence set up for it, if it sprang from that formulated distrust of the energetic rational judgment in comparison with the emotional, affective, contemplative parts of man, which underlies the various forms of religious mysticism. If you look closely into our present mood, it is seen to be the product mainly and above all of a shrinking deference to the *status quo*, not merely as having a claim not to be lightly dealt with, which every serious man concedes, but as being the last word and final test of truth and justice. Physical science is allowed to be the sphere of accurate reasoning and distinct conclusions, but in morals and politics, instead of admitting that these subjects have equally a logic of their own, we silently suspect all first principles, and practically deny the strict inferences from demonstrated premisses. Faith in the soundness of given general theories of right and wrong melts away before the first momentary triumph of wrong, or the first passing discouragement in enforcing right.

Our robust political sense, which has discovered so many of the secrets of good government, which has given us freedom with order, and popular administration without corruption, and unalterable respect for law along with indelible respect for individual right, this, which has so long been our strong point, is fast becoming our weakness and undoing. For the extension of the ways of thinking which are proper in politics, to other than political matter, means at the same time the depravation of the political sense itself. Not only is social expediency effacing the many other points of view that men ought to take of the various facts of life and thought: the idea of social expediency itself is becoming a dwarfed and pinched idea. Ours is the country where love of constant improvement ought to be greater than anywhere else, because fear of revolution is less. Yet the art of politics is growing to be as meanly conceived as all the rest. At elections the national candidate has not often a chance against the local candidate, nor the man of a principle against the man of a class. In parliament, we are admonished on high authority that 'the policy of a party is not the carrying out of the opinion of any section of it, but the general consensus of the whole,' which seems to be a hierophantic manner of saying that the policy of a party is one thing, and the principle which makes it a party is another thing, and that men who care very strongly about anything are to surrender that and the hope of it, for the sake of succeeding in something about which they care very little or not at all. This is our modern way of giving politicians heart for their voyage, of inspiring them with resoluteness and self-respect, with confidence in the worth of their cause and enthusiasm for its success. Thoroughness is a mistake, and nailing your flag to the mast a bit of delusive heroics. Think wholly of to-day, and not at all of to-morrow. Beware of the high and hold fast to the safe. Dismiss conviction, and study general consensus. No zeal, no faith, no intellectual trenchancy, but as much low-minded geniality and trivial complaisance as you please.

Of course, all these characteristics of our own society mark tendencies that are common enough in all societies. They often spring from an indolence and enervation that besets a certain number of people, however invigorating the general mental climate may be. What we are now saying is that the general mental climate itself has, outside of the domain of physical science, ceased to be invigorating; that, on the contrary, it fosters the more inglorious predispositions of men, and encourages a native willingness, already so strong, to acquiesce in a lazy accommodation with error, an ignoble economy of truth, and a vicious compromise of the permanent gains of adhering to a sound general principle, for the sake of the temporary gains of departing from it.

Without attempting an elaborate analysis of the causes that have brought about this debilitation of mental tone, we may shortly remind ourselves of one or two facts in the political history, in the intellectual history, and in the religious history of this generation, which perhaps help us to understand a phenomenon that we have all so keen an interest both in understanding and in modifying.

To begin with what lies nearest to the surface. The most obvious agency at work in the present exaggeration of the political standard as the universal test of truth, is to be found in some contemporary incidents. The influence of France upon England since the revolution of 1848 has tended wholly to the discredit of abstract theory and general reasoning among us, in all that relates to politics, morals, and religion. In 1848, not in 1789, questions affecting the fundamental structure and organic condition of the social union came for the first time into formidable prominence. For the first time these questions and the answers to them were stated in articulate formulas and distinct theories. They were not merely written in books; they so fascinated the imagination and inflamed the hopes of the time, that thousands of men were willing actually to go down into the streets and to shed their blood for the realisation of their generous dream of a renovated society. The same sight has been seen since, and even when we do not see it, we are perfectly aware that the same temper is smouldering. Those were premature attempts to convert a crude aspiration into a political reality, and to found a new social order on a number of uncompromising deductions from abstract principles of the common weal. They have had the natural effect of deepening the English dislike of a general theory, even when such a theory did no more than profess to announce a remote object of desire, and not the present goal of immediate effort.

It is not only the Socialists who are responsible for the low esteem into which a spirit of political generalisation has fallen in other countries, in consequence of French experience. Mr. Mill has described in a well-known passage the characteristic vice of the leaders of all French parties, and not of the democratic party more than any other. 'The commonplaces of politics in France,' he says, 'are large and sweeping practical maxims, from which, as ultimate premisses, men reason downwards to particular applications, and this they call being logical and consistent. For instance, they are perpetually arguing that such and such a measure ought to be adopted, because it is a consequence of the principle on which the form of government is founded; of the principle of legitimacy, or the principle of the sovereignty of the people. To which it may be answered that if these be really practical principles, they must rest on speculative grounds; the sovereignty of the people (for example) must be a right foundation for government, because a government thus constituted tends to produce certain beneficial effects. Inasmuch, however, as no government produces all possible beneficial effects, but all are attended with more or fewer inconveniences; and since these cannot be combated by means drawn from the very causes which produce them, it would often be a much stronger recommendation of some practical arrangement that it does not follow from what is called the general principle of the government, than that it does.'[2]

---

2 *System of Logic*, bk vi, ch. xi.

The English feeling for compromise is on its better side the result of a shrewd and practical, though informal, recognition of a truth which the writer has here expressed in terms of Method. The disregard which the political action of France has repeatedly betrayed of a principle really so important, has hitherto strengthened our own regard for it, until it has not only made us look on its importance as exclusive and final, but has extended our respect for the right kind of compromise to wrong and injurious kinds.

A minor event, which now looks much less important than it did not many years ago, but which still had real influence in deteriorating moral judgment, was the career of a late sovereign of France.† Some apparent advantages followed for a season from a rule which had its origin in a violent and perfidious usurpation, and which was upheld by all the arts of moral corruption, political enervation, and military repression. The advantages lasted long enough to create in this country a steady and powerful opinion that Napoleon the Third's early crime was redeemed by the seeming prosperity which followed. The shocking prematureness of this shallow condonation is now too glaringly visible for any one to deny it. Not often in history has the great truth that 'morality is the nature of things' received corroboration so prompt and timely. We need not commit ourselves to the optimistic or sentimental hypothesis that wickedness always fares ill in the world, or on the other hand that whoso hearkens diligently to the divine voice, and observes all the commandments to do them, shall be blessed in his basket and his store and all the work of his hand. The claims of morality to our allegiance, so far as its precepts are solidly established, rest on the same positive base as our faith in the truth of physical laws. Moral principles, when they are true, are at bottom only registered generalisations from experience. They record certain uniformities of antecedence and consequence in the region of human conduct. Want of faith in the persistency of these uniformities is only a little less fatuous in the moral order than a corresponding want of faith would instantly disclose itself to be in the purely physical order. In both orders alike there is only too much of this kind of fatuousness, this readiness to believe that for once in our favour the stream shall flow up hill, that we may live in miasmatic air unpoisoned, that a government may depress the energy, the self-reliance, the public spirit of its citizens, and yet be able to count on these qualities whenever the government itself may have broken down, and left the country to make the best of such resources as are left after so severe and prolonged a drain. This is the sense in which morality is the nature of things. The system of the Second

Empire was in the same sense an immoral system. Unless all the lessons of human experience were futile, and all the principles of political morality mere articles of pedantry, such a system must inevitably bring disaster, as we might have seen that it was sowing the seeds of disaster. Yet because the catastrophe lingered, opinion in England began to admit the possibility of evil being for this once good, and to treat any reference to the moral and political principles which condemned the imperial system, and all systems like it, beyond hope or appeal, as simply the pretext of a mutinous or utopian impatience.

This, however, is only one of the more superficial influences which have helped and fallen in with the working of profounder causes of weakened aspiration and impoverished moral energy, and of the substitution of latitudinarian acquiescence and faltering conviction for the whole-hearted assurance of better times. Of these deeper causes, the most important in the intellectual development of the prevailing forms of thought and sentiment is the growth of the Historic Method. Let us consider very shortly how the abuse of this method, and an unauthorised extension and interpretation of its conclusions, are likely to have had something to do with the enervation of opinion.

The Historic Method may be described as the comparison of the forms of an idea, or a usage, or a belief, at any given time, with the earlier forms from which they were evolved, or the later forms into which they were developed, and the establishment, from such a comparison, of an ascending and descending order among the facts. It consists in the explanation of existing parts in the frame of society by connecting them with corresponding parts in some earlier frame; in the identification of present forms in the past, and past forms in the present. Its main process is the detection of corresponding customs, opinions, laws, beliefs, among different communities, and a grouping of them into general classes with reference to some one common feature. It is a certain way of seeking answers to various questions of origin, resting on the same general doctrine of evolution, applied to moral and social forms, as that which is being applied with so much ingenuity to the series of organic matter. The historic conception is a reference of every state of society to a particular stage in the evolution of its general conditions. Ideas of law, of virtue, of religion, of the physical universe, of history, of the social union itself, all march in a harmonious and inter-dependent order.

Curiosity with reference to origins is for various reasons the most marked element among modern scientific tendencies. It covers the whole field, moral, intellectual, and physical, from the smile or the frown on a man's face, up to the most complex of the ideas in his mind; from the expression of his emotions, to their root and relations with one another in his inmost organisation. As an ingenious writer, too soon lost to our political literature, has put it: – 'If we wanted to describe one of the most marked results, perhaps the most marked result, of late thought, we should say that by it everything is made *an antiquity*. When in former times our ancestors thought of an antiquarian, they described him as occupied with coins and medals and Druids' stones. But now there are other relics; indeed all matter is become such. Man himself has to the eye of science become an antiquity. She tries to read, is beginning to read, knows she ought to read, in the frame of each man the result of a whole history of all his life, and what he is and what makes him so.'[3] Character is considered less with reference to its absolute qualities than as an interesting scene strewn with scattered rudiments, survivals, inherited predispositions. Opinions are counted rather as phenomena to be explained than as matters of truth and falsehood. Of usages, we are beginning first of all to think where they came from, and secondarily whether they are the most fitting and convenient that men could be got to accept. In the last century men asked of a belief or a story, Is it true? We now ask, How did men come to take it for true?† In short the relations among social phenomena which now engage most attention, are relations of original source, rather than those of actual consistency in theory and actual fitness in practice. The devotees of the current method are more concerned with the pedigree and genealogical connections of a custom or an idea than with its own proper goodness or badness, its strength or its weakness.

Though there is no necessary or truly logical association between systematic use of this method rightly limited, and a slack and slipshod preference of vague general forms over definite ideas, yet every one can see its tendency, if uncorrected, to make men shrink from importing anything like absolute quality into their propositions. We can see also, what is still worse, its tendency to place individual robustness and initiative in the light of superfluities, with which a world that goes by evolution can very well dispense. Men easily come to consider clearness and positiveness in their opinions, staunchness in holding and defending them, and fervour in carrying them into action, as equivocal virtues of very doubtful perfection, in a state of things where every abuse has after all had a defensible origin; where every error has, we must confess,

---

3 Bagehot.

once been true relatively to other parts of belief in those who held the error; and where all parts of life are so bound up with one another, that it is of no avail to attack one evil, unless you attack many more at the same time. This is a caricature of the real teaching of the Historic Method, of which we shall have to speak presently; but it is one of those caricatures which the natural sloth in such matters, and the indigenous intellectual haziness of the majority of men, make them very willing to take for the true philosophy of things.

Then there is the newspaper press, that huge engine for keeping discussion on a low level, and making the political test final. To take off the taxes on knowledge was to place a heavy tax on broad and independent opinion.† The multiplication of journals 'delivering brawling judgments unashamed on all things all day long,' has done much to deaden the small stock of individuality in public verdicts. It has done much to make vulgar ways of looking at things and vulgar ways of speaking of them stronger and stronger, by formulating and repeating and stereotyping them incessantly from morning until afternoon, and from year's end to year's end. For a newspaper must live, and to live it must please, and its conductors suppose, perhaps not altogether rightly, that it can only please by being very cheerful towards prejudices, very chilly to general theories, loftily disdainful to the men of a principle. Their one cry to an advocate of improvement is some sagacious silliness about recognising the limits of the practicable in politics, and seeing the necessity of adapting theories to facts. As if the fact of taking a broader and wiser view than the common crowd disqualifies a man from knowing what the view of the common crowd happens to be, and from estimating it at the proper value for practical purposes. Why are the men who despair of improvement to be the only persons endowed with the gift of discerning the practicable? It is, however, only too easy to understand how a journal, existing for a day, should limit its view to the possibilities of the day, and how, being most closely affected by the particular, it should coldly turn its back upon all that is general. And it is easy, too, to understand the reaction of this intellectual timorousness upon the minds of ordinary readers, who have too little natural force and too little cultivation to be able to resist the narrowing and deadly effect of the daily iteration of short-sighted commonplaces.

Far the most penetrating of all the influences that are impairing the moral and intellectual nerve of our generation, remain still to be mentioned. The first of these is the immense increase of material prosperity, and the second is the immense decline in sincerity of spiritual interest. The evil wrought by the one fills up the measure of the evil wrought by the other. We have been, in spite of momentary declensions, on a flood tide of high profits and a roaring trade, and there is nothing like a roaring trade for engendering latitudinarians. The effect of many possessions, especially if they be newly acquired, in slackening moral vigour, is a proverb. Our new wealth is hardly leavened by any tradition of public duty such as lingers among the English nobles, nor as yet by any common custom of devotion to public causes, such as seems to live and grow in the United States. Under such conditions, with new wealth come luxury and love of ease and that fatal readiness to believe that God has placed us in the best of possible worlds, which so lowers men's aims and unstrings their firmness of purpose. Pleasure saps high interests, and the weakening of high interests leaves more undisputed room for pleasure. Management and compromise appear among the permitted arts, because they tend to comfort, and comfort is the end of ends, comprehending all ends. Not truth is the standard, but the politic and the reputable. Are we to suppose that it is firm persuasion of the greater scripturalness of episcopacy that turns the second generation of dissenting manufacturers in our busy Lancashire into churchmen? Certainly such conversions do no violence to the conscience of the proselyte, for he is intellectually indifferent, a spiritual neuter.

That brings us to the root of the matter, the serious side of a revolution that in this social consequence is so unspeakably ignoble. This root of the matter is the slow transformation now at work of the whole spiritual basis of thought. Every age is in some sort an age of transition, but our own is characteristically and cardinally an epoch of transition in the very foundations of belief and conduct. The old hopes have grown pale, the old fears dim; strong sanctions are become weak, and once vivid faiths very numb. Religion, whatever destinies may be in store for it, is at least for the present hardly any longer an organic power. It is not that supreme, penetrating, controlling, decisive part of a man's life, which it has been, and will be again. The work of destruction is all the more perturbing to timorous spirits, and more harassing even to doughtier spirits, for being done impalpably, indirectly, almost silently and as if by unseen hands. Those who dwell in the tower of ancient faiths look about them in constant apprehension, misgiving, and wonder, with the hurried uneasy mien of people living amid earthquakes. The air seems to their alarms to be full of missiles, and all is doubt, hesitation, and shivering expectancy. Hence a decisive reluctance to commit one's self. Conscience has lost its strong and on-pressing energy, and the sense of personal responsibility lacks sharpness of edge. The native hue of spiritual resolution is sicklied o'er with the pale cast of distracted, wavering, confused thought. The souls of men have become void. Into the void have entered in triumph the seven devils of Secularity.

And all this hesitancy, this tampering with conviction for fear of its consequences, this want of faithful dealing in the highest matters, is being intensified, aggravated, driven inwards like a fatal disorder toward the vital parts, by the existence of a State Church. While thought stirs and knowledge extends, she remains fast moored by ancient formularies. While the spirit of man expands in search after new light, and feels energetically for new truth, the spirit of the Church is eternally entombed within the four corners of acts of parliament. Her ministers vow almost before they have crossed the threshold of manhood that they will search no more. They virtually swear that they will to the end of their days believe what they believe then, before they have had time either to think or to know the thoughts of others. They take oath, in other words, to lead mutilated lives. If they cannot keep this solemn promise, they have at least every inducement that ordinary human motives can supply, to conceal their breach of it. The same system which begins by making mental indolence a virtue and intellectual narrowness a part of sanctity, ends by putting a premium on something too like hypocrisy. Consider the seriousness of fastening up in these bonds some thousands of the most instructed and intelligent classes in the country, the very men who would otherwise be best fitted from position and opportunities for aiding a little in the long, difficult, and plainly inevitable work of transforming opinion. Consider the waste of intelligence, and what is assuredly not less grave, the positive deadweight and thick obstruction, by which an official hierarchy so organized must paralyse mental independence in a community.

We know the kind of man whom this system delights to honour. He was described for us five and thirty years ago by a master hand. 'Mistiness is the mother of wisdom. A man who can set down half a dozen general propositions which escape from destroying one another only by being diluted into truisms; who can hold the balance between opposites so skilfully as to do without fulcrum or beam; who never enunciates a truth without guarding himself against being supposed to exclude the contradictory, – who holds that scripture is the only authority, yet that the Church is to be deferred to, that faith only justifies, yet that it does not justify without works, that grace does not depend upon the sacraments, yet is not given without them, that bishops are a divine ordinance, yet that those who have them not are in the same religious condition as those who have, – this is your safe man and the hope of the Church; this is what the Church is said to want, not party men, but sensible, temperate, sober, well-judging persons, to guide it through the channel of no meaning, between the Scylla and Charybdis of Aye and No.'[4] The writer then thought that such a type could not endure, and that the Church must become more real. On the contrary, her reality is more phantom-like now than it was then. She is the sovereign pattern and exemplar of management, of the triumph of the political method in spiritual things, and of the subordination of ideas to the *status quo*.

It is true that all other organized priesthoods are also bodies which move within formularies even more inelastic than those of the Establishment. But then they have not the same immense social power, nor the same temptations to make all sacrifices to preserve it. They affect the intellectual temper of large numbers of people, but the people whom they affect are not so strongly identified with the greater organs of the national life. The State Church is bound up in the minds of the most powerful classes with a given ordering of social arrangements, and the consequence of this is that the teachers of the Church have reflected back upon them a sense of responsibility for these arrangements, which obscures their spirituality, clogs their intellectual energy and mental openness, and turns them into a political army of obstruction to new ideas. They feel themselves to a certain extent discharged from the necessity of recognising the tremendous conflict in the region of belief that goes on around them, just as if they were purely civil administrators, concerned only with the maintenance of the present order. None of this is true of the private Churches. Their teachers and members regard belief as something wholly independent of the civil ordering of things. However little enlightened in some respects, however hostile to certain of the ideas by which it is sought to replace their own, they are at least representatives of the momentous principle of our individual responsibility for the truth of our opinions. They may bring their judgments to conclusions that are less in accord with modern tendencies than those of one or two schools that still see their way to subscribing Anglican articles and administering Anglican rites. At any rate, they admit that the use of his judgment is a duty incumbent on the individual, and a duty to be discharged without reference to any

---

4   Dr J. H. Newman's *Essays Critical and Historical*, vol. i, p. 301.

external considerations whatever, political or otherwise. This is an elevating, an exhilarating principle, however deficiencies of culture may have narrowed the sphere of its operations. It is because a State Church is by its very conception hostile to such a principle, that we are justified in counting it apart from the private Churches with all their faults, and placing it among the agencies that weaken the vigour of a national conscience and check the free play and access of intellectual light.

Here we may leave the conditions that have made an inquiry as to some of the limits of compromise, which must always be an interesting and important subject, one of especial interest and importance to ourselves at present. Is any renovation of the sacredness of principle a possible remedy for some of these elements of national deterioration? They will not disappear until the world has grown into possession of a new doctrine. When that comes, all other good things will follow. What we have to remember is that the new doctrine itself will never come, except to spirits predisposed to their own liberation. Our day of small calculations and petty utilities must first pass away; our vision of the true expediencies must reach further and deeper; our resolution to search for the highest verities, to give up all and follow them, must first become the supreme part of ourselves.†

Chapter II

Of the Possible Utility of Error

Das Wahre fördert; aus dem Irrthum entwickelt sich nichts, er verwickeltuns nur. –

GOETHE.

At the outset of an inquiry how far existing facts ought to be allowed to overrule ideas and principles that are at variance with them, a preliminary question lies in our way, about which it may be well to say something. This is the question of a dual doctrine. In plainer words, the question whether it is expedient that the more enlightened classes in a community should upon system not only possess their light in silence, but whether they should openly encourage a doctrine for the less enlightened classes which they do not believe to be true for themselves, while they regard it as indispensably useful in the case of less fortunate people. An eminent teacher tells us how after he had once succeeded in presenting the principle of Necessity to his own mind in a shape which seemed to bring with it all the advantages of the principle of Free Will, he 'no longer suffered under the burden so heavy to one who aims at being a reformer in opinions, of thinking one doctrine true, and the contrary doctrine morally beneficial.' [1] The discrepancy which this writer thought a heavy burden has struck others as the basis of a satisfactory solution.

> Nil dulcius est bene quam munita tenere
> Edita doctrina sapientum templa serena,
> Despicere unde queas alios passimque videre
> Errare atque viam palantes quærere vitæ.

The learned are to hold the true doctrine; the unlearned are to be taught its morally beneficial contrary. 'Let the Church,' it has been said, 'admit two descriptions of believers, those who are for the letter,

---

[1] Mill's *Autobiography*, p. 170.

and those who hold by the spirit. At a certain point in rational culture, belief in the supernatural becomes for many an impossibility; do not force such persons to wear a cowl of lead. Do not you meddle with what we teach or write, and then we will not dispute the common people with you; do not contest our place in the school and the academy, and then we will surrender to your hands the country school.'[2] This is only a very courageous and definite way of saying what a great many less accomplished persons than M. Renan have silently in their hearts, and in England quite as extensively as in France. They do not believe in hell, for instance, but they think hell a useful fiction for the lower classes. They would deeply regret any change in the spirit or the machinery of public instruction which would release the lower classes from so wholesome an error. And as with hell, so with other articles of the supernatural system; the existence of a Being who will distribute rewards and penalties in a future state, the permanent sentience of each human personality, the vigilant supervision of our conduct, as well as our inmost thoughts and desires, by the heavenly powers; and so forth.

Let us discuss this matter impersonally, without reference to our own opinions and without reference to the evidence for or against their truth. I am not speaking now of those who hold all these ideas to be certainly true, or highly probable, and who at the same time incidentally insist on the great usefulness of such ideas in confirming morality and producing virtuous types of character. With such persons, of course, there is no question of a dual doctrine. They entertain certain convictions themselves, and naturally desire to have their influence extended over others. The proposition which we have to consider is of another kind. It expresses the notions of those who – to take the most important kind of illustration – think untrue the popular ideas of supernatural interference in our obscure human affairs; who think untrue the notion of the prolongation of our existence after death to fulfil the purpose of the supernatural powers; or at least who think them so extremely improbable that no reasonable man or woman, once awakened to a conviction of this improbability, would thenceforth be capable of receiving effective check or guidance from beliefs, that would have sunk slowly down to the level of doubtful guesses. We have now to deal with those who while taking this view of certain doctrines, still declare them to be indispensable for restraining from anti-social conduct all who are not acute or instructed enough to see through them. In other

2 M. Renan's *Réforme Intellectuelle et Morale de la France*, p. 98.

words, they think error useful, and that it may be the best thing for society that masses of men should cheat and deceive themselves in their most fervent aspirations and their deepest assurances. This is the furthest extreme to which the empire of existing facts over principles can well be imagined to go. It lies at the root of every discussion upon the limits which separate lawful compromise or accommodation from palpable hypocrisy.

It will probably be said that according to the theory of the school of which M. Renan is the most eloquent representative, the common people are not really cheating themselves or being cheated. Indeed M. Renan himself has expatiated on the charm of seeing figures of the ideal in the cottages of the poor, images representing no reality, and so forth. 'What a delight,' he cries, 'for the man who is borne down by six days of toil to come on the seventh to rest upon his knees, to contemplate the tall columns, a vault, arches, an altar; to listen to the chanting, to hear moral and consoling words!'[3] The dogmas which criticism attacks are not for these poor people 'the object of an explicit affirmation,' and therefore there is no harm in them; 'it is the privilege of pure sentiment to be invulnerable, and to play with poison without being hurt by it.' In other words, the dogmas are false, but the liturgy, as a performance stirring the senses of awe, reverence, susceptibility to beauty of various kinds, appeals to and satisfies a sentiment that is both true and indispensable in the human mind. More than this, in the two or three supreme moments of life to which men look forward and on which they look back, – at birth, at the passing of the threshold into fulness of life, at marriage, at death, – the Church is present to invest the hour with a certain solemn and dignified charm. That is the way in which the instructed are to look at the services of a Church, after they have themselves ceased to believe its faith, as a true account of various matters which it professes to account for truly.

It will be perceived that this is not exactly the ground of those who think a number of what they confess to be untruths, wholesome for the common people for reasons of police, and who would maintain churches on the same principle on which they maintain the county constabulary. It is a psychological, not a political ground. It is on the whole a more true, as well as a far more exalted position. The human soul, they say, has these lovely and elevating aspirations; not to satisfy them is to leave man a dwarfed creature. Why quarrel with a system that leaves you to satisfy them in the true way, and does much to satisfy

[3] *Etudes d'Histoire Religieuse*, Preface, p. xvi.

them in a false but not very harmful way among those who unfortunately have to sit in the darkness of the outer court?

This is not a proper occasion for saying anything about the adequateness of the catholic, or any other special manner of fostering and solacing the religious impulses of men. We have to assume that the instructed class believe the catholic dogmas to be untrue, and yet wishes the uninstructed to be handed over to a system that reposes on the theory that these dogmas are superlatively true. What then is to be said of the tenableness of such a position? To the plain man it looks like a deliberate connivance at a plan for the propagation of error – assuming, as I say, for the moment, that these articles of belief are erroneous and contrary to fact and evidence. Ah, but, we are told, the people make no explicit affirmation of dogma; that does nothing for them; they are indifferent to it. A great variety of things might be said to this statement. We might ask, for instance, whether the people ever made an explicit affirmation of dogma in the past, or whether it was always the hazy indifferent matter which it is supposed to be now. If so, whether we shall not have to re-cast our most fundamental notions of the way in which Christian civilisation has been evolved. If not, and if people did once explicitly affirm dogma, when exactly was it that they ceased to do so?

The answers to these questions would all go to show that at the time when religion was the great controlling and organising force in conduct, the prime elemental dogmas were accepted with the most vivid conviction of reality. I do not pretend that the common people followed all the inferences which the intellectual subtlety of the master-spirits of theology drew so industriously from the simple premisses of scripture and tradition. But assuredly dogma was at the foundation of the whole structure. When did it cease to be so? How was the structure supported, after you had altered this condition of things?

Apart from this historic issue, the main question one would like to put to the upholder of duality of religion on this plea, is the simple one, whether the power of the ceremonial which charms him so much is not actually at this moment drawn wholly from dogma and the tradition of dogma; whether its truth is not explicitly affirmed to the unlettered man, and whether the inseparable connection between the dogma and the ceremonial is not constantly impressed upon him by the spiritual teachers to whom the dual system hands him and his order over for all time? If any one of these philosophic critics will take the trouble to listen to a few courses of sermons at the present day, and the remark applies not less to protestant than to catholic churches, he will find that instead of that '*parole morale et consolante*' which is so soothing to think of, the pulpit is now the home of fervid controversy and often exacerbated declamation in favour of ancient dogma against modern science. We do not say whether this is or is not the wisest line for the clergy to follow. We only press the fact against those who wish us to believe that dogma counts for nothing in the popular faith, and that therefore we need not be uneasy as to its effects.

Next, one would say to those who think that all will go well if you divide the community into two classes, one privileged to use its own mind, the other privileged to have its mind used by a priesthood, that they overlook the momentous circumstance of these professional upholders of dogmatic systems being also possessed of a vast social influence in questions that naturally belong to another sphere. There is hardly a single great controversy in modern politics, where the statesman does not find himself in immediate contact with the real or supposed interests, and with the active or passive sentiment, of one of these religious systems.[†] Therefore if the instructed or intellectually privileged class cheerfully leave the field open to men who, *ex hypothesi*, are presumed to be less instructed, narrower, more impenetrable by reason, and the partisans of the letter against the spirit, then this result follows. They are deliberately strengthening the hands of the persons least fitted by judgment, experience, and temper, for using such power rightly. And they are strengthening them not merely in dealing with religious matters, but, what is of more importance, in dealing with an endless variety of the gravest social and political matters. It is impossible to map out the exact dimensions of the field in which a man shall exercise his influence, and to which he is to be rigorously confined. Give men influence in one matter, especially if that be such a matter as religious belief and ceremonial, and it is simply impossible that this influence shall not extend with more or less effect over as much of the whole sphere of conduct as they may choose to claim. This is no discredit to them; on the contrary it is to their honour. So, in short, in surrendering the common people without dispute or effort to organised priesthoods for religious purposes, you would be inevitably including a vast number of other purposes in the self-same destination. This does not in the least prejudice practical ways of dealing with certain existing circumstances, such as the propriety or justice of allowing a catholic people to have a catholic university. It is only an argument against erecting into a complete and definite formula the division of a society into two great castes, the one with a religion of the spirit, the other with a creed of the letter.

Again, supposing that the enlightened caste were to consent to abandon the common people to what are assumed to be lower and narrower forms of truth, – which is after all little more than a fine phrase for forms of falsehood, – what can be more futile than to suppose that such a compromise will be listened to for a single moment by a caste whose first principle is that they are the possessors and ministers, not of an inferior or superior form of truth, but of the very truth itself, absolute, final, complete, divinely sent, infallibly interpreted? The disciples of the relative may afford to compromise. The disciples of the absolute, never.

We shall see other objections as we go on to this state of things, in which a minority holds true opinions and abandons the majority to false ones. At the bottom of the advocacy of a dual doctrine slumbers the idea that there is no harm in men being mistaken, or at least only so little harm as is more than compensated for by the marked tranquillity in which their mistake may wrap them. This is not an idea merely that intellectual error is a pathological necessity of the mind, no more to be escaped than the pathological necessities which afflict and finally dissolve the body. That is historically true. It is an idea that error somehow in certain stages, where there is enough of it, actually does good, like vaccination. Well, the thesis of the present chapter is that erroneous opinion or belief, in itself and as such, can never be useful. This may seem a truism which everybody is willing to accept without demur. But it is one of those truisms which persons habitually forget and repudiate in practice, just because they have never made it real to themselves by considering and answering the objections that may be brought against it. We see this repudiation before our eyes every day. Thus for instance, parents theoretically take it for granted that error cannot be useful, while they are teaching or allowing others to teach their children what they, the parents, believe to be untrue. Thus husbands who think the common theology baseless and unmeaning, are found to prefer that their wives shall not question this theology nor neglect its rites. These are only two out of a hundred examples of the daily admission that error may be very useful to other people. I need hardly say that to deny this, as the commonplace to which this chapter is devoted denies it, is a different thing from denying the expediency of letting errors alone at a given time. That is another question, to be discussed afterwards. You may have a thoroughly vicious and dangerous enemy, and yet it may be expedient to choose your own hour and occasion for attacking him. 'The passage from error to truth,' in the words of Condorcet, 'may be accompanied by certain evils. Every great change necessarily brings some of these in its train; and though they may be always far below the evil you are for destroying, yet it ought to do what is possible to diminish them. It is not enough to do good; one must do it in a good way. No doubt we should destroy all errors, but as it is impossible to destroy them all in an instant, we should imitate a prudent architect who, when obliged to destroy a building, and knowing how its parts are united together, sets about its demolition in such a way as to prevent its fall from being dangerous.'[4]

Those, let us note by the way, who are accustomed to think the moral tone of the eighteenth century low and gross compared with that of the nineteenth, may usefully contrast these just and prudent words of caution in extirpating error, with M. Renan's invitation to men whom he considers wrong in their interpretation of religion, to plant their error as widely and deeply as they can; and who are moreover themselves supposed to be demoralised, or else they would not be likely to acquiesce in a previous surrender of the universities to men whom they think in mortal error. Apart however from M. Renan, Condorcet's words merely assert the duty of setting to work to help on the change from false to true opinions with prudence, and this every sensible man admits. Our position is that in estimating the situation, in counting up and balancing the expediencies of an attack upon error at this or that point, nothing is to be set to the credit of error as such, nor is there anything in its own operations or effects to entitle it to a moment's respite. Every one would admit this at once in the case of physical

---

[4] In 1779 the Academy of Prussia announced this as the question for their annual prize essay: – '*S'il est utile au peuple d'être trompé.*' They received thirty-three essays; twenty showing that it is not useful, thirteen showing that it is. The Academy, with an impartiality that caused much amusement in Paris and Berlin, awarded two prizes, one to the best proof of the negative answer, another to the best proof of the affirmative. See Bartholmess, *Hist. Philosophique de l'Académie de Prusse*, i. 231, and ii. 273. Condorcet did not actually compete for the prize, but he wrote a very acute piece, suggested by the theme, which was printed in 1790. *Œuv.* v. 343.

To illustrate the common fact of certain currents of thought being in the air at given times, we may mention that in 1770 was published the posthumous work of another Frenchman, Chesneau du Marsais (1676–1756) entitled: – '*Essai sur les Préjugés; ou de l'influence des Opinions sur les Mœurs et sur le Bonheur des Hommes.*' The principal prejudices to which he refers are classed under Antiquity – Ancestry – Native Country – Religion – Respect for Wealth. Some of the reasoning is almost verbally identical with Condorcet's. For an account of Du Marsais, see D'Alembert, *Œuv.* iii. 481.†

truths, though there are those who say that some of the time spent in the investigation of physical truths might be more advantageously devoted to social problems. But in the case of moral and religious truths or errors, people, if they admit that nothing is to be set to the credit of error as such, still constantly have a subtle and practically mischievous confusion in their minds between the possible usefulness of error, and the possible expediency of leaving it temporarily undisturbed.† What happens in consequence of such a confusion is this. Men leave error undisturbed, because they accept in a loose way the proposition that a belief may be 'morally useful without being intellectually sustainable.' They disguise their own dissent from popular opinions, because they regard such opinions as useful to other people. We are not now discussing the case of those who embrace a creed for themselves, on the ground that, though they cannot demonstrate its truth to the understanding, yet they find it pregnant with moralising and elevating characteristics. We are thinking of a very different attitude – that, namely, of persons who believe a creed to be not more morally useful than it is intellectually sustainable, so far as they themselves are concerned. To them it is pure and uncompensated error. Yet from a vague and general idea that what is useless error to them may be useful to others, they insist on doing their best to perpetuate the system which spreads and consecrates the error. And how do they settle the question? They reckon up the advantages, and forget the drawbacks. They detect and dwell on one or two elements of utility in the false belief or the worn-out institution, and leave out of all account the elements that make in the other direction.

Considering how much influence this vague persuasion has in encouraging a well-meaning hypocrisy in individuals, and a profound stagnation in societies, it may be well to examine the matter somewhat generally. Let us try to measure the force of some of the most usual pleas for error.

I. A false opinion, it may be said, is frequently found to have clustering around it a multitude of excellent associations, which do far more good than the false opinion that supports them does harm. In the middle ages, for instance, there was a belief that a holy man had the gift of routing demons, of healing the sick, and of working divers other miracles. Supposing that this belief was untrue, supposing that it was an error to attribute the sudden death of an incredible multitude of troublesome flies in a church to the fact of Saint Bernard having excommunicated them, what then? The mistaken opinion was still associated with a deep reverence for virtue and sanctity, and this was more valuable, than the error of the explanation of the death of the flies was noxious or degrading.

The answer to this seems to be as follows. First, in making false notions the proofs or close associates of true ones, you are exposing the latter to the ruin which awaits the former. For example, if you have in the minds of children or servants associated honesty, industry, truthfulness, with the fear of hell-fire, then supposing this fear to become extinct in their minds, – which, being unfounded in truth, it is in constant risk of doing – the virtues associated with it are likely to be weakened exactly in proportion as that association was strong.

Second, for all good habits in thought or conduct there are good and real reasons in the nature of things. To leave such habits attached to false opinions is to lessen the weight of these natural or spontaneous reasons, and so to do more harm in the long run than effacement of them seems for a time to do good. Most excellences in human character have a spontaneous root in our nature. Moreover if they had not, and where they have not, there is always a valid and real external defence for them. The unreal defence must be weaker than the real one, and the substitution of a weak for a strong defence, where both are to be had, is not useful but the very opposite.

II. It is true, the objector would probably continue, that there is a rational defence for all excellences of conduct, as there is for all that is worthy and fitting in institutions. But the force of a rational defence lies in the rationality of the man to whom it is proffered. The arguments which persuade one trained in scientific habits of thought, only touch persons of the same kind. Character is not all pure reason. That fitness of things which you pronounce to be the foundation of good habits, may be borne in upon men, and may speak to them, through other channels than the syllogism. You assume a community of highly trained wranglers and proficient sophisters. The plain fact is that, for the mass of men, use and wont, rude or gracious symbols, blind custom, prejudices, superstitions, – however erroneous in themselves, however inadequate to the conveyance of the best truth, – are the only safe guardians of the common virtues. In this sense, then, error may have its usefulness.

A hundred years ago this apology for error was met by those high-minded and interesting men, the French believers in human perfectibility, with their characteristic dogma, – of which Rousseau was the ardent expounder, – that man is born with a clear and unsophisticated spirit, perfectly able to discern all the simple truths necessary for common conduct by its own unaided light. His motives are all pure and unselfish and his intelligence is unclouded, until priests and tyrants mutilate the one and corrupt the other. We who have the benefit of the historic method, and have to take into account the medium that surrounds a human creature the moment it comes into the world, to say nothing of all the inheritance from the past which it brings within it into the world at the same moment, cannot take up this ground. We cannot maintain that everybody is born with light enough to see the rational defences of things for himself, without the education of institutions. What we do maintain is – and this is the answer to the plea for error at present under consideration – that whatever impairs the brightness of such light as a man has, is not useful but hurtful. Our reply to those who contend for the usefulness of error on the ground of the comparative impotence of rationality over ordinary minds, is something of this kind. Superstition, blind obedience to custom, and the other substitutes for a right and independent use of the mind, may accidentally and in some few respects impress good ideas upon persons who are too darkened to accept these ideas on their real merits. But then superstition itself is the main cause of this very darkness. To hold error is in so far to foster erroneous ways of thinking on all subjects; is to make the intelligence less and less ready to receive truth in all matters whatever. Men are made incapable of perceiving the rational defences, and of feeling rational motives, for good habits, – so far as they are thus incapable, – by the very errors which we are asked silently to countenance as useful substitutes for right reason. 'Erroneous motives,' as Condorcet has expressed this matter, 'have an additional drawback attached to them, the habit which they strengthen of reasoning ill. The more important the subject on which you reason ill, and the more you busy yourself about it, by so much the more dangerous do the influences of such a habit become. It is especially on subjects analogous to that on which you reason wrongly, or which you connect with it by habit, that such a defect extends most powerfully and most rapidly. Hence it is extremely hard for the man who believes himself obliged to conform in his conduct to what he considers truths useful to men, but who attributes the obligation to erroneous motives, to reason very correctly on the truths themselves; the more attention he pays to such motives, and the more importance he comes to attach to them, the more likely he will be to go wrong.'[5] So, in short, superstition does an immense harm by enfeebling rational ways of thinking; it does a little good by accidentally endorsing rational conclusions in one or

5 *Œuv.* v. 354.

two matters. And yet, though the evil which it is said to repair is a trifle beside the evil which it is admitted to inflict, the balance of expediencies is after all declared to be such as to warrant us in calling errors useful!

III. A third objection now presents itself to me, which I wish to state as strongly as possible. 'Even if a false opinion cannot in itself be more useful than a true one, whatever good habits may seem to be connected with it, yet,' it may be contended, 'relatively to the general mental attitude of a set of men, to their other notions and maxims, the false opinion may entail less harm than would be wrought by its mere demolition. There are false opinions so intimately bound up with the whole way of thinking and feeling, that to introduce one or two detached true opinions in their stead, would, even if it were possible, only serve to break up that coherency of character and conduct which it is one of the chief objects of moralists and the great art of living to produce. For a true opinion does not necessarily bring in its train all the other true opinions that are logically connected with it. On the contrary, it is only too notorious a fact in the history of belief, that not merely individuals but whole societies are capable of holding at one and the same time contradictory opinions and mutually destructive principles. On the other hand, neither does a false opinion involve practically all the evil consequences deducible from it. For the results of human inconsistency are not all unhappy, and if we do not always act up to virtuous principle, no more do we always work out to its remotest inference every vicious principle. Not insincerity, but inconsistency, has constantly turned the adherents of persecuting precepts into friends of tolerant practice.'

'It is a comparatively small thing to persuade a superstitious person to abandon this or that article of his superstition. You have no security that the rejection of the one article which you have displaced will lead to the rejection of any other, and it is quite possible that it may lead to all the more fervid an adhesion to what remains behind. Error, therefore, in view of such considerations may surely be allowed to have at least a provisional utility.'

Now undoubtedly the repudiation of error is not at all the same thing as embracing truth. People are often able to see the force of arguments that destroy a given opinion, without being able to see the force of arguments for the positive opinion that ought to replace it. They can only be quite sure of seeing both, when they have acquired not merely a conviction that one notion is false and another true, but have furthermore exchanged a generally erroneous way of thinking for a generally correct way. Hence the truly important object with every one who holds opinions which he deems it of the highest moment that others should accept, must obviously be to reach people's general ways of thinking; to stir their love of truth; to penetrate them with a sense of the difference in the quality of evidence; to make them willing to listen to criticism and new opinion; and perhaps above all to teach them to take ungrudging and daily trouble to clear up in their minds the exact sense of the terms they use.

If this be so, a false opinion, like an erroneous motive, can hardly have even a provisional usefulness. For how can you attack an erroneous way of thinking except in detail, that is to say through the sides of this or that single wrong opinion? Each of these wrong opinions is an illustration and type, as it is a standing support and abettor, of some kind of wrong reasoning, though they are not all on the same scale nor all of them equally instructive. It is precisely by this method of gradual displacement of error step by step, that the few stages of progress which the race has yet traversed, have been actually achieved. Even if the place of the erroneous idea is not immediately taken by the corresponding true one, or by the idea which is at least one or two degrees nearer to the true one, still the removal of error in this purely negative way amounts to a positive gain. Why? For the excellent reason that it is the removal of a bad element which otherwise tends to propagate itself, or even if it fails to do that, tends at the best to make the surrounding mass of error more inveterate. All error is what physiologists term fissiparous, and in exterminating one false opinion you may be hindering the growth of an uncounted brood of false opinions.

Then as to the maintenance of that coherency, interdependence, and systematisation of opinions and motives, which is said to make character organic, and is therefore so highly prized by some schools of thought. No doubt the loosening of this or that part of the fabric of heterogeneous origin, which constitutes the character of a man or woman, tends to loosen the whole. But do not let us feed ourselves upon phrases. This organic coherency, what does it come to? It signifies in a general way, to describe it briefly, a harmony between the intellectual, the moral, and the practical parts of human nature; an undisturbed co-operation between reason, affection, and will; the reason prescribing nothing against which the affections revolt, and proscribing nothing which they crave; and the will obeying the joint impulses of these two directing forces, without liability to capricious or extravagant disturbance of their direction. Well, if the reason were perfect in information and method, and the affections faultless in their impulse, then organic unity of character would be the final consummation of all human improvement, and it would be criminal, even if it were possible, to undermine a structure of such priceless value. But short of this there can be no value in coherency and harmonious consistency as such. So long as error is an element in it, then for so long the whole product is vitiated. Undeniably and most fortunately, social virtues are found side by side with speculative mistakes and the gravest intellectual imperfections. We may apply to humanity the idea which, as Hebrew students tell us, is imputed in the Talmud to the Supreme Being. *God prays*, the Talmud says; and his prayer is this, – 'Be it my will that my mercy overpower my justice.' And so with men, with or without their will, their mercifulness overpowers their logic. And not their mercifulness only, but all their good impulses overpower their logic. To repeat the words which I have put into the objector's mouth, we do not always work out every vicious principle to its remotest inference. What, however, is this but to say that in such cases character is saved, not by its coherency, but by the opposite; to say not that error is useful, but what is a very different thing, that its mischievousness is sometimes capable of being averted or minimised?

The apologist may retort that he did not mean logical coherency, but a kind of practical everyday coherency, which may be open to a thousand abstract objections, yet which still secures both to the individual and to society a number of advantages that might be endangered by any disturbance of opinion or motive. No doubt, and the method and season of chasing erroneous opinions and motives out of the mind must always be a matter of much careful and far-seeing consideration. Only in the course of such consideration, let us not admit the notion in any form that error can have even provisional utility. For it is not the error which confers the advantages that we desire to preserve, but some true opinion or just motive or high or honest sentiment, which exists and thrives and operates in spite of the error and in face of it, springing from man's spontaneous and unformulated recognition of the real relations of things. This recognition is very faint in the beginnings of society. It grows clearer and firmer with each step forward. And in a tolerably civilised age it has become a force on which you can fairly lean with a considerable degree of assurance.

And this leads to the central point of the answer to the argument from coherency of conduct. In measuring utility you have to take into account not merely the service rendered to the objects of the present hour, but the contribution to growth, progress, and the future. From this point of view most of the talk about unity of character is not much more than a glorifying of stagnation. It leaves out of sight the conditions necessary for the continuance of the unending task of human improvement. Now whatever ease may be given to an individual or a generation by social or religious error, such error at any rate can conduce nothing to further advancement. That, at least, is not one of its possible utilities.

This is also one of the answers to the following plea. 'Though the knowledge of every positive truth is an useful acquisition, this doctrine cannot without reservation be applied to negative truth. When the only truth ascertainable is that nothing can be known, we do not, by this knowledge, gain any new fact by which to guide ourselves.'[6] But the negative truth that nothing can be known is in fact a truth that guides us. It leads us away from sterile and irreclaimable tracts of thought and emotion, and so inevitably compels the energies which would otherwise have been wasted, to feel after a more profitable direction. By leaving the old guide-marks undisturbed, you may give ease to an existing generation, but the present ease is purchased at the cost of future growth. To have been deprived of the faith of the old dispensation, is the first condition of strenuous endeavour after the new.†

No doubt history abounds with cases in which a false opinion on moral or religious subjects, or an erroneous motive in conduct, has seemed to be a stepping-stone to truth. But this is in no sense a demonstration of the utility of error. For in all such cases the erroneous opinion or motive was far from being wholly erroneous, or wholly without elements of truth and reality. If it helped to quicken the speed or mend the direction of progress, that must have been by virtue of some such elements within it. All that was error in it was pure waste, or worse than waste. It is true that the religious sentiment has clothed itself in a great number of unworthy, inadequate, depressing, and otherwise misleading shapes, dogmatic and liturgic. Yet on the whole the religious sentiment has conferred enormous benefits on civilisation. This is no proof of the utility of the mistaken direction which these dogmatic or liturgic shapes imposed upon it. On the contrary, the effect of the false dogmas and enervating liturgies is so much that has to be deducted from the advantages conferred by a sentiment in itself valuable and of priceless capability.[7]

---

6 Mill's *Three Essays on Religion*, p. 73. I have offered some criticisms on the whole passage in *Critical Miscellanies, Second Series*, pp. 300–304.
7 'Enfin, supposons pour un instant que le dogme de l'autre vie soit de quelqu'utilité, et qu'il retienne vraiment un petit nombre d'individus, qu'est-ce que ces foibles avantages comparés à la foule de maux que l'on en voir découler?

Yes, it will be urged, but from the historic conditions of the time, truth could only be conveyed in erroneous forms, and motives of permanent price for humanity could only be secured in these mistaken expressions. Here I would again press the point of this necessity for erroneous forms and mistaken expressions being, in a great many of the most important instances, itself derivative, one among other ill consequences of previous moral and religious error. 'It was gravely said,' Bacon tells us, 'by some of the prelates in the Council of Trent, where the doctrines of the Schoolmen have great sway; that the schoolmen were like Astronomers, which did faigne Eccentricks and Epicycles and Engines of Orbs to save the Phenomena; though they knew there were no such Things; and in like manner that the Schoolmen had framed a number of subtile and intricate Axioms and Theorems, to save the practice of the Church.'† This is true of much else besides scholastic axioms and theorems. Subordinate error was made necessary and invented, by reason of some pre-existent main stock of error, and to save the practice of the Church. Thus we are often referred to the consolation which this or that doctrine has brought to the human spirit. But what if the same system had produced the terror which made absence of consolation intolerable? How much of the necessity for expressing the enlarged humanity of the Church in the doctrine of purgatory, arose from the existence of the older unsoftened doctrine of eternal hell?

Again, how much of this alleged necessity of error, as alloy for the too pure metal of sterling truth, is to be explained by the interest which powerful castes or corporations have had in preserving the erroneous forms, even when they could not resist, or did not wish to resist, their impregnation by newer and better doctrine? This interest was not deliberately sinister or malignant. It may be more correctly as well as more charitably explained by that infirmity of human nature, which makes us very ready to believe what it is on other grounds convenient to us to believe. Nobody attributes to pure malevolence the heartiness with which the great corporation of lawyers, for example, resist the removal of superfluous and obstructive forms in their practice; they have come to look on such forms as indispensable safeguards. Hence

---

note 7 continued

Contre un homme timide que cette idée contient, il en est des millions qu'elle ne peut contenir; il en est des millions qu'elle rend insensés, farouches, fanatiques, inutiles et méchants; il en est des millions qu'elle détourne de leurs devoirs envers la société; il en est une infinité qu'elle afflige et qu'elle trouble, sans aucun bien réel pour leurs associés.' – *Système de la Nature*, i. xiii.†

powerful teachers and preachers of all kinds have been spontaneously inclined to suppose a necessity, which had no real existence, of preserving as much as was possible of what we know to be error, even while introducing wholesome modification of it. This is the honest, though mischievous, conservatism of the human mind. We have no right to condemn our foregoers; far less to lavish on them the evil names of impostor, charlatan, and brigand, which the zealous unhistoric school of the last century used so profusely. But we have a right to say of them, as we say of those who imitate their policy now, that their conservatism is no additional proof of the utility of error. Least of all is it any justification for those who wish to have impressed upon the people a complete system of religious opinion which men of culture have avowedly put away.† And, moreover, the very priests must, I should think, be supposed to have put it away also. Else they would hardly be invited deliberately to abdicate their teaching functions in the very seats where teaching is of the weightiest and most far-spreading influence.

Meanwhile our point is that the reforms in opinion which have been effected on the plan of pouring the new wine of truth into the old bottles of superstition – though not dishonourable to the sincerity of the reformers – are no testimony to even the temporary usefulness of error. Those who think otherwise do not look far enough in front of the event. They forget the evil wrought by the prolonged duration of the error, to which the added particle of truth may have given new vitality. They overlook the ultimate enervation that is so often the price paid for the temporary exaltation.

Nor, finally, can they know the truths which the error thus prolonged has hindered from coming to the birth. A strenuous disputant has recently asserted against me that 'the region of the *might have been* lies beyond the limits of sane speculation.'[8] It is surely extending optimism too far to insist on carrying it back right through the ages. To me at any rate the history of mankind is a huge *pis-aller*, just as our present society is; a prodigious wasteful experiment, from which a certain number of precious results have been extracted, but which is not now, nor ever has been at any other time, a final measure of all the possibilities of the time. This is not inconsistent with the scientific conception of history; it is not to deny the great law that society has a certain order of progress; but only to urge that within that, the only possible order, there is always room for all kinds and degrees of invention, improvement, and happy or unhappy accident. There is no discoverable law

---

8 Sir J. F. Stephen's *Liberty, Equality, and Fraternity*, 2nd ed., p. 19, *note*.

fixing precisely the more or the less of these; nor how much of each of them a community shall meet with, nor exactly when it shall meet with them. We have to distinguish between possibility and necessity. Only certain steps in advance are possible at a given time; but it is not inevitable that these potential advances should all be realised. Does anybody suppose that humanity has had the profit of all the inventive and improving capacity born into the world? That Turgot, for example, was the only man that ever lived, who might have done more for society than he was allowed to do, and spared society a cataclysm? No, – history is a *pis-aller*.† It has assuredly not moved without the relation of cause and effect; it is a record of social growth and its conditions; but it is also a record of interruption and misadventure and perturbation. You trace the long chain which has made us what we are in this aspect and that. But where are the dropped links that might have made all the difference? *Ubi sunt eorum tabulæ qui post vota nuncupata perierunt?* Where is the fruit of those multitudinous gifts which came into the world in untimely seasons? We accept the past for the same reason that we accept the laws of the solar system, though, as Comte says, 'we can easily conceive them improved in certain respects.' The past, like the solar system, is beyond reach of modification at our hands, and we cannot help it. But it is surely the mere midsummer madness of philosophic complacency to think that we have come by the shortest and easiest of all imaginable routes to our present point in the march; to suppose that we have wasted nothing, lost nothing, cruelly destroyed nothing, on the road. What we have lost is all in the region of the 'might have been,' and we are justified in taking this into account, and thinking much of it, and in trying to find causes for the loss. One of them has been want of liberty for the human intelligence; and another, to return to our proper subject, has been the prolonged existence of superstition, of false opinions, and of attachment to gross symbols, beyond the time when they might have been successfully attacked, and would have fallen into decay but for the mistaken political notion of their utility. In making a just estimate of this utility, if we see reason to believe that these false opinions, narrow superstitions, gross symbols, have been an impediment to the free exercise of the intelligence and a worthier culture of the emotions, then we are justified in placing the unknown loss as a real and most weighty item in the account against them.

In short, then, the utmost that can be said on behalf of errors in opinion and motive, is that they are inevitable elements in human growth. But the inevitable does not coincide with the useful. Pain can be avoided by none of the sons of men, yet the horrible and uncompensated subtraction which it makes from the value and usefulness of human life, is one of the most formidable obstacles to the smoother progress of the world. And as with pain, so with error. The moral of our contention has reference to the temper in which practically we ought to regard false doctrine and ill-directed motive. It goes to show that if we have satisfied ourselves on good grounds that the doctrine is false, or the motive ill directed, then the only question that we need ask ourselves turns solely upon the possibility of breaking it up and dispersing it, by methods compatible with the doctrine of liberty. Any embarrassment in dealing with it, due to a semi-latent notion that it may be useful to some one else, is a weakness that hinders social progress.†

Chapter III

Intellectual Responsibility and the Political Spirit

We have been considering the position of those who would fain divide the community into two great castes; the one of thoughtful and instructed persons using their minds freely, but guarding their conclusions in strict reserve; the other of the illiterate or unreflecting, who should have certain opinions and practices taught them, not because they are true or are really what their votaries are made to believe them to be, but because the intellectual superiors of the community think the inculcation of such a belief useful in all cases save their own. Nor is this a mere theory. On the contrary, it is a fair description of an existing state of things. We have the old *disciplina arcani* among us in as full force as in the primitive church, but with an all-important difference. The Christian fathers practised reserve for the sake of leading the acolyte the more surely to the fulness of truth. The modern economiser keeps back his opinions, or dissembles the grounds of them, for the sake of leaving his neighbours the more at their ease in the peaceful sloughs of prejudice and superstition and low ideals. We quote Saint Paul when he talked of making himself all things to all men, and of becoming to the Jews a Jew, and as without the Law to the heathen.† But then we do so with a view to justifying ourselves for leaving the Jew to remain a Jew, and the heathen to remain heathen. We imitate the same apostle in accepting old timeworn altars dedicated to the Unknown God.† We forget that he made the ancient symbol the starting-point of a revolutionised doctrine. There is, as anybody can see, a whole world of difference between the reserve of sagacious apostleship, on the one hand, dealing tenderly with scruple and fearfulness and fine sensibility of conscience, and the reserve of intellectual cowardice on the other hand, dealing hypocritically with narrow minds in the supposed interests of social peace and quietness. The old *disciplina arcani* signified the disclosure of a little light with a view to the disclosure of more. The new means the dissimulation of truth with a view to the perpetuation of error. Consider the difference between these two fashions of compromise, in their effects upon the mind and character of the person compromising. The one is fully compatible with fervour and hopefulness and devotion to great causes. The other stamps a man with artifice, and hinders the free eagerness of his vision, and wraps him about with mediocrity, – not always of understanding, but that still worse thing, mediocrity of aspiration and purpose.

The coarsest and most revolting shape† which the doctrine of conformity can assume, and its degrading consequences to the character of the conformer, may be conveniently illustrated by a passage in the life of Hume. He looked at things in a more practical manner than would find favour with the sentimental champions of compromise in nearer times. There is a well-known letter of Hume's, in which he recommends a young man to become a clergyman, on the ground that it was very hard to get any tolerable civil employment, and that as Lord Bute was then all powerful, his friend would be certain of preferment. In answer to the young man's scruples as to the Articles and the rest, Hume says: –

'It is putting too great a respect on the vulgar and their superstitions to pique one's self on sincerity with regard to them. If the thing were worthy of being treated gravely, I should tell him [the young man] that the Pythian oracle with the approbation of Xenophon advised every one to worship the gods – νόμῳ πόλεως. I wish it were still in my power to be a hypocrite in this particular. The common duties of society usually require it; and the ecclesiastical profession only adds a little more to an innocent dissimulation, or rather simulation, without which it is impossible to pass through the world.'[1]

This is a singularly straightforward way of stating a view which silently influences a much greater number of men than it is pleasant to think of. They would shrink from throwing their conduct into so gross a formula. They will lift up their hands at this quotation, so strangely blind are we to the hiding-places of our own hearts, even when others flash upon them the terrible illumination that comes of calling conduct and motives by plain names. Now it is not merely the moral improbity of these cases which revolts us – the improbity of making in solemn form a number of false statements for the sake of earning a livelihood; of saying in order to get money or social position that you accept a number of propositions which in fact you utterly reject; of declaring expressly that you trust you are inwardly moved to take upon you this office and ministration by the Holy Ghost, when the real motive is a desire not to miss the chance of making something

---

[1] Burton's *Life of Hume*, ii. 186–188.

out of the Earl of Bute. This side of such dissimulation is shocking enough. And it is not any more shocking to the most devout believer than it is to people who doubt whether there be any Holy Ghost or not. Those who no longer place their highest faith in powers above and beyond men, are for that very reason more deeply interested than others in cherishing the integrity and worthiness of man himself. Apart, however, from the immorality of such reasoned hypocrisy, which no man with a particle of honesty will attempt to blink, there is the intellectual improbity which it brings in its train, the infidelity to truth, the disloyalty to one's own intelligence. Gifts of understanding are numbed and enfeebled in a man, who has once played such a trick with his own conscience as to persuade himself that, because the vulgar are superstitious, it is right for the learned to earn money by turning themselves into the ministers and accomplices of superstition. If he is clever enough to see through the vulgar and their beliefs, he is tolerably sure to be clever enough from time to time and in his better moments to see through himself. He begins to suspect himself of being an impostor. That suspicion gradually unmans him when he comes to use his mind in the sphere of his own enlightenment. One of really superior power cannot escape these better moments and the remorse that they bring. As he advances in life, as his powers ought to be coming to fuller maturity and his intellectual productiveness to its prime, just in the same degree the increasing seriousness of life multiplies such moments and deepens their remorse, and so the light of intellectual promise slowly goes out in impotent endeavour, or else in taking comfort that much goods are laid up, or, what is deadliest of all, in a soulless cynicism.

We do not find out until it is too late that the intellect too, at least where it is capable of being exercised on the higher objects, has its sensitiveness. It loses its colour and potency and finer fragrance in an atmosphere of mean purpose and low conception of the sacredness of fact and reality. Who has not observed inferior original power achieving greater results even in the intellectual field itself, where the superior understanding happens to have been unequally yoked with a self-seeking character, ever scenting the expedient? If Hume had been in the early productive part of his life the hypocrite which he wished it were in his power to show himself in its latter part, we may be tolerably sure that European philosophy would have missed one of its foremost figures. It has been often said that he who begins life by stifling his convictions, is in a fair way for ending it without any convictions to stifle. We may, perhaps, add that he who sets out with the notion that the difference between truth and falsehood is a thing of no concern to the vulgar, is very likely sooner or later to come to the kindred notion that it is not a thing of any supreme concern to himself.

Let thus much have been said as to those who deliberately and knowingly sell their intellectual birthright for a mess of pottage, making a brazen compromise with what they hold despicable, lest they should have to win their bread honourably. Men need to expend no declamatory indignation upon them. They have a hell of their own; words can add no bitterness to it. It is no light thing to have secured a livelihood on condition of going through life masked and gagged. To be compelled, week after week, and year after year, to recite the symbols of ancient faith and lift up his voice in the echoes of old hopes, with the blighting thought in his soul that the faith is a lie, and the hope no more than the folly of the crowd; to read hundreds of times in a twelvemonth with solemn unction as the inspired word of the Supreme what to him are meaningless as the Abracadabras of the conjuror in a booth; to go on to the end of his days administering to simple folk holy rites of commemoration and solace, when he has in his mind at each phrase what dupes are these simple folk and how wearisomely counterfeit their rites: and to know through all that this is really to be the one business of his prostituted life, that so dreary and hateful a piece of play-acting will make the desperate retrospect of his last hours – of a truth here is the very $\beta\delta\epsilon\lambda\upsilon\gamma\mu\alpha$ $\tau\eta s$ $\epsilon\rho\eta\mu\omega\sigma\omega s$, the abomination of desolation of the human spirit indeed.

No one will suppose that this is designed for the normal type of priest. But it is well to study tendencies in their extreme catastrophe. This is only the catastrophe, in one of its many shapes, of the fatal doctrine that money, position, power, philanthropy, or any of the thousand seductive masks of the pseudo-expedient, may carry a man away from love of truth and yet leave him internally unharmed. The depravation that follows the trucking for money of intellectual freedom and self-respect, attends in its degree each other departure from disinterested following of truth, and each other substitution of convenience, whether public or private, in its place. And both parties to such a compromise are losers. The world which offers gifts and tacitly undertakes to ask no questions as to the real state of the timeserver's inner mind, loses no less than the timeserver himself who receives the gifts and promises to hold his peace. It is as though a society placed penalties on mechanical inventions and the exploration of new material resources, and offered bounties for the steadiest adherence to all ancient processes in culture and production. The injury to wealth in the one case would not be any deeper than the injury to morality is in the other.†

To pass on to less sinister forms of this abnegation of intellectual responsibility. In the opening sentences of the first chapter we spoke of a wise suspense in forming opinions, a wise reserve in expressing them, and a wise tardiness in trying to realise them. Thus we meant to mark out the three independent provinces of compromise, each of them being the subject of considerations that either do not apply at all to the other two, or else apply in a different degree. Disingenuousness or self-illusion, arising from a depressing deference to the existing state of things, or to what is immediately practicable, or to what other people would think of us if they knew our thoughts, is the result of compromising truth in the matter of forming and holding opinions. Secondly, positive simulation is what comes of an unlawful willingness to compromise in the matter of avowing and publishing them. Finally, pusillanimity or want of faith is the vice that belongs to unlawful compromise in the department of action and realisation. This is not merely a division arranged for convenience of discussion. It goes to the root of conduct and character, and is the key to the present mood of our society. It is always a hardy thing to attempt to throw a complex matter into very simple form, but we should say that the want of energy and definiteness in contemporary opinions, of which we first complained, is due mainly to the following notion; that if a subject is not ripe for practical treatment, you and I are therefore entirely relieved from the duty of having clear ideas about it. If the majority cling to an opinion, why should we ask whether that is the sound and right opinion or the reverse? Now this notion, which springs from a confusion of the three fields of compromise with one another, quietly reigns almost without dispute. The devotion to the practical aspect of truth is in such excess, as to make people habitually deny that it can be worth while to form an opinion, when it happens at the moment to be incapable of realisation, for the reason that there is no direct prospect of inducing a sufficient number of persons to share it. 'We are quite willing to think that your view is the right one, and would produce all the improvements for which you hope; but then there is not the smallest chance of persuading the only persons able to carry out such a view; why therefore discuss it?' No talk is more familiar to us than this. As if the mere possibility of the view being a right one did not obviously entitle it to discussion; discussion being the only process by which people are likely to be induced to accept it, or else to find good grounds for finally dismissing it.

It is precisely because we believe that opinion, and nothing but opinion, can effect great permanent changes, that we ought to be careful to keep this most potent force honest, wholesome, fearless, and independent. Take the political field. Politicians and newspapers almost systematically refuse to talk about a new idea, which is not capable of being at once embodied in a bill, and receiving the royal assent before the following August. There is something rather contemptible, seen from the ordinary standards of intellectual integrity, in the position of a minister who waits to make up his mind whether a given measure, say the disestablishment of the Irish Church, is in itself and on the merits desirable, until the official who runs diligently up and down the backstairs of the party, tells him that the measure is practicable and required in the interests of the band. On the one hand, a leader is lavishly panegyrised for his highmindedness, in suffering himself to be driven into his convictions by his party. On the other, a party is extolled for its political tact, in suffering itself to be forced out of its convictions by its leader. It is hard to decide which is the more discreditable and demoralising sight. The education of chiefs by followers, and of followers by chiefs, into the abandonment in a month of the traditions of centuries or the principles of a lifetime may conduce to the rapid and easy working of the machine. It certainly marks a triumph of the political spirit which the author of *The Prince* might have admired. It is assuredly mortal to habits of intellectual self-respect in the society which allows itself to be amused by the cajolery and legerdemain and self-sophistication of its rulers.

Of course there are excellent reasons why a statesman immersed in the actual conduct of affairs, should confine his attention to the work which his hands find to do. But the fact that leading statesmen are of necessity so absorbed in the tasks of the hour furnishes all the better reason why as many other people as possible should busy themselves in helping to prepare opinion for the practical application of unfamiliar but weighty and promising suggestions, by constant and ready discussion of them upon their merits. As a matter of fact it is not the men most occupied who are usually most deaf to new ideas. It is the loungers of politics, the quidnuncs, gossips, bustling idlers, who are most industrious in stifling discussion by protests against the waste of time and the loss of force involved in talking about proposals which are not exactly ready to be voted on. As it is, everybody knows that questions are inadequately discussed, or often not discussed at all, on the ground that the time is not yet come for their solution. Then when some unforeseen perturbation, or the natural course of things, forces on the time for their solution, they are settled in a slovenly, imperfect, and often downright vicious manner, from the fact that opinion has not been prepared for solving them in an efficient and perfect manner. The so-called settlement of the question of national education is the most recent and most deplorable illustration of what comes of refusing to examine ideas alleged to be impracticable. Perhaps we may venture to prophesy that the disendowment of the national church will supply the next illustration on an imposing scale. Gratuitous primary instruction, and the redistribution of electoral power, are other matters of signal importance, which comparatively few men will consent to discuss seriously and patiently, and for our indifference to which we shall one day surely smart. A judicious and cool writer has said that 'an opinion gravely professed by a man of sense and education demands always respectful consideration – demands and actually receives it from those whose own sense and education give them a correlative right; and whoever offends against this sort of courtesy may fairly be deemed to have forfeited the privileges it secures.'² That is the least part of the matter. The serious mischief is the eventual miscarriage and loss and prodigal waste of good ideas.

The evil of which we have been speaking comes of not seeing the great truth, that it is worth while to take pains to find out the best way of doing a given task, even if you have strong grounds for suspecting that it will ultimately be done in a worse way. And so also in spheres of thought away from the political sphere, it is worth while 'to scorn delights and live laborious days'† in order to make as sure as we can of having the best opinion, even if we know that this opinion has an infinitely small chance of being speedily or ever accepted by the majority, or by anybody but ourselves. Truth and wisdom have to bide their time, and then take their chance after all. The most that the individual can do is to seek them for himself, even if he seek alone. And if it is the most, it is also the least. Yet in our present mood we seem not to feel this. We misunderstand the considerations which should rightly lead us in practice to surrender some of what we desire, in order to secure the rest; and rightly make us acquiesce in a second-best course of action, in order to avoid stagnation or retrogression. We misunderstand all this, and go on to suppose that there are the same grounds why we should in our own minds acquiesce in second-best opinions; why we should mix a little alloy of conventional expression with the too fine ore of conviction; why we should adopt beliefs that

---

2 Isaac Taylor's *Natural History of Enthusiasm*, p. 226.

we suspect in our hearts to be of more than equivocal authenticity, but into whose antecedents we do not greatly care to inquire, because they stand so well with the general public. This is compromise or economy or management of the first of the three kinds of which we are talking. It is economy applied to the formation of opinion; compromise or management in making up one's mind.

The lawfulness or expediency of it turns mainly, as with the other two kinds of compromise, upon the relative rights of the majority and the minority, and upon the respect which is owing from the latter to the former. It is a very easy thing for people endowed with the fanatical temperament, or demoralised by the habit of looking at society exclusively from the juridical point of view, to insist that no respect at all, except the respect that arises from being too weak to have your own way, is due from either to the other. This shallow and mischievous notion rests either on a misinterpretation of the experience of civilised societies, or else on nothing more creditable than an arbitrary and unreflecting temper. Those who have thought most carefully and disinterestedly about the matter, are agreed that in advanced societies the expedient course is that no portion of the community should insist on imposing its own will upon any other portion, except in matters which are vitally connected with the maintenance of the social union. The question where this vital connection begins is open to much discussion. The line defining the sphere of legitimate interference may be drawn variously, whether at self-regarding acts, or in some other condition and element of conduct. Wherever this line may be best taken, not only abstract speculation, but the practical and spontaneous tact of the world, has decided that there are limits, alike in the interest of majority and minority, to the rights of either to disturb the other. In other words, it is expedient in certain affairs that the will of the majority should be absolutely binding, while in affairs of a different order it should count for nothing, or as nearly nothing as the sociable dependence of a man on his fellows will permit.

Our thesis is this. In the positive endeavour to realise an opinion, to convert a theory into practice, it may be, and very often is, highly expedient to defer to the prejudices of the majority, to move very slowly, to bow to the conditions of the *status quo*, to practise the very utmost sobriety, self-restraint, and conciliatoriness. The mere expression of opinion, in the next place, the avowal of dissent from received notions, the refusal to conform to language which implies the acceptance of such notions, – this rests on a different footing. Here the reasons for respecting the wishes and sentiments of the majority are far less strong, though, as we shall presently see, such reasons certainly exist, and will weigh with all well-considering men. Finally, in the formation of an opinion as to the abstract preferableness of one course of action over another, or as to the truth or falsehood or right significance of a proposition, the fact that the majority of one's contemporaries lean in the other direction is naught, and no more than dust in the balance. In making up our minds as to what would be the wisest line of policy if it were practicable, we have nothing to do with the circumstance that it is not practicable. And in settling with ourselves whether propositions purporting to state matters of fact are true or not, we have to consider how far they are conformable to the evidence. We have nothing to do with the comfort and solace which they would be likely to bring to others or ourselves, if they were taken as true.

A nominal assent to this truth will be instantly given even by those who in practice systematically disregard it. The difficulty of transforming that nominal assent into a reality is enormous in such a community as ours. Of all societies since the Roman Republic, and not even excepting the Roman Republic, England has been the most emphatically and essentially political.† She has passed through military phases and through religious phases, but they have been transitory, and the great central stream of national life has flowed in political channels. The political life has been stronger than any other, deeper, wider, more persistent, more successful. The wars which built up our far-spreading empire were not waged with designs of military conquest; they were mostly wars for a market. The great spiritual emancipation of the sixteenth and seventeenth centuries figures in our history partly as an accident, partly as an intrigue, partly as a raid of nobles in search of spoil. It was hardly until the reformed doctrine became associated with analogous ideas and corresponding precepts in government, that people felt at home with it, and became really interested in it.

One great tap-root of our national increase has been the growth of self-government, or government by deliberative bodies, representing opposed principles and conflicting interests. With the system of self-government has grown the habit – not of tolerance precisely, for Englishmen when in earnest are as little in love with tolerance as Frenchmen or any other people, but – of giving way to the will of the majority, so long as they remain a majority. This has come to pass for the simple reason that, on any other terms, the participation of large numbers of people in the control and arrangement of public affairs immediately becomes unworkable. The gradual concentration of power in the hands of a supreme deliberative body, the active share of so many thousands of persons in choosing and controlling its members, the close attention with which the proceedings of parliament are followed and watched, the kind of dignity that has been lent to parliamentary methods by the great importance of the transactions, have all tended in the same direction. They have all helped both to fix our strongest and most constant interests upon politics, and to ingrain the mental habits proper to politics, far more deeply than any other, into our general constitution and inmost character.

Thus the political spirit has grown to be the strongest element in our national life; the dominant force, extending its influence over all our ways of thinking in matters that have least to do with politics, or even nothing at all to do with them. There has thus been engendered among us the real sense of political responsibility. In a corresponding degree has been discouraged, what it is the object of the present chapter to urge, the sense of intellectual responsibility. If it were inevitable that one of these two should always enfeeble or exclude the other, if the price of the mental alacrity and open-mindedness of the age of Pericles must always be paid in the political incompetence of the age of Demosthenes, it would be hard to settle which quality ought to be most eagerly encouraged by those who have most to do with the spiritual direction of a community. No doubt the tone of a long-enduring and imperial society, such as Rome was, must be conservative, drastic, positive, hostile to the death to every speculative novelty. But then, after all, the permanence of Roman power was only valuable to mankind because it ensured the spread of certain civilising ideas. And these ideas had originated among people so characteristically devoid of the sovereign faculty of political coherency, as were the Greeks and the Jews. In the Greeks, it is true, we find not only ideas of the highest speculative fertility, but actual political institutions. Still we should hardly point to Greek history for the most favourable examples of their stable working. Practically and as a matter of history, a society is seldom at the same time successfully energetic both in temporals and spirituals; seldom prosperous alike in seeking abstract truth and nursing the political spirit. There is a decisive preponderance in one direction or the other, and the equal balance between free and active thinking, and coherent practical energy in a community, seems too hard to sustain. The vast military and political strength of Germany, for instance, did not exist, and was scarcely anticipated in men's minds, during the time of her most strenuous passion for abstract truth and deeper learning and new criticism. In France never was political and national interest so debilitated, so extinct, as it was during the reign of Lewis the

Fifteenth: her intellectual interest was never so vivid, so fruitful, or so widely felt.

Yet it is at least well, and more than that, it is an indispensable condition of social wellbeing, that the divorce between political responsibility and intellectual responsibility, between respect for what is instantly practicable and search after what is only important in thought, should not be too complete and universal. Even if there were no other objection, the undisputed predominance of the political spirit has a plain tendency to limit the subjects in which the men animated by it can take a real interest. All matters fall out of sight, or at least fall into a secondary place, which do not bear more or less directly and patently upon the material and structural welfare of the community. In this way the members of the community miss the most bracing, widening, and elevated of the whole range of influences that create great characters. First, they lose sincere concern about the larger questions which the human mind has raised up for itself. Second, they lose a fearless desire to reach the true answers to them, or if no certain answers should prove to be within reach, then at any rate to be satisfied on good grounds that this is so. Such questions are not immediately discerned by commonplace minds to be of social import. Consequently they, and all else that is not obviously connected with the machinery of society, give way in the public consideration to what is so connected with it, in a manner that cannot be mistaken.

Again, even minds that are not commonplace are affected for the worse by the same spirit. They are aware of the existence of the great speculative subjects and of their importance, but the pressure of the political spirit on such men makes them afraid of the conclusions to which free inquiry might bring them. Accordingly they abstain from inquiry, and dread nothing so much as making up their minds. They see reasons for thinking that, if they applied themselves seriously to the formation of true opinions in this or that department, they would come to conclusions which, though likely to make their way in the course of some centuries, are wholly unpopular now, and which might ruin the influence of anybody suspected of accepting, or even of so much as leaning towards, them. Life, they reflect, is short; missionaries do not pass for a very agreeable class, nor martyrs for a very sensible class; one can only do a trifling amount of good in the world, at best; it is moral suicide to throw away any chance of achieving even that trifle; and therefore it is best not only not to express, but not to take the trouble to acquire, right views in this quarter or that, and to draw clear away from such or such a region of thought, for the sake of keeping peace on earth and superficial good will among men.

It would be too harsh to stigmatise such a train of thought as self-seeking and hypocritical. It is the natural product of the political spirit, which is incessantly thinking of present consequences and the immediately feasible. There is nothing in the mere dread of losing it, to hinder influence from being well employed, so far as it goes. But one can hardly overrate the ill consequences of this particular kind of management, this unspoken bargaining with the little circle of his fellows which constitutes the world of a man. If he may retain his place among them as preacher or teacher, he is willing to forego his birthright of free explanation; he consents to be blind to the duty which attaches to every intelligent man of having some clear ideas, even though only provisional ones, upon the greatest subjects of human interest, and of deliberately preferring these, whatever they may be, to their opposites. Either an individual or a community is fatally dwarfed by any such limitation of the field in which one is free to use his mind. For it is a limitation, not prescribed by absorption in one set of subjects rather than another, nor by insufficient preparation for the discussion of certain subjects, nor by indolence nor incuriousness, but solely by apprehension of the conclusions to which such use of the mind might bring the too courageous seeker. If there were no other ill effect, this kind of limitation would at least have the radical disadvantage of dulling the edge of responsibility, of deadening the sharp sense of personal answerableness either to a God, or to society, or to a man's own conscience and intellectual self-respect.

How momentous a disadvantage this is, we can best know by contemplating the characters which have sometimes lighted up the old times. Men were then devoutly persuaded that their eternal salvation depended on their having true beliefs. Any slackness in finding out which beliefs are the true ones would have to be answered for before the throne of Almighty God, at the sure risk and peril of everlasting damnation. To what quarter in the large historic firmament can we turn our eyes with such certainty of being stirred and elevated, of thinking better of human life and the worth of those who have been most deeply penetrated by its seriousness, as to the annals of the intrepid spirits whom the protestant doctrine of indefeasible personal responsibility brought to the front in Germany in the sixteenth century, and in England and Scotland in the seventeenth? It is not their fanaticism, still less is it their theology, which makes the great Puritan chiefs of England and the stern Covenanters of Scotland so heroic in our sight.

It is the fact that they sought truth and ensued it, not thinking of the practicable nor cautiously counting majorities and minorities, but each man pondering and searching so 'as ever in the great Taskmaster's eye.'†

It is no adequate answer to urge that this awful consciousness of a divine presence and supervision has ceased to be the living fact it once was. That partly explains, but it certainly does not justify, our present lassitude. For the ever-wakeful eye of celestial power is not the only conceivable stimulus to responsibility. To pass from those grim heroes of protestantism to the French philosophers of the last century is a wide leap in a hundred respects, yet they too were pricked by the œstrus of intellectual responsibility. Their doctrine was dismally insufficient, and sometimes, as the present writer has often pointed out, it was directly vicious. Their daily lives were surrounded by much shabbiness and many meannesses. But, after all, no temptation and no menace, no pains or penalties for thinking about certain subjects, and no rewards for turning to think about something else, could divert such men as Voltaire and Diderot from their alert and strenuous search after such truth as could be vouchsafed to their imperfect lights. A catastrophe followed, it is true, but the misfortunes which attended it were due more to the champions of tradition and authority, than to the soldiers of emancipation. Even in the case of the latter, they were due to an inadequate doctrine, and not at all either to their sense of the necessity of free speculation and inquiry, or to the intrepidity with which they obeyed the promptings of that ennobling sense.

Perhaps the latest attempt of a considerable kind to suppress the political spirit in non-political concerns was the famous movement which had its birth a generation ago among the grey quadrangles and ancient gardens of Oxford, 'the sweet city with her dreaming spires,'† where there has ever been so much detachment from the world, alongside of the coarsest and fiercest hunt after the grosser prizes of the world. No one has much less sympathy with the direction of the tractarian revival than the present writer, in whose Oxford days the star of Newman had set, and the sun of Mill had risen in its stead. And it is needful to distinguish the fervid and strong spirits with whom the revival began from the mimics of our later day. No doubt the mere occasion of tractarianism was political. Its leaders were alarmed at the designs imputed to the newly reformed parliament of disestablishing the Anglican Church. They asked themselves the question, which I will put in their own words (*Tract* i.) – 'Should the government of the country so far forget their God as to cut off the Church, to deprive it of its temporal honours and substance, on what will you rest the claims to respect and attention which you make upon your flock?' In answering this question they speedily found themselves, as might have been expected, at the opposite pole of thought from things political. The whole strength of their appeal to members of the Church lay in men's weariness of the high and dry optimism, which presents the existing order of things as the noblest possible, and the undisturbed way of the majority as the way of salvation. Apostolical succession and Sacramentalism may not have been in themselves progressive ideas. The spirit which welcomed them had at least the virtue of taking away from Cæsar the things that are not Cæsar's.

Glaring as were the intellectual faults of the Oxford movement, it was at any rate a recognition in a very forcible way of the doctrine that spiritual matters are not to be settled by the dicta of a political council. It acknowledged that a man is answerable at his own peril for having found or lost the truth. It was a warning that he must reckon with a judge who will not account the *status quo*, nor the convenience of a cabinet, a good plea for indolent acquiescence in theological error. It ended, in the case of its most vigorous champions, in a final and deliberate putting out of the eyes of the understanding. The last act of assertion of personal responsibility was a headlong acceptance of the responsibility of tradition and the Church. This was deplorable enough. But apart from other advantages incidental to the tractarian movement, such as the attention which it was the means of drawing to history and the organic connection between present and past, it had, we repeat, the merit of being an effective protest against what may be called the House of Commons' view of human life – a view excellent in its place, but most blighting and dwarfing out of it. It was, what every sincere uprising of the better spirit in men and women must always be, an effective protest against the leaden tyranny of the man of the world and the so-called practical person. The man of the world despises catholics for taking their religious opinions on trust and being the slaves of tradition. As if he had himself formed his own most important opinions either in religion or anything else. He laughs at them for their superstitious awe of the Church. As if his own inward awe of the Greater Number were one whit less of a superstition. He mocks their deference for the past. As if his own absorbing deference to the present were one tittle better bottomed or a jot more respectable. The modern emancipation will profit us very little if the *status quo* is to be fastened round our necks with the despotic authority of a heavenly dispensation, and if in the stead of ancient Scriptures we are to accept the plenary inspiration of Majorities.

It may be urged that if, as it is the object of the present chapter to state, there are opinions which a man should form for himself, and which it may yet be expedient that he should not only be slow to attempt to realise in practical life, but sometimes even slow to express, – then we are demanding from him the performance of a troublesome duty, while we are taking from him the only motives which could really induce him to perform it. If, it may be asked, I am not to carry my notions into practice, nor try to induce others to accept them, nor even boldly publish them, why in the name of all economy of force should I take so much pains in forming opinions which are, after all, on these conditions so very likely to come to naught? The answer to this is that opinions do not come to naught, even if the man who holds them should never think fit to publish them. For one thing, as we shall see in our next division, the conditions which make against frank declaration of our convictions are of rare occurrence. And, apart from this, convictions may well exert a most decisive influence over our conduct, even if reasons exist, or seem to exist, for not pressing them on others. Though themselves invisible to the outer world, they may yet operate with magnetic force both upon other parts of our belief which the outer world does see, and upon the whole of our dealings with it. Whether we are good or bad, it is only a broken and incoherent fragment of our whole personality that even those who are intimate with us, much less the common world, can ever come into contact with. The important thing is that the personality itself should be as little as possible broken, incoherent, and fragmentary; that reasoned and consistent opinions should back a firm will, and independent convictions inspire the intellectual self-respect and strenuous self-possession which the clamour of majorities and the silent yet ever-pressing force of the *status quo* are equally powerless to shake.

Character is doubtless of far more importance than mere intellectual opinion. We only too often see highly rationalised convictions in persons of weak purpose or low motives. But while fully recognising this, and the sort of possible reality which lies at the root of such a phrase as 'godless intellect' or 'intellectual devils' – though the phrase has no reality when it is used by self-seeking politicians or prelates – yet it is well to remember the very obvious truth that opinions are at least an extremely important part of character. As it is sometimes put, what we think has a prodigiously close connection with what we are. The consciousness of having reflected seriously and conclusively on important questions, whether social or spiritual, augments dignity while it does not lessen humility. In this sense, taking thought can and does add a cubit to our stature. Opinions which we may not feel bound or even permitted to press on other people, are not the less forces for being latent. They shape ideals, and it is ideals that inspire conduct. They do this, though from afar, and though he who possesses them may not presume to take the world into his confidence. Finally, unless a man follows out ideas to their full conclusion without fear what the conclusion may be, whether he thinks it expedient to make his thought and its goal fully known or not, it is impossible that he should acquire a commanding grasp of principles. And a commanding grasp of principles, whether they are public or not, is at the very root of coherency of character. It raises mediocrity near to a level with the highest talents, if these talents are in company with a disposition that allows the little prudences of the hour incessantly to obscure the persistent laws of things. These persistencies, if a man has once satisfied himself of their direction and mastered their bearings and application, are just as cogent and valuable a guide to conduct, whether he publishes them *ad urbem et orbem*, or esteems them too strong meat for people who have, through indurated use and wont, lost the courage of facing unexpected truths.

One conspicuous result of the failure to see that our opinions have roots to them, independently of the feelings which either majorities or other portions of the people around us may entertain about them, is that neither political matters nor any other serious branches of opinion, engage us in their loftiest or most deep-reaching forms. The advocate of a given theory of government or society is so misled by a wrong understanding of the practice of just and wise compromise in applying it, as to forget the noblest and most inspiring shape which his theory can be made to assume. It is the worst of political blunders to insist on carrying an ideal set of principles into execution, where others have rights of dissent, and those others persons whose assent is as indispensable to success, as it is impossible to attain. But to be afraid or ashamed of holding such an ideal set of principles in one's mind in their highest and most abstract expression, does more than any one other cause to stunt or petrify those elements in character to which life should owe most of its savour.

If a man happens to be a Conservative, for instance, it is pitiful that he should think so much more of what other people on his side or the other think, than of the widest and highest of the ideas on which a conservative philosophy of life and human society reposes. Such ideas are these, – that the social union is the express creation and ordering of the Deity: that its movements follow his mysterious and fixed dispensation: that the church and the state are convertible terms, and each citizen of the latter is an incorporated member of the former: that conscience, if perversely and misguidedly self-asserting, has no rights against the decrees of the conscience of the nation: that it is the most detestable of crimes to perturb the pacific order of society either by active agitation or speculative restlessness: that descent from a long line of ancestors in great station adds an element of dignity to life, and imposes many high obligations. We do not say that these and the rest of the propositions which make up the true theoretic basis of a conservative creed, are proper for the hustings, or expedient in an election address or a speech in parliament. We do say that if these high and not unintelligible principles, which alone can give to reactionary professions any worth or significance, were present in the minds of men who speak reactionary language, the country would be spared the ignominy of seeing certain real truths of society degraded at the hands of aristocratic adventurers and plutocratic parasites into some miserable process of 'dishing Whigs.'†

This impoverishment of aims and depravation of principles by the triumph of the political spirit outside of its proper sphere, cannot unfortunately be restricted to any one set of people in the state. It is something in the very atmosphere, which no sanitary cordon can limit. Liberalism, too, would be something more generous, more attractive – yes, and more practically effective, if its professors and champions could allow their sense of what is feasible to be refreshed and widened by a more free recognition, however private and undemonstrative, of the theoretic ideas which give their social creed whatever life and consistency it may have. Such ideas are these: That the conditions of the social union are not a mystery, only to be touched by miracle, but the results of explicable causes, and susceptible of constant modification: that the thoughts of wise and patriotic men should be perpetually turned towards the improvement of these conditions in every direction: that contented acquiescence in the ordering that has come down to us from the past is selfish and anti-social, because amid the ceaseless change that is inevitable in a growing organism, the institutions of the past demand progressive re-adaptations: that such improvements are most likely to be secured in the greatest abundance by limiting the sphere of authority, extending that of free individuality, and steadily striving after the bestowal, so far as the nature of things will ever permit it, of equality of opportunity: that while there is dignity in ancestry, a modern society is only safe in proportion as it summons capacity to its public counsels and enterprises: that such a society to endure must progress: that progress on its political side means more than anything else the substitution of Justice as a governing idea, instead of Privilege, and that the best guarantee for justice in public dealings is the participation in their own government of the people most likely to suffer from injustice. This is not an exhaustive account of the progressive doctrine, and we have here nothing to say as to its soundness. We only submit that if those who use the watchwords of Liberalism were to return upon its principles, instead of dwelling exclusively on practical compromises, the tone of public life would be immeasurably raised. The cause of social improvement would be less systematically balked of the victories that are best worth gaining. Progress would mean something more than mere entrances and exits on the theatre of office. We should not see in the mass of parliamentary candidates – and they are important people, because nearly every Englishman with any ambition is a parliamentary candidate, actual or potential – that grave anxiety, that sober rigour, that immense caution, which are all so really laughable, because so many of these men are only anxious lest they should make a mistake in finding out what the majority of their constituents would like them to think; only rigorous against those who are indiscreet enough to press a principle against the beck of a whip or a wire-puller; and only very cautious not so much lest their opinion should be wrong, as lest it should not pay.†

Indolence and timidity have united to popularise among us a flaccid latitudinarianism, which thinks itself a benign tolerance for the opinions of others. It is in truth only a pretentious form of being without settled opinions of our own, and without any desire to settle them. No one can complain of the want of speculative activity at the present time in a certain way. The air, at a certain social elevation, is as full as it has ever been of ideas, theories, problems, possible solutions, suggested questions, and proffered answers. But then they are at large, without cohesion, and very apt to be the objects even in the more instructed minds of not much more than dilettante interest. We see in solution an immense number of notions, which people think it quite unnecessary to precipitate in the form of convictions. We constantly hear the age lauded for its tolerance, for its candour, for its openness of mind, for the readiness with which a hearing is given to ideas that forty years ago, or even less than that, would have excluded persons suspected of holding them from decent society, and in fact did so exclude them. Before, however, we congratulate ourselves too warmly on this, let us be quite sure that we are not mistaking for tolerance what is really nothing more creditable than indifference. These two attitudes of mind, which are so vitally unlike in their real quality, are so hard to distinguish in their outer seeming.

One is led to suspect that carelessness is the right name for what looks like reasoned toleration, by such a line of consideration as the following. It is justly said that at the bottom of all the great discussions of modern society lie the two momentous questions, first whether there is a God, and second whether the soul is immortal. In other words, whether our fellow-creatures are the highest beings who take an interest in us, or in whom we need take an interest; and, then, whether life in this world is the only life of which we shall ever be conscious. It is true of most people that when they are talking of evolution, and the origin of species, and the experiential or intuitional source of ideas, and the utilitarian or transcendental basis of moral obligation, these are the questions which they really have in their minds. Now, in spite of the scientific activity of the day, nobody is likely to contend that men are pressed keenly in their souls by any poignant stress of spiritual tribulation in the face of the two supreme enigmas. Nobody will say that there is much of that striving and wrestling and bitter agonising, which whole societies of men have felt before now on questions of far less tremendous import. Ours, as has been truly said, is 'a time of loud disputes and weak convictions.' In a generation deeply impressed by a sense of intellectual responsibility this could not be. As it is, even superior men are better pleased to play about the height of these great arguments, to fly in busy intellectual sport from side to side, from aspect to aspect, than they are intent on resolving what it is, after all, that the discussion comes to and to which solution, when everything has been said and heard, the balance of truth really seems to incline. There are too many giggling epigrams; people are too willing to look on collections of mutually hostile opinions with the same kind of curiosity which they bestow on a collection of mutually hostile beasts in a menagerie. They have very faint predilections for one rather than another. If they were truly alive to the duty of conclusiveness, or to the inexpressible magnitude of the subjects which nominally occupy their minds, but really only exercise their tongues, this elegant Pyrrhonism would be impossible, and this lighthearted neutrality most unendurable.

Well has the illustrious Pascal said with reference to one of the two great issues of the modern controversy: – 'The immortality of the soul is a thing that concerns us so closely and touches us so profoundly, that one must have lost all feeling to be indifferent as to knowing how the matter is. All our actions and all our thoughts must follow such different paths, according as there are eternal goods to hope for or are not, that it is impossible to take a step with sense and judgment, without regulating it in view of this point, which ought to be our first object.... I can have nothing but compassion for those who groan and travail in this doubt with all sincerity, who look on it as the worst of misfortunes, and who, sparing no pains to escape from it, make of this search their chief and most serious employment.... But he who doubts and searches not is at the same time a grievous wrongdoer, and a grievously unfortunate man. If along with this he is tranquil and self-satisfied, if he publishes his contentment to the world and plumes himself upon it, and if it is this very state of doubt which he makes the subject of his joy and vanity – I have no terms in which to describe so extravagant a creature.'[3] Who, except a member of the school of extravagant creatures themselves, would deny that Pascal's irritation is most wholesome and righteous?

Perhaps in reply to this, we may be confronted by our own doctrine of intellectual responsibility interpreted in a directly opposite sense. We may be reminded of the long array of difficulties that interfere between us and knowledge in that tremendous matter, and of objections that rise in such perplexing force to an answer either one way or the other. And finally we may be dispatched with a eulogy of caution and a censure of too great heat after certainty. The answer is that there is a kind of Doubt not without search, but after and at the end of search, which is not open to Pascal's just reproaches against the more ignoble and frivolous kind. And this too has been described for us by a subtle doctor of Pascal's communion. 'Are there pleasures of Doubt, as well as of Inference and Assent? In one sense there are. Not indeed if doubt means ignorance, uncertainty, or hopeless suspense; but there is a certain grave acquiescence in ignorance, a recognition of our impotence to solve momentous and urgent questions, which has a satisfaction of its own. After high aspirations, after renewed endeavours, after bootless toil, after long wanderings, after hope, effort, weariness, failure, painfully alternating and recurring, it is an immense relief to the exhausted mind to be able to say, "At length I know that I can know nothing about anything." ... Ignorance remains the evil which it ever was, but something of the peace of certitude is gained in knowing the worst, and in having reconciled the mind to the endurance of it.'[4] Precisely, and what one would say of our own age is that it will not deliberately

3 *Pensées*, II. Art. ii.
4 Dr. Newman's *Grammar of Assent*, p. 201.

face this knowledge of the worst. So it misses the peace of certitude, and not only its peace, but the strength and coherency that follow strict acceptance of the worst, when the worst is after all the best within reach.

Those who are in earnest when they blame too great haste after certainty, do in reality mean us to embrace certainty, but in favour of the vulgar opinions. They only see the prodigious difficulties of the controversy when you do not incline to their own side in it. They only panegyrise caution and the strictly provisional when they suspect that intrepidity and love of the conclusive would lead them to unwelcome shores. These persons, however, whether fortunately or unfortunately, have no longer much influence over the most active part of the national intelligence. Whether permanently or not, resolute orthodoxy, however prosperous it may seem among many of the uncultivated rich, has lost its hold upon thought. For thought has become dispersive, and the centrifugal forces of the human mind, among those who think seriously, have for the time become dominant and supreme. No one, I suppose, imagines that the singular ecclesiastical revival which is now going on, is accompanied by any revival of real and reasoned belief; or that the opulent manufacturers who subscribe so generously for restored cathedral fabrics and the like, have been moved by the apologetics of *Aids to Faith* and the Christian Evidence Society.

Obviously only three ways of dealing with the great problems of which we have spoken are compatible with a strong and well-bottomed character. We may affirm that there is a deity with definable attributes; and that there is a conscious state and continued personality after the dissolution of the body. Or we may deny. Or we may assure ourselves that we have no faculties enabling us on good evidence either to deny or affirm. Intellectual self-respect and all the qualities that are derived from that, may well go with any one of these three courses, decisively followed and consistently applied in framing a rule of life and a settled scheme of its aims and motives. Why do we say that intellectual self-respect is not vigorous, nor the sense of intellectual responsibility and truthfulness and coherency quick and wakeful among us? Because so many people, even among those who might be expected to know better, insist on the futile attempt to reconcile all those courses, instead of fixing on one and steadily abiding in it. They speak as if they affirmed, and they act as if they denied, and in their hearts they cherish a slovenly sort of suspicion that we can neither deny nor affirm. It may be said that this comes to much the same thing as if they had formally decided in the last or neutral sense. It is not so. This illegitimate union of three contradictories fritters character away, breaks it up into discordant parts, and dissolves into mercurial fluidity that leavening sincerity and free and cheerful boldness, which come of harmonious principles of faith and action, and without which men can never walk as confident lovers of justice and truth.

Ambrose's famous saying, that 'it hath not pleased the Lord to give his people salvation in dialectic,' has a profound meaning far beyond its application to theology. It is deeply true that our ruling convictions are less the product of ratiocination than of sympathy, imagination, usage, tradition. But from this it does not follow that the reasoning faculties are to be further discouraged. On the contrary, just because the other elements are so strong that they can be trusted to take care of themselves, it is expedient to give special countenance to the intellectual habits, which alone can check and rectify the constantly aberrating tendencies of sentiment on the one side, and custom on the other. This remark brings us to another type, of whom it is not irrelevant to speak shortly in this place. The consequences of the strength of the political spirit are not all direct, nor does its strength by any means spring solely from its indulgence to the less respectable elements of character, such as languor, extreme pliableness, superficiality. On the contrary, it has an indirect influence in removing the only effective restraint on the excesses of some qualities which, when duly directed and limited, are among the most precious parts of our mental constitution. The political spirit is the great force in throwing love of truth and accurate reasoning into a secondary place. The evil does not stop here. This achievement has indirectly countenanced the postponement of intellectual methods, and the diminution of the sense of intellectual responsibility, by a school that is anything rather than political.

Theology has borrowed, and coloured for her own use, the principles which were first brought into vogue in politics. If in the one field it is the fashion to consider convenience first and truth second, in the other there is a corresponding fashion of placing truth second and emotional comfort first.† If there are some who compromise their real opinions, or the chance of reaching truth, for the sake of gain, there are far more who shrink from giving their intelligence free play, for the sake of keeping undisturbed certain luxurious spiritual sensibilities. This choice of emotional gratification before truth and upright dealing with one's own understanding, creates a character that is certainly far less unlovely than those who sacrifice their intellectual integrity to mere material convenience. The moral flaw is less palpable and less gross. Yet here too there is the stain of intellectual improbity, and it is perhaps all the more mischievous for being partly hidden under the mien of spiritual exaltation.

There is in literature no more seductive illustration of this seductive type than Rousseau's renowned character of the Savoyard Vicar – penetrated with scepticism as to the attributes of the deity, the meaning of the holy rites, the authenticity of the sacred documents; yet full of reverence, and ever respecting in silence what he could neither reject nor understand. 'The essential worship,' he says, 'is the worship of the heart. God never rejects this homage, under whatever form it be offered to him. In old days I used to say mass with the levity which in time infects even the gravest things when we do them too often. Since acquiring my new principles [of reverential scepticism] I celebrate it with more veneration: I am overcome by the majesty of the Supreme Being, by his presence, by the insufficiency of the human mind, which conceives so ill what pertains to its author. When I approach the moment of consecration, I collect myself for performing the act with all the feelings required by the church and the majesty of the sacrament. I strive to annihilate my reason before the Supreme Intelligence, saying, Who art thou that thou shouldst measure infinite power?'[5]

The Savoyard Vicar is not imaginary. The acquiescence in indefinite ideas for the sake of comforted emotions, and the abnegation of strong convictions in order to make room for free and plenteous effusion, have for us all the marks of a too familiar reality. Such a doctrine is an everyday plea for self-deception, and a current justification for illusion even among some of the finer spirits. They have persuaded themselves not only that the life of the religious emotions is the highest life, but that it is independent of the intellectual forms with which history happens to have associated it. And so they refine and sophisticate and make havoc with plain and honest interpretation, in order to preserve a soft serenity of soul unperturbed.

Now, we are not at all concerned to dispute such positions as that Feeling is the right starting-point of moral education; that in forming character appeal should be to the heart rather than to the understanding; that the only basis on which our faculties can be harmoniously ordered is the preponderance of affection over reason. These propositions open much grave and complex discussion, and they are not to our present purpose. We only desire to state the evil of the notion that a man is warranted in comforting himself with dogmas and formularies, which

[5] *Emile*, bk. iv.

he has first to empty of all definite, precise, and clearly determinable significance, before he can get them out of the way of his religious sensibilities. Whether Reason or Affection is to have the empire in the society of the future, when Reason may possibly have no more to discover for us in the region of morals and religion, and so will have become *emeritus* and taken a lower place, as of a tutor whose services the human family, being now grown up, no longer requires, – however this may be, it is at least certain that in the meantime the spiritual life of man needs direction quite as much as it needs impulse, and light quite as much as force. This direction and light can only be safely procured by the free and vigorous use of the intelligence. But the intelligence is not free in the presence of a mortal fear lest its conclusions should trouble soft tranquillity of spirit. There is always hope of a man so long as he dwells in the region of the direct categorical proposition and the unambiguous term; so long as he does not deny the rightly drawn conclusion after accepting the major and minor premisses. This may seem a scanty virtue and very easy grace. Yet experience shows it to be too hard of attainment for those who tamper with disinterestedness of conviction, for the sake of luxuriating in the softness of spiritual transport without interruption from a syllogism. It is true that there are now and then in life as in history noble and fair natures, that by the silent teaching and unconscious example of their inborn purity, star-like constancy, and great devotion, do carry the world about them to further heights of living than can be attained by ratiocination. But these, the blameless and loved saints of the earth, rise too rarely on our dull horizons to make a rule for the world. The law of things is that they who tamper with veracity, from whatever motive, are tampering with the vital force of human progress. Our comfort and the delight of the religious imagination are no better than forms of self-indulgence, when they are secured at the cost of that love of truth on which, more than on anything else, the increase of light and happiness among men must depend. We have to fight and do lifelong battle against the forces of darkness, and anything that turns the edge of reason blunts the surest and most potent of our weapons.[†]

Chapter IV

Religious Conformity†

The main field of discussion touching Compromise in expression and avowal lies in the region of religious belief. In politics no one seriously contends that respect for the feelings and prejudices of other people requires us to be silent about our opinions. A republican, for instance, is at perfect liberty to declare himself so. Nobody will say that he is not within his rights if he should think it worth while to practise this liberty, though of course he will have to face the obloquy which attends all opinion that is not shared by the more demonstrative and vocal portions of the public. It is true that in every stable society a general conviction prevails of the extreme undesirableness of constantly laying bare the foundations of government. Incessant discussion of the theoretical bases of the social union is naturally considered worse than idle. It is felt by many wise men that the chief business of the political thinker is to interest himself in generalisations of such a sort as leads with tolerable straightness to practical improvements of a far-reaching and durable kind. Even among those, however, who thus feel it not to be worth while to be for ever handling the abstract principles which are, after all, only clumsy expressions of the real conditions that bring and keep men together in society, yet nobody of any consideration pretends to silence or limit the free discussion of these principles. Although a man is not likely to be thanked who calls attention to the vast discrepancies between the theory and practice of the constitution, yet nobody now would countenance the notion of an inner doctrine in politics. We smile at the line that Hume took in speaking of the doctrine of non-resistance. He did not deny that the right of resistance to a tyrannical sovereign does actually belong to a nation. But, he said, 'if ever on any occasion it were laudable to conceal truth from the populace, it must be confessed that the doctrine of resistance affords such an example; and that all speculative reasoners ought to observe with regard to this principle the same cautious silence which the laws, in every species of government, have ever prescribed to themselves.' As if the cautious silence of the political writer could prevent a populace from feeling the heaviness of an oppressor's hand, and striving to find relief from unjust burdens. As if any nation endowed with enough of the spirit of independence to assent to the right of resistance when offered to them as a speculative theorem, would not infallibly be led by the same spirit to assert the right without the speculative theorem. That so acute a head as Hume's should have failed to perceive these very plain considerations, and that he should moreover have perpetrated the absurdity of declaring the right of resistance, in the same breath in which he declares the laudableness of keeping it a secret, only shows how carefully a man need steer after he has once involved himself in the labyrinths of Economy.¹

In religion the unreasonableness of imposing a similar cautious silence is not yet fully established, nor the vicious effects of practising it clearly recognised. In these high matters an amount of economy and management is held praiseworthy, which in any other subject would be universally condemned as cowardly and ignoble. Indeed the preliminary stage has scarcely been reached – the stage in which public opinion grants to every one the unrestricted right of shaping his own beliefs, independently of those of the people who surround him. Any woman, for instance, suspected of having cast behind her the Bible and all practices of devotion and the elementary articles of the common creed, would be distrustfully regarded even by those who wink at the same kind of mental boldness in men. Nay, she would be so regarded even by some of the very men who have themselves discarded as superstition what they still wish women to retain for law and gospel. So long as any class of adults are effectually discouraged in the free use of their minds upon the most important subjects, we are warranted in saying that the era of free thought, which naturally precedes the era of free speech, is still imperfectly developed.

The duties and rights of free speech are by no means identical with those of independent thought. One general reason for this is tolerably

---

1 It may be said that Hume meant no more than this: that of two equally oppressed nations, the one which had been taught to assent to the doctrine of resistance would be more likely to practise 'the sacred duty of insurrection' than the other, from whom the doctrine had been concealed. Or, in other words, that the first would rise against oppression, when the oppression had reached a pitch which to the second would still seem bearable. The answer to Hume's proposition, interpreted in this way, would be that if the doctrine of resistance he presented to the populace in its true shape, – if it be 'truth,' as he admits, – then the application of it in practice should be as little likely to prove mischievous as that of any other truth. If the gist of the remark be that this is a truth which the populace is especially likely to apply wrongly, in consequence of its ignorance, passion, and heedlessness, we may answer by appealing to history, which is rather a record of excessive patience in the various nations of the earth than of excessive petulance.†

plain. The expression of opinion directly affects other people, while its mere formation directly affects no one but ourselves. Therefore the limits of compromise in expression are less widely and freely placed, because the rights and interests of all who may be made listeners to our spoken or written words are immediately concerned. In forming opinions, a man or woman owes no consideration to any person or persons whatever. Truth is the single object. It is truth that in the forum of conscience claims an undivided allegiance. The publication of opinion stands on another footing. That is an external act, with possible consequences, like all other external acts, both to the doer and to every one within the sphere of his influence. And, besides these, it has possible consequences to the prosperity of the opinion itself.[2]

A hundred questions of fitness, of seasonableness, of conflicting expediencies, present themselves in this connection, and nothing gives more anxiety to a sensible man who holds notions opposed to the current prejudices, than to hit the right mark where intellectual integrity and prudence, firmness and wise reserve, are in exact accord. When we come to declaring opinions that are, however foolishly and unreasonably, associated with pain and even a kind of turpitude in the minds of those who strongly object to them, then some of our most powerful sympathies are naturally engaged. We wonder whether duty to truth can possibly require us to inflict keen distress on those to whom we are bound by the tenderest and most consecrated ties. This is so wholly honourable a sentiment, that no one who has not made himself drunk with the thin sour wine of a crude and absolute logic will refuse to consider it. Before, however, attempting to illustrate cases of conscience in this order, we venture to make a short digression into the region of the matter, as distinct from the manner of free speech. One or two changes of great importance in the way in which men think about religion, bear directly upon the conditions on which they may permit themselves and others to speak about it.

The peculiar character of all the best kinds of dissent from the nominal creed of the time, makes it rather less difficult for us to try to reconcile

[2] There is another ground for the distinction between the conditions of holding and those of expressing opinion. This depends upon the psychological proposition that belief is independent of the will. Though this or any other state of the understanding may be involuntary, the manifestation of such a state is not so, but is a voluntary act, and, 'being neutral in itself, may be commendable or reprehensible according to the circumstances in which it takes place' (Bailey's *Essay on Formation of Opinion*, § 7).[†]

unflinching honesty with a just and becoming regard for the feelings of those who have claims upon our forbearance, than would have been the case a hundred years ago. 'It is not now with a polite sneer,' as a high ecclesiastical authority lately admitted, 'still less with a rude buffet or coarse words, that Christianity is assailed.'[†] Before churchmen congratulate themselves too warmly on this improvement in the nature of the attack, perhaps they ought to ask themselves how far it is due to the change in the position of the defending party. The truth is that the coarse and realistic criticism of which Voltaire was the consummate master, has done its work. It has driven the defenders of the old faith into the milder and more genial climate of non-natural interpretations, and the historic sense, and a certain elastic relativity of dogma. The old criticism was victorious, but after victory it vanished. One reason of this was that the coarse and realistic forms of belief had either vanished before it, or else they forsook their ancient pretensions and clothed themselves in more modest robes. The consequence of this, and of other causes which might be named, is that the modern attack, while fully as serious and much more radical, has a certain gravity, decorum, and worthiness of form. No one of any sense or knowledge now thinks the Christian religion had its origin in deliberate imposture. The modern freethinker does not attack it; he explains it. And what is more, he explains it by referring its growth to the better, and not to the worse part of human nature. He traces it to men's cravings for a higher morality. He finds its source in their aspirations after nobler expression of that feeling for the incommensurable things, which is in truth under so many varieties of inwoven pattern the common universal web of religious faith.

The result of this way of looking at a creed which a man no longer accepts, is that he is able to speak of it with patience and historic respect. He can openly mark his dissent from it, without exacerbating the orthodox sentiment by galling pleasantries or bitter animadversion upon details. We are now awake to the all-important truth that belief in this or that detail of superstition is the result of an irrational state of mind, and flows logically from superstitious premisses. We see that it is to begin at the wrong end, to assail the deductions as impossible, instead of sedulously building up a state of mind in which their impossibility would become spontaneously visible.

Besides the great change which such a point of view makes in men's way of speaking of a religion, whose dogmas and documents they reject, there is this further consideration leaning in the same direction. The tendency of modern free thought is more and more visibly towards the extraction of the first and more permanent elements of the old faith, to make the purified material of the new. When Dr. Congreve met the famous epigram about Comte's system being Catholicism minus Christianity, by the reply that it is Catholicism plus Science,† he gave an ingenious expression to the direction which is almost necessarily taken by all who attempt, in however informal a manner, to construct for themselves some working system of faith, in place of the faith which science and criticism have sapped. In what ultimate form, acceptable to great multitudes of men, these attempts will at last issue, no one can now tell. For we, like the Hebrews of old, shall all have to live and die in faith, 'not having received the promises, but having seen them afar off, and being persuaded of them, and embracing them, and confessing that we are strangers and pilgrims on the earth.'† Meanwhile, after the first great glow and passion of the just and necessary revolt of reason against superstition have slowly lost the exciting splendour of the dawn, and become diffused in the colourless space of a rather bleak noonday, the mind gradually collects again some of the ideas of the old religion of the West, and willingly, or even joyfully, suffers itself to be once more breathed upon by something of its spirit. Christianity was the last great religious synthesis. It is the one nearest to us. Nothing is more natural than that those who cannot rest content with intellectual analysis, while awaiting the advent of the Saint Paul of the humanitarian faith of the future, should gather up provisionally such fragmentary illustrations of this new faith as are to be found in the records of the old. Whatever form may be ultimately imposed on our vague religious aspirations by some prophet to come, who shall unite sublime depth of feeling and lofty purity of life with strong intellectual grasp and the gift of a noble eloquence, we may at least be sure of this, that it will stand as closely related to Christianity as Christianity stood closely related to the old Judaic dispensation. It is commonly assumed that the rejecters of the popular religion stand in face of it, as the Christians stood in face of the pagan belief and pagan rites in the Empire. The analogy is inexact. The modern denier, if he is anything better than that, or entertains hopes of a creed to come, is nearer to the position of the Christianising Jew.³

3 The following words, illustrating the continuity between the Christian and Jewish churches, are not without instruction to those who meditate on the possible continuity between the Christian church and that which is one day to [gr]ow into the place of it: – 'Not only do forms and ordinances remain under [the] Gospel equally as before; but, what was in use before is not so much [sup]erseded by the Gospel ordinances as changed into them. What took place [und]er the Law is a pattern, what was commanded is a rule, under the Gospel.

Science, when she has accomplished all her triumphs in her own order, will still have to go back, when the time comes, to assist in the building up of a new creed by which men can live. The builders will have to seek material in the purified and sublimated ideas, of which the confessions and rites of the Christian churches have been the grosser expression. Just as what was once the new dispensation was preached *a Judæis ad Judæos apud Judæos*,† so must the new, that is to be, find a Christian teacher and Christian hearers. It can hardly be other than an expansion. a development, a re-adaptation, of all the moral and spiritual truth that lay hidden under the worn-out forms. It must be such a harmonising of the truth with our intellectual conceptions, as shall fit it to be an active guide to conduct. In a world '*where men sit and hear each other groan, where but to think is to be full of sorrow*,' † it is hard to imagine a time when we shall be indifferent to that sovereign legend of Pity. We have to incorporate it in some wider gospel of Justice and Progress.

I shall not, I hope, be suspected of any desire to prophesy too smooth things. It is no object of ours to bridge over the gulf between belief in the vulgar theology and disbelief. Nor for a single moment do we pretend that, when all the points of contact between virtuous belief and virtuous disbelief are made the most of that good faith will allow, there will not still and after all remain a terrible controversy between those who cling passionately to all the consolations, mysteries, personalities, of the orthodox faith, and us who have made up our minds to face the worst, and to shape, as best we can, a life in which the cardinal verities of the common creed shall have no place. The future faith, like the faith of the past, brings not peace but a sword. It is a tale not of concord, but of households divided against themselves. Those who are incessantly striving to make the old bottles hold the new wine, to

note 3 continued
The substance remains, the use, the meaning, the circumstances, the benefit is changed; grace is added, life is infused: "the body is of Christ;" but it is in great measure that same body which was in being before He came. The Gospel has not put aside, it has incorporated into itself the revelation which went before it. It avails itself of the Old Testament, as a great gift to Christian as well as to Jew. It does not dispense with it, but it dispenses it. Persons sometimes urge that there is no code of duty in the New Testament, no ceremonial, no rules for Church polity. Certainly not; they are unnecessary; they are already given in the Old. Why should the Old Testament remain in the Christian church but to be used? *There* we are to look for our forms, our rites, our polity; only illustrated, tempered, spiritualised by the Gospel. The precepts remain, the observance of them is changed.' – Dr. J. H. Newman: *Sermon on Subjects of the Day*, p. 205.†

reconcile the irreconcilable, to bring the Bible and the dogmas of the churches to be good friends with history and criticism, are prompted by the humanest intention.[4] One sympathises with this amiable anxiety to soften shocks, and break the rudeness of a vital transition. In this essay, at any rate, there is no such attempt. We know that it is the son against the father, and the mother-in-law against the daughter-in-law. No softness of speech will disguise the portentous differences between those who admit a supernatural revelation and those who deny it. No charity nor goodwill can narrow the intellectual breach between those who declare that a world without an ever-present Creator with intelligible attributes would be to them empty and void, and those who insist that none of the attributes of a Creator can ever be grasped by the finite intelligence of men.[5] Our object in urging the purpose, semi-conservative, and almost sympathetic quality, which distinguishes the unbelief of to-day from the unbelief of a hundred years ago, is only to show that the most strenuous and upright of plain-speakers is less likely to shock and wound the lawful sensibilities of devout persons than he would have been so long as unbelief went no further than bitter attack on small details. In short, all save the purely negative and purely destructive school of freethinkers, are now able to deal with the beliefs from which they dissent, in a way which makes patient and disinterested controversy not wholly impossible.

One more point of much importance ought to be mentioned. The

---

4 There is a set of most acute and searching criticisms on this matter in Mr. Leslie Stephen's *Essays on Free-Thinking and Plain-Speaking* (Longmans, 1873). The last essay in the volume, *An Apology for Plain-Speaking*, is a decisive and remarkable exposition of the treacherous playing with words, which underlies even the most vigorous efforts to make the phrases and formulæ of the old creed hold the reality of new faith.†

5 Upon this sentence the following criticism has been made: – 'Surely both of these so-called contradictions are deliberately affirmed by the vast majority of all thinkers upon the subject. What orthodox asserter of the omnipresence of a "Creator with intelligible attributes" ever maintained that these attributes could be "grasped by men"?' – The orthodox asserter, no doubt, *says* that he does not maintain that the divine attributes can be grasped by men; but his habitual treatment of them as intelligible, and as the subjects of propositions made in language that is designed to be intelligible, shows that his first reservation is merely nominal, as it is certainly inconsistent with his general position. Religious people who warn you most solemnly that man who is a worm and the son of a worm cannot possibly compass in his puny understanding the attributes of the Divine Being, will yet – as an eminent divine not in holy orders has truly said – tell you all about him, as if he were the man who lives in the next street.†

belief that heresy is the result of wilful depravity is fast dying out. People no longer seriously think that speculative error is bound up with moral iniquity, or that mistaken thinking is either the result or the cause of wicked living. Even the official mouthpieces of established beliefs now usually represent a bad heart as only one among other possible causes of unbelief. It divides the curse with ignorance, intellectual shallowness, the unfortunate influence of plausible heresiarchs, and other alternative roots of evil. They thus leave a way of escape, by which the person who does not share their own convictions may still be credited with a good moral character. Some persons, it is true, 'cannot see how a man who deliberately rejects the Roman Catholic religion can, in the eyes of those who earnestly believe it, be other than a rebel against God.' They assure us that, 'as opinions become better marked and more distinctly connected with action, the truth that decided dissent from them implies more or less of a reproach upon those who hold them decidedly, becomes so obvious that every one perceives it.' No doubt a protestant or a sceptic regards the beliefs of a catholic as a reproach upon the believer's understanding. So the man whose whole faith rests on the miraculous and on acts of special intervention, regards the strictly positive and scientific thinker as the dupe of a crude and narrow logic. But this now carries with it no implication of moral obliquity. De Maistre's rather grotesque conviction that infidels always die of horrible diseases with special names, could now only be held among the very dregs of the ecclesiastical world.

Nor is it correct to say that 'when religious differences come to be, and are regarded as, mere differences of opinion, it is because the controversy is really decided in the sceptical sense.' Those who agree with the present writer, for example, are not sceptics. They positively, absolutely, and without reserve, reject as false the whole system of objective propositions which make up the popular belief of the day, in one and all of its theological expressions. They look upon that system as mischievous in its consequences to society, for many reasons, – among others because it tends to divert and misdirect the most energetic faculties of human nature. This, however, does not make them suspect the motives or the habitual morality of those who remain in the creed in which they were nurtured. The difference is a difference of opinion, as purely as if we refused to accept the undulatory theory of light; and we treat it as such. Then reverse this. Why is it any more impossible for those who remain in the theological stage, who are not in the smallest degree sceptical, who in their heart of hearts embrace without a shadow of misgiving all the mysteries of the faith, why is it any more impossible for them than for us, whose convictions are as strong as theirs, to treat the most radical dissidence as that and nothing other or worse? Logically, it perhaps might not be hard to convict them of inconsistency, but then, as has been so often said, inconsistency is a totally different thing from insincerity, or doubting adherence, or silent scepticism. The beliefs of an ordinary man are a complex structure of very subtle materials, all compacted into a whole, not by logic, but by lack of logic; not by syllogism or sorites, but by the vague.

As a plain matter of fact and observation, we may all perceive that dissent from religious opinion less and less implies reproach in any serious sense. We all of us know in the flesh liberal catholics and latitudinarian protestants, who hold the very considerable number of beliefs that remain to them, quite as firmly and undoubtingly as believers who are neither liberal nor latitudinarian. The compatibility of error in faith with virtue in conduct is to them only a mystery the more, a branch of the insoluble problem of Evil, permitted by a Being at once all-powerful and all-benevolent. Stringent logic may make short work of either fact, – a benevolent author of evil, or a virtuous despiser of divine truth. But in an atmosphere of mystery, logical contradictions melt away. Faith gives a sanction to that tolerant and charitable judgment of the character of heretics, which has its real springs partly in common human sympathy whereby we are all bound to one another, and partly in experience, which teaches us that practical righteousness and speculative orthodoxy do not always have their roots in the same soil. The world is every day growing larger. The range of the facts of the human race is being enormously extended by naturalists, by historians, by philologists, by travellers, by critics. The manifold past experiences of humanity are daily opening out to us in vaster and at the same time more ordered proportions. And so even those who hold fast to Christianity as the noblest, strongest, and only final conclusion of these experiences, are yet constrained to admit that it is no more than a single term in a very long and intricate series.

The object of the foregoing digression is to show some cause for thinking that dissent from the current beliefs is less and less likely to inflict upon those who retain them any very intolerable kind or degree of mental pain. Therefore it is in so far all the plainer, as well as easier, a duty not to conceal such dissent. What we have been saying comes to this. If a believer finds that his son, for instance, has ceased to believe, he no longer has this disbelief thrust upon him in gross and irreverent forms. Nor does he any longer suppose that the unbelieving son must necessarily be a profligate. And moreover, in ninety-nine cases out of a hundred, he no longer supposes that infidels, of his own family or acquaintance at any rate, will consume for eternal ages in lakes of burning marl.

Let us add another consideration. One reason why so many persons are really shocked and pained by the avowal of heretical opinions is the very fact that such avowal is uncommon. If unbelievers and doubters were more courageous, believers would be less timorous. It is because they live in an enervating fool's paradise of seeming assent and conformity, that the breath of an honest and outspoken word strikes so eager and nipping on their sensibilities. If they were not encouraged to suppose that all the world is of their own mind, if they were forced out of that atmosphere of self-indulgent silences and hypocritical reserves, which is systematically poured round them, they would acquire a robuster mental habit. They would learn to take dissents for what they are worth. They would be led either to strengthen or to discard their own opinions, if the dissents happened to be weighty or instructive; either to refute or neglect such dissents as should be ill-founded or insignificant. They will remain valetudinarians, so long as a curtain of compromise shelters them from the real belief of those of their neighbours who have ventured to use their minds with some measure of independence. A very brief contact with people who, when the occasion comes, do not shrink from saying what they think, is enough to modify that excessive liability to be shocked at truth-speaking, which is only so common because truth-speaking itself is so unfamiliar.

Now, however great the pain inflicted by the avowal of unbelief, it seems to the present writer that one relationship in life, and one only, justifies us in being silent where otherwise it would be right to speak. This relationship is that between child and parents. Those parents are wisest who train their sons and daughters in the utmost liberty both of thought and speech; who do not instil dogmas into them, but inculcate upon them the sovereign importance of correct ways of forming opinions; who, while never dissembling the great fact that if one opinion is true, its contradictory cannot be true also, but must be a lie and must partake of all the evil qualities of a lie, yet always set them the example of listening to unwelcome opinions with patience and candour. Still all parents are not wise. They cannot all endure to hear of any religious opinions except their own. Where it would give them sincere and deep pain to hear a son or daughter avow disbelief in the inspiration of the Bible and so forth, then it seems that the younger person is warranted in refraining from saying that he or she does not accept such and such doctrines. This, of course, only where the son or daughter feels a tender and genuine attachment to the parent. Where the parent has not earned this attachment, has been selfish, indifferent, or cruel, the title to the special kind of forbearance of which we are speaking can hardly exist. In an ordinary way, however, a parent has a claim on us which no other person in the world can have, and a man's self-respect ought scarcely to be injured if he finds himself shrinking from playing the apostle to his own father and mother.

One can indeed imagine circumstances where this would not be true. If you are persuaded that you have had revealed to you a glorious gospel of light and blessedness, it is impossible not to thirst to impart such tidings most eagerly to those who are closest about your heart. We are not in that position. We have as yet no magnificent vision, so definite, so touching, so 'clothed with the beauty of a thousand stars,'[†] as to make us eager, for the sake of it, to murder all the sweetnesses of filial piety in an aggressive eristic. This much one concedes. Yet let us ever remember that those elders are of nobler type who have kept their minds in a generous freedom, and have made themselves strong with that magnanimous confidence in truth, which the Hebrew expressed in old phrase, that if counsel or work be of men it will come to nought, but if it be of God ye cannot overthrow it.[†]

Even in the case of parents, and even though our new creed is but rudimentary, there can be no good reason why we should go further in the way of economy than mere silence. Neither they nor any other human being can possibly have a right to expect us, not merely to abstain from the open expression of dissents, but positively to profess unreal and feigned assents. No fear of giving pain, no wish to soothe the alarms of those to whom we owe much, no respect for the natural clinging of the old to the faith which has accompanied them through honourable lives, can warrant us in saying that we believe to be true what we are convinced is false. The most lax moralist counts a lie wrong, even when the motive is unselfish and springs from the desire to give pleasure to those whom it is our duty to please. A deliberate lie avowedly does not cease to be one because it concerns spiritual things. Nor is it the less wrong because it is uttered by one to whom all spiritual things have become indifferent. Filial affection is a motive which would, if any motive could, remove some of the taint of meanness with which pious lying, like every other kind of lying, tends to infect character. The motive may no doubt ennoble the act, though the act remains in the category of forbidden things. But the motive of these complaisant assents and false affirmations, taken at their very best, is still comparatively a poor motive. No real elevation of spirit is possible for a man who is willing to subordinate his convictions to his domestic affections, and to bring himself to a habit of viewing falsehood lightly, lest the truth should shock the illegitimate and over-exacting sensibilities either of his parents or any one else. We may understand what is meant by the logic of the feelings, and accept it as the proper corrective for a too intense egoism. But when the logic of the feelings is invoked to substitute the egoism of the family for the slightly narrower egoism of the individual, it can hardly be more than a fine name for self-indulgence and a callous indifference to all the largest human interests.†

This brings us to consider the case of another no less momentous relationship, and the kind of compromise in the matter of religious conformity which it justifies or imposes. It constantly happens that the husband has wholly ceased to believe the religion to which his wife clings with unshaken faith. We need not enter into the causes why women remain in bondage to opinions which so many cultivated men either reject or else hold in a transcendental and non-natural sense. The only question with which we are concerned is the amount of free assertion of his own convictions which a man should claim and practise, when he knows that such convictions are distasteful to his wife. Is it lawful, as it seems to be in dealing with parents, to hold his conviction silently? Is it lawful either positively or by implication to lead his wife to suppose that he shares her opinions, when in truth he rejects them?

If it were not for the maxims and practice in daily use among men otherwise honourable, one would not suppose it possible that two answers could be given to these questions by any one with the smallest pretence of principle or self-respect. As it is, we all of us know men who deliberately reject the entire Christian system, and still think it compatible with uprightness to summon their whole establishments round them at morning and evening, and on their knees to offer up elaborately formulated prayers, which have just as much meaning to them as the entrails of the sacrificial victim had to an infidel haruspex.† We see the same men diligently attending religious services; uttering assents to confessions of which they really reject every syllable; kneeling, rising, bowing, with deceptive solemnity; even partaking of the sacrament with a consummate devoutness that is very edifying to all who are not in the secret, and who do not know that they are acting a part, and making a mock both of their own reason and their own probity, merely to please persons whose delusions they pity and despise from the bottom of their hearts.

On the surface there is certainly nothing to distinguish this kind of conduct from the grossest hypocrisy. Is there anything under the surface to relieve it from this complexion? Is there any weight in the sort of answer which such men make to the accusation that their conformity is a very degrading form of deceit, and a singularly mischievous kind of treachery? Is the plea of a wish to spare mental discomfort to others an admissible and valid plea? It seems to us to be none of these things, and for the following among other reasons.

If a man drew his wife by lot, or by any other method over which neither he nor she has any control, as in the case of parents, perhaps he might with some plausibleness contend that he owed her certain limited deferences and reserves, just as we admit that he may owe them to his parents. But this is not the case. Marriage, in this country at least, is the result of mutual choice. If men and women do as a matter of fact usually make this choice hastily and on wofully imperfect information of one another's characters, that is no warrant for a resort to unlawful expedients to remedy the blunder. If a woman cares ardently enough about religion to feel keen distress at the idea of dissent from it on the part of those closely connected with her, she surely may be expected to take reasonable pains to ascertain beforehand the religious attitude of one with whom she is about to unite herself for life. On the other hand, if a man sets any value on his own opinions, if they are in any real sense a part of himself, he must be guilty of something like deliberate and systematic duplicity during the acquaintance preceding marriage, if his dissent has remained unsuspected. Certainly if men go through society before marriage under false colours, and feign beliefs which they do not hold, they have only themselves to thank for the degradation of having to keep up the imposture afterwards. Suppose a protestant were to pass himself off for a catholic, because he happened to meet a catholic lady whom he desired to marry. Everybody would agree in calling such a man by a very harsh name. It is hard to see why a freethinker, who by reticence and conformity passes himself off for a believer, should be more leniently judged. The differences between a catholic and a protestant are assuredly not any greater than those between a believer and an unbeliever. We all admit the baseness of dissimulation in the former case. Why is it any less base in the latter?

Marriages, however, are often made in haste, or heedlessly, or early in life, before either man or woman has come to feel very deeply about religion either one way or another. The woman does not know how much she will need religion, nor what comfort it may bring to her.

The man does not know all the objections to it which may disclose themselves to his understanding as the years ripen. There is always at work that most unfortunate maxim, tacitly held and acted upon in ninety-nine marriages out of a hundred, that money is of importance, and social position is of importance, and good connections are of importance, and health and manners and comely looks, and that the only thing which is of no importance whatever is opinion and intellectual quality and temper.† Now granting that both man and woman are indifferent at the time of their union, is that any reason why upon either of them acquiring serious convictions, the other should be expected, out of mere complaisance, to make a false and hypocritical pretence of sharing them? To see how flimsy is this plea of fearing to give pain to the religious sensitiveness of women, we have only to imagine one or two cases which go beyond the common experience, yet which ought not to strain the plea, if it be valid.

Thus, if my wife turns catholic, am I to pretend to turn catholic too, to save her the horrible distress of thinking that I am doomed to eternal perdition? Or if she chooses to embrace the doctrine of direct illumination from heaven, and to hear voices bidding her to go or come, to do or abstain from doing, am I too to shape my conduct after these fancied monitions? Or if it comes into her mind to serve tables, and to listen in all faith to the miracles of spiritualism, am I, lest I should pain her, to feign a surrender of all my notions of evidence, to pretend a transformation of all my ideas of worthiness in life and beyond life, and to go to séances with the same regularity and seriousness with which you go to church? Of course in each of these cases everybody who does not happen to share the given peculiarity of belief, will agree that however severely a husband's dissent might pain the wife, whatever distress and discomfort it might inflict upon her, yet he would be bound to let her suffer, rather than sacrifice his veracity and self-respect. Why then is it any less discreditable to practise an insincere conformity in more ordinary circumstances? If the principle of such conformity is good for anything at all, it ought to cover these less usual cases as completely as the others which are more usual. Indeed there would be more to be said on behalf of conformity for politeness' sake, where the woman had gone through some great process of change, for then one might suppose that her heart was deeply set on the matter. Even then the plea would be worthless, but it is more indisputably worthless still where the sentiment which we are bidden to respect at the cost of our own freedom of speech is nothing more laudable than a fear of moving out of the common groove of religious opinion, or an intolerant and unreasoned bigotry, or mere stupidity and silliness of the vulgarest type.⁶

Ah, it is said, you forget that women cannot live without religion. The present writer is equally of this opinion that women cannot be happy without a religion, nor men either.† That is not the question. It does not follow because a woman cannot be happy without a religion, that therefore she cannot be happy unless her husband is of the same religion. Still less, that she would be made happy by his insincerely pretending to be of the same religion. And least of all is it true, if both these propositions were credible, that even then for the sake of her happiness he is bound not merely to live a life of imposture, but in so doing to augment the general forces of imposture in the world, and to make the chances of truth, light, and human improvement more and more unfavourable. Women are at present far less likely than men to possess a sound intelligence and a habit of correct judgment. They will remain so, while they have less ready access than men to the best kinds of literary and scientific training, and – what is far more important – while social arrangements exclude them from all those kinds of public activity, which are such powerful agents both in fitting men to judge soundly, and in forming in them the sense of responsibility for their judgments being sound.†

It may be contended that this alleged stronger religiosity of women, however coarse and poor in its formulæ, is yet of constant value as a protest in favour of the maintenance of the religious element in human character and life, and that this is a far more important thing for us all than the greater or less truth of the dogmas with which such religiosity happens to be associated. In reply to this, without tediously labouring

---

6 That able man, the late J. E. Cairnes, suggested the following objection to this paragraph. When two persons marry, there is a reasonable expectation, almost amounting to an understanding, that they will both of them adhere to their religion, just as both of them tacitly agree to follow the ways of the world in the host of minor social matters. If, therefore, either of them turns to some other creed, the person so turning has, so to speak, broken the contract. The utmost he or she can contend for is forbearance. If a woman embraces catholicism, she may seek tolerance, but she has no right to exact conformity. If the man becomes an unbeliever, he in like manner breaks the bargain, and may be justly asked not to flaunt his misdemeanour.

My answer to this would turn upon the absolute inexpediency of such silent bargains being assumed by public opinion. In the present state of opinion, where the whole air is alive with the spirit of change, nobody who takes his life or her life seriously, could allow an assumption which means reduction of one of the most important parts of character, the love of truth, to a nullity.†

the argument, I venture to make the following observations. In the first place, it is an untenable idea that religiosity or devoutness of spirit is valuable in itself, without reference to the goodness or badness of the dogmatic forms and the practices in which it clothes itself. A fakir would hardly be an estimable figure in our society, merely because his way of living happens to be a manifestation of the religious spirit. If the religious spirit leads to a worthy and beautiful life, if it shows itself in cheerfulness, in pity, in charity and tolerance, in forgiveness, in a sense of the largeness and the mystery of things, in a lifting up of the soul in gratitude and awe to some supreme power and sovereign force, then whatever drawback there may be in the way of superstitious dogma, still such a spirit is on the whole a good thing. If not, not. It would be better without the superstition: even with the superstition it is good.† But if the religious spirit is only a fine name for narrowness of understanding, for stubborn intolerance, for mere social formality, for a dread of losing that poor respectability which means thinking and doing exactly as the people around us think and do, then the religious spirit is not a good thing, but a thoroughly bad and hateful thing. To that we owe no management of any kind. Any one who suppresses his real opinions, and feigns others, out of deference to such a spirit as this in his household, ought to say plainly both to himself and to us that he cares more for his own ease and undisturbed comfort than he cares for truth and uprightness. For it is that, and not any tenderness for holy things, which is the real ground of his hypocrisy.†

Now with reference to the religious spirit in its nobler form, it is difficult to believe that any one genuinely animated by it would be soothed by the knowledge that her dearest companion is going through life with a mask on, quietly playing a part, uttering untrue professions, doing his best to cheat her and the rest of the world by a monstrous spiritual make-believe. One would suppose that instead of having her religious feeling gratified by conformity on these terms, nothing could wound it so bitterly nor outrage it so unpardonably. To know that her sensibility is destroying the entireness of the man's nature, its loyalty alike to herself and to truth, its freedom and singleness and courage – surely this can hardly be less distressing to a fine spirit, than the suspicion that his heresies may bring him to the pit, or than the void of going through life without even the semblance of religious sympathy between them. If it be urged that the woman would never discover the piety of the man to be a counterfeit, we reply that unless her own piety were of the merely formal kind, she would be sure to make the discovery. The congregation in the old story were untouched by the disguised devil's eloquence on behalf of religion: it lacked unction.† The verbal conformity of the unbeliever lacks unction, and its hollowness is speedily revealed to the quick apprehension of true faith.⁷

Let us not be supposed to be arguing in favour of incessant battle of high dialectic in the household. Nothing could be more destructive of the gracious composure and mental harmony, of which household life ought to be, but perhaps seldom is, the great organ and instrument. Still less are we pleading for the freethinker's right at every hour of day or night to mock, sneer, and gibe at the sincere beliefs and conscientiously performed rites of those, whether men or women, whether strangers or kinsfolk, from whose religion he disagrees. 'It is not ancient impressions only,' said Pascal, 'which are capable of abusing us. The charm of novelty has the same power.' The prate of new-born scepticism may be as tiresome and as odious as the cant of grey orthodoxy. Religious discussion is not to be foisted upon us at every turn either by defenders or assailants. All we plead for is that when the opportunity meets the freethinker full in front, he is called upon to speak as freely as he thinks. Not more than this. A plain man has no trouble in acquiring this tact of seasonableness. We may all write what we please, because it is in the discretion of the rest of the world whether they will hearken or not. But in the family this is not so. If a man systematically intrudes disrespectful and unwelcome criticism upon a woman who retains the ancient belief, he is only showing that freethinker may be no more than bigot differently writ. It ought to be essential to no one's self-respect that he cannot consent to live with people who do not think as he thinks. We may be sure that there is something shallow and convulsive about the beliefs of a man who cannot allow his house-mates to possess their own beliefs in peace.

On the other hand, it is essential to the self-respect of every one with the least love of truth that he should be free to express his opinions

---

7 The reader remembers how Wolmar, the atheistic husband of Julie in Rousseau's *New Heloïsa*, is distressed by the chagrin which his unbelief inflicts on the piety of his wife. 'He told me that he had been frequently tempted to make a feint of yielding to her arguments, and to pretend, for the sake of calming her, sentiments that he did not really hold. But such baseness of soul is too far from him. Without for a moment imposing on Julie, such dissimulation would only have been a new torment to her. The good faith, the frankness, the union of heart, that console for so many troubles, would have been eclipsed between them. Was it by lessening his wife's esteem for him that he could reassure her? Instead of using any disguise, he tells her sincerely what he thinks, but he says it in so simple a tone,' etc. – V. v. 126.†

on every occasion, where silence would be taken for an assent which he does not really give. Still more unquestionably, he should be free from any obligation to forswear himself either directly, as by false professions, or by implication, as when he attend services, public or private, which are to him the symbol of superstition and mere spiritual phantasmagoria. The vindication of this simple right of living one's life honestly can hardly demand any heroic virtue. A little of the straightforwardness which men are accustomed to call manly, is the only quality that is needed; a little of that frank courage and determination in spiritual things, which men are usually so ready to practise towards their wives in temporal things. It must be a keen delight to a cynic to see a man who owns that he cannot bear to pain his wife by not going to church and saying prayers, yet insisting on having his own way, fearlessly thwarting her wishes, and contradicting her opinions, in every other detail, small and great, of the domestic economy.

The truth of the matter is that the painful element in companionship is not difference of opinion, but discord of temperament. The important thing is not that two people should be inspired by the same convictions, but rather that each of them should hold his and her own convictions in a high and worthy spirit. Harmony of aim, not identity of conclusion, is the secret of the sympathetic life; to stand on the same moral plane, and that, if possible, a high one; to find satisfaction in different explanations of the purpose and significance of life and the universe, and yet the same satisfaction. It is certainly not less possible to disbelieve religiously than to believe religiously. This accord of mind, this emulation in freedom and loftiness of soul, this kindred sense of the awful depth of the enigma which the one believes to be answered, and the other suspects to be for ever unanswerable – here, and not in a degrading and hypocritical conformity, is the true gratification of those spiritual sensibilities which are alleged to be so much higher in women than in men. Where such an accord exists, there may still be solicitude left in the mind of either at the superstition or the incredulity of the other, but it will be solicitude of that magnanimous sort which is in some shape or other the inevitable and not unfruitful portion of every better nature.

If there are women who petulantly or sourly insist on more than this kind of harmony, it is probable that their system of divinity is little better than a special manifestation of shrewishness. The man is as much bound to resist that, as he is bound to resist extravagance in spending money, or any other vice of character. If he does not resist it, if he suppresses his opinions, and practises a hypocritical conformity, it must be from weakness of will and principle. Against this we have nothing to say. A considerable proportion of people, men no less than women, are born invertebrate, and they must get on as they best can.† But let us at least bargain that they shall not erect the maxims of their own feebleness into a rule for those who are braver and of stronger principle than themselves. And do not let the accidental exigencies of a personal mistake be made the foundation of a general doctrine. It is a poor saying, that the world is to become void of spiritual sincerity, because Xanthippe has a turn for respectable theology.

One or two words should perhaps be said in this place as to conformity to common religious belief in the education of children. Where the parents differ, the one being an unbeliever, the other a believer, it is almost impossible for anybody to lay down a general rule. The present writer certainly has no ambition to attempt the thorny task of compiling a manual for mixed marriages. It is perhaps enough to say that all would depend upon the nature of the beliefs which the religious person wished to inculcate. Considering that the woman has an absolutely equal moral right with the man to decide in what faith the child shall be brought up, and considering how important it is that the mother should take an active part in the development of the child's affections and impulses, the most resolute of deniers may perhaps think that the advantages of leaving the matter to her, outweigh the disadvantages of having a superstitious bias given to the young mind. In these complex cases an honest and fair-minded man's own instincts are more likely to lead him right than any hard and fast rule. Two reserves in assenting to the wife's control of early teaching will probably suggest themselves to everybody who is in earnest about religion. First, if the theology which the woman desires to instil contains any of those wicked and depraving doctrines which neither Catholicism nor Calvinism is without, in the hands of some professors, the husband is as much justified in pressing his legal rights over the child to the uttermost, as he would be if the proposed religion demanded physical mutilation. Secondly, he will not himself take part in baptismal or other ceremonies which are to him no better than mere mummeries, nor will he ever do anything to lead his children at any age to suppose that he believes what he does not believe. Such limitations as these are commended by all considerations alike of morality and good sense.

To turn to the more normal case where either the man has had the wise forethought not to yoke himself unequally with a person of ardent belief which he does not share, or where both parents dissent from the popular creed. Here, whatever difficulties may attend its application, the principle is surely as clear as the sun at noonday. There can be no good plea for the deliberate and formal inculcation upon the young of a number of propositions which you believe to be false. To do this is to sow tares not in your enemy's field, but in the very ground which is most precious of all others to you and most full of hope for the future. To allow it to be done merely that children may grow up in the stereotyped mould, is simply to perpetuate in new generations the present thick-sighted and dead-heavy state of our spirits. It is to do one's best to keep society for an indefinite time sapped by hollow and void professions, instead of being nourished by sincerity and wholeheartedness.[8]

Nor here, more than elsewhere in this chapter, are we trying to turn the family into a field of ceaseless polemic. No one who knows the stuff of which life is made, the pressure of material cares, the play of passion, the busy energising of the affections, the anxieties of health, and all the other solicitudes, generous or ignoble, which naturally absorb the days of the common multitude of men – is likely to think such an ideal either desirable or attainable. Least of all is it desirable to give character a strong set in this polemical direction in its most plastic days. The controversial and denying humour is a different thing from

---

8 The common reason alleged by freethinkers for having their children brought up in the orthodox ways is that, if they were not so brought up, they would be looked on as contaminating agents whom other parents would take care to keep away from the companionship of their children. This excuse may have had some force at another time. At the present day, when belief is so weak, we doubt whether the young would be excluded from the companionship of their equals in age, merely because they had not been trained in some of the conventional shibboleths. Even if it were so, there are certainly some ways of compensating for the disadvantages of exclusion from orthodox circles.

I have heard of a more interesting reason; namely, that the historic position of the young, relatively to the time in which they are placed, is in some sort falsified, unless they have gone through a training in the current beliefs of their age: unless they have undergone that, they miss, as it were, some of the normal antecedents. I do not think this plea will hold good. However desirable it may be that the young should know all sorts of erroneous beliefs and opinions as products of the past, it can hardly be in any degree desirable that they should take them for truths. If there were no other objection, there would be this, that the disturbance and waste of force involved in shaking off in their riper years the erroneous opinions which had been instilled into them in childhood, would more than counterbalance any advantages, whatever their precise nature may be, to be derived from having shared in their own proper persons the ungrounded notions of others.†

the habit of being careful to know what we mean by the words we use, and what evidence there is for the beliefs we hold. It is possible to foster the latter habit without creating the former. And it is possible to bring up the young in dissent from the common beliefs around them, or in indifference to them, without engendering any of that pride in eccentricity for its own sake, which is so little likable a quality in either young or old. There is, however, little risk of an excess in this direction. The young tremble even more than the old at the penalties of nonconformity. There is more excuse for them in this. Such penalties in their case usually come closer and in more stringent forms. Neither have they had time to find out, as their elders have or ought to have found out, what a very moderate degree of fortitude enables us to bear up against social disapproval, when we know that it is nothing more than the common form of convention.

The great object is to keep the minds of the young as open as possible in the matter of religion; to breed in them a certain simplicity and freedom from self-consciousness, in finding themselves without the religious beliefs and customs of those around them; to make them regard differences in these respects as very natural and ordinary matters, susceptible of an easy explanation. It is of course inevitable, unless they are brought up in cloistered seclusion, that they should hear much of the various articles of belief which we are anxious that they should not share. They will ask you whether the story of the creation of the universe is true; whether such and such miracles really happened; whether this person or that actually lived, and actually did all that he is said to have done. Plainly the right course is to tell them, without any agitation or excess or vehemence or too much elaboration, the simple truth in such matters exactly as it appears to one's own mind. There is no reason why they should not know the best parts of the Bible as well as they know the Iliad or Herodotus. There are many reasons why they should know them better. But one most important condition of this is constantly overlooked by people, who like to satisfy their intellectual vanity by scepticism, and at the same time to make their comfort safe by external conformity. If the Bible is to be taught only because it is a noble and most majestic monument of literature, it should be taught as that and no more. That a man who regards it solely as supreme literature, should impress it upon the young as the supernaturally inspired word of God and the accurate record of objective occurrences, is a piece of the plainest and most shocking dishonesty. Let a youth be trained in simple and straightforward recognition of the truth that we can know, and can conjecture, nothing with any assurance as to the ultimate mysteries of things. Let his imagination and his sense of awe be fed from those springs, which are none the less bounteous because they flow in natural rather than supernatural channels. Let him be taught the historic place and source of the religions which he is not bound to accept, unless the evidence for their authority by and by brings him to another mind. A boy or girl trained in this way has an infinitely better chance of growing up with the true spirit and leanings of religion implanted in the character, than if they had been educated in formulæ which they could not understand, by people who do not believe them.

The most common illustration of a personal mistake being made the base of a general doctrine, is found in the case of those who, after committing themselves for life to the profession of a given creed, awake to the shocking discovery that the creed has ceased to be true for them. The action of a popular modern story, Mrs. Gaskell's *North and South*, turns upon the case of a clergyman whose faith is overthrown, and who in consequence abandons his calling, to his own serious material detriment and under circumstances of severe suffering to his family. I am afraid that current opinion, especially among the cultivated class, would condemn such a sacrifice as a piece of misplaced scrupulosity. No man, it would be said, is called upon to proclaim his opinions, when to do so will cost him the means of subsistence. This will depend upon the value which he sets upon the opinions that he has to proclaim. If such a proposition is true, the world must efface its habit of admiration for the martyrs and heroes of the past, who embraced violent death rather than defile themselves by a lying confession. Or is present heroism ridiculous, and only past heroism admirable? However, nobody has a right to demand the heroic from all the world; and if to publish his dissent from the opinions which he nominally holds would reduce a man to beggary, human charity bids us say as little as may be. We may leave such men to their unfortunate destiny, hoping that they will make what good use of it may be possible. *Non ragioniam di lor*. These cases only show the essential and profound immorality of the priestly profession – in all its forms, and no matter in connection with what church or what dogma – which makes a man's living depend on his abstaining from using his mind, or concealing the conclusions to which use of his mind has brought him. The time will come when society will look back on the doctrine, that they who serve the altar should live by the altar, as a doctrine of barbarism and degradation.[†]

But if one, by refusing to offer a pinch of incense to the elder gods, should thus strip himself of a marked opportunity of exerting an undoubtedly useful influence over public opinion, or over a certain section of society, is he not justified in compromising to the extent necessary to preserve this influence? Instead of answering this directly, we would make the following remarks. First, it can seldom be clear in times like our own that religious heterodoxy must involve the loss of influence in other than religious spheres. The apprehension that it will do so is due rather to timorousness and a desire to find a fair reason for the comforts of silence and reserve. If a teacher has anything to tell the world in science, philosophy, history, the world will not be deterred from listening to him by knowing that he does not walk in the paths of conventional theology. Second, what influence can a man exert, that should seem to him more useful than that of a protester against what he counts false opinions, in the most decisive and important of all regions of thought? Surely if any one is persuaded, whether rightly or wrongly, that his fellows are expending the best part of their imaginations and feelings on a dream and a delusion, and that by so doing moreover they are retarding to an indefinite degree the wider spread of light and happiness, then nothing that he can tell them about chemistry or psychology or history can in his eyes be comparable in importance to the duty of telling them this. There is no advantage nor honest delight in influence, if it is only to be exerted in the sphere of secondary objects, and at the cost of the objects which ought to be foremost in the eyes of serious people. In truth the men who have done most for the world have taken very little heed of influence. They have sought light, and left their influence to fare as it might list. Can we not imagine the mingled mystification and disdain with which a Spinoza or a Descartes, a Luther or a Pascal, would have listened to an exhortation in our persuasive modern manner on the niceties of the politic and the social obligation of pious fraud? It is not given to many to perform the achievements of such giants as these, but every one may help to keep the standard of intellectual honesty at a lofty pitch, and what better service can a man render than to furnish the world with an example of faithful dealing with his own conscience and with his fellows? This at least is the one talent that is placed in the hands of the obscurest of us all.[9]

9 Miss Martineau has an excellent protest against 'the dereliction of principle shown in supposing that any "Cause" can be of so much importance as fidelity to truth, or can be important at all otherwise than in its relation to truth which wants vindicating. It reminds me of an incident which happened when I was in America, at the time of the severest trials of the Abolitionists. A pastor from

And what is this smile of the world, to win which we are bidden to sacrifice our moral manhood; this frown of the world, whose terrors are more awful than the withering up of truth and the slow going out of light within the souls of us? Consider the triviality of life and conversation and purpose, in the bulk of those whose approval is held out for our prize and the mark of our high calling. Measure, if you can, the empire over them of prejudice unadulterated by a single element of rationality, and weigh, if you can, the huge burden of custom, unrelieved by a single leavening particle of fresh thought. Ponder the share which selfishness and love of ease have in the vitality and the maintenance of the opinions that we are forbidden to dispute. Then how pitiful a thing seems the approval or disapproval of these creatures of the conventions of the hour, as one figures the merciless vastness of the universe of matter sweeping us headlong through viewless space; as one hears the wail of misery that is for ever ascending to the deaf gods; as one counts the little tale of the years that separate us from eternal silence. In the light of these things, a man should surely dare to live his small span of life with little heed of the common speech upon him or his life, only caring that his days may be full of reality, and his conversation of truth-speaking and wholeness.

Those who think conformity in the matters of which we have been speaking harmless and unimportant, must do so either from indifference or else from despair. It is difficult to convince any one who is possessed by either one or other of these two evil spirits. Men who have once accepted them, do not easily relinquish philosophies that relieve their professors from disagreeable obligations of courage and endeavour. To the indifferent person one can say nothing. We can only acquiesce in that deep and terrible scripture, 'He that is filthy, let him be filthy still.' To those who despair of human improvement or the spread of

note 9 continued
the southern States lamented to a brother clergyman in the North the introduction of the Anti-slavery question, because the views of their sect were "getting on so well before!" "Getting on!" cried the northern minister. "What is the use of getting your vessel on when you have thrown both captain and cargo overboard?" Thus, what signifies the pursuit of any one reform, like those specified, – Anti-slavery and the Woman question, – when the freedom which is the very soul of the controversy, the very principle of the movement, – is mourned over in any other of its many manifestations? The only effectual advocates of such reforms as those are people who follow truth wherever it leads.' – *Autobiography*, ii. 442.[†]

light in the face of the huge mass of brute prejudice, we can only urge that the enormous weight and the firm hold of baseless prejudice and false commonplace are the very reasons which make it so important that those who are not of the night nor of the darkness should the more strenuously insist on living their own lives in the daylight. To those, finally, who do not despair, but think that the new faith will come so slowly that it is not worth while for the poor mortal of a day to make himself a martyr, we may suggest that the new faith when it comes will be of little worth, unless it has been shaped by generations of honest and fearless men, and unless it finds in those who are to receive it an honest and fearless temper. Our plea is not for a life of perverse disputings or busy proselytising, but only that we should learn to look at one another with a clear and steadfast eye, and march forward along the paths we choose with firm step and erect front. The first advance towards either the renovation of one faith or the growth of another, must be the abandonment of those habits of hypocritical conformity and compliance which have filled the air of the England of to-day with gross and obscuring mists.[†]

Chapter V

The Realisation of Opinion[†]

A person who takes the trouble to form his own opinions and beliefs will feel that he owes no responsibility to the majority for his conclusions. If he is a genuine lover of truth, if he is inspired by the divine passion for seeing things as they are, and a divine abhorrence of holding ideas which do not conform to the facts, he will be wholly independent of the approval or assent of the persons around him. When he proceeds to apply his beliefs in the practical conduct of life, the position is different. There are now good reasons why his attitude should be in some ways less inflexible. The society in which he is placed is a very ancient and composite growth. The people from whom he dissents have not come by their opinions, customs, and institutions by a process of mere haphazard. These opinions and customs all had their origin in a certain real or supposed fitness. They have a certain depth of root in the lives of a proportion of the existing generation. Their fitness for satisfying human needs may have vanished, and their congruity with one another may have come to an end. That is only one side of the truth. The most zealous propagandism cannot penetrate to them. The quality of bearing to be transplanted from one kind of soil and climate to another is not very common, and it is far from being inexhaustible even where it exists.

In common language we speak of a generation as something possessed of a kind of exact unity, with all its parts and members one and homogeneous. Yet very plainly it is not this. It is a whole, but a whole in a state of constant flux. Its factors and elements are eternally shifting. It is not one, but many generations. Each of the seven ages of man is neighbour to all the rest.[†] The column of the veterans is already staggering over into the last abyss, while the column of the newest recruits is forming with all its nameless and uncounted hopes. To each its tradition, its tendency, its possibilities. Only a proportion of each in one society can have nerve enough to grasp the banner of a new truth, and endurance enough to bear it along rugged and untrodden ways.

And then, as we have said, one must remember the stuff of which life is made. One must consider what an overwhelming preponderance of the most tenacious energies and most concentrated interests of a society must be absorbed between material cares and the solicitude of the affections. It is obviously unreasonable to lose patience and quarrel with one's time, because it is tardy in throwing off its institutions and beliefs, and slow to achieve the transformation which is the problem in front of it. Men and women have to live. The task for most of them is arduous enough to make them well pleased with even such imperfect shelter as they find in the use and wont of daily existence. To insist on a whole community being made at once to submit to the reign of new practices and new ideas, which have just begun to commend themselves to the most advanced speculative intelligence of the time, – this, even if it were a possible process, would do much to make life impracticable and to hurry on social dissolution.

'It cannot be too emphatically asserted,' as has been said by one of the most influential of modern thinkers, 'that this policy of compromise, alike in institutions, in actions, and in beliefs, which especially characterises English life, is a policy essential to a society going through the transitions caused by continued growth and development. Ideas and institutions proper to a past social state, but incongruous with the new social state that has grown out of it, surviving into this new social state they have made possible, and disappearing only as this new social state establishes its own ideas and institutions, are necessarily, during their survival, in conflict with these new ideas and institutions – necessarily furnish elements of contradiction in men's thoughts and deeds. And yet, as for the carrying on of social life, the old must continue so long as the new is not ready, this perpetual compromise is an indispensable accompaniment of a normal development.'[1]

Yet we must not press this argument, and the state of feeling that belongs to it, further than they may be fairly made to go. The danger in most natures lies on this side, for on this side our love of ease works, and our prejudices. The writer in the passage we have just quoted is describing compromise as a natural state of things, the resultant of divergent forces. He is not professing to define its conditions or limits as a practical duty. Nor is there anything in his words, or in the doctrine of social evolution of which he is the most elaborate and systematic expounder, to favour that deliberate sacrifice of truth, either in search or in expression, against which our two previous chapters were meant to protest.[2] When Mr. Spencer talks of a new social state establishing

---

1 *The Study of Sociology*, p. 396.
2 No one, for instance, has given more forcible or decisive expression than Mr. Spencer has done to the duty of not passively accepting the current

its own ideas, of course he means, and can only mean, that men and women establish their own ideas, and to do that, it is obvious that they must at one time or another have conceived them without any special friendliness of reference to the old ideas, which they were in the fulness of time to supersede. Still less, of course, can a new social state ever establish its ideas, unless the persons who hold them confess them openly, and give to them an honest and effective adherence.

Every discussion of the more fundamental principles of conduct must contain, expressly or by implication, some general theory of the nature and constitution of the social union. Let us state in a few words that which seems to command the greatest amount both of direct and analogical evidence in our time. It is perhaps all the more important to discuss our subject with immediate and express reference to this theory, because it has become in some minds a plea for a kind of philosophic indifference towards any policy of Thorough, as well as an excuse for systematic abstention from vigorous and downright courses of action.

A progressive society is now constantly and justly compared to a growing organism. Its vitality in this aspect consists of a series of changes in ideas and institutions. These changes arise spontaneously from the operation of the whole body of social conditions, external and internal. The understanding and the affections and desires are always acting on the domestic, political, and economic ordering. They influence the religious sentiment. They touch relations with societies outside. In turn they are constantly being acted on by all these elements. In a society progressing in a normal and uninterrupted course, this play and inter-action is the sign and essence of life. It is, as we are so often told, a long process of new adaptations and re-adaptations; of the modification of tradition and usage by truer ideas and improved institutions. There may be, and there are, epochs of rest, when this modification in its active and demonstrative shape slackens or ceases to be visible. But even then the modifying forces are only latent. Further progress depends on the revival of their energy, before there has been time for the social structure to become ossified and inelastic. The history of civilisation is the history of the displacement of old conceptions by new

note 2 continued
theology. See his *First Principles*, pt. i. ch. vi. § 34; paragraph beginning, – 'Whoever hesitates to utter that which he thinks the highest truth, lest it should be too much in advance of the time, may reassure himself by looking at his acts from an impersonal point of view,' etc.

ones more conformable to the facts. It is the record of the removal of old institutions and ways of living, in favour of others of greater convenience and ampler capacity, at once multiplying and satisfying human requirements.

Now compromise, in view of the foregoing theory of social advance, may be of two kinds, and of these two kinds one is legitimate and the other not. It may stand for two distinct attitudes of mind, one of them obstructive and the other not. It may mean the deliberate suppression or mutilation of an idea, in order to make it congruous with the traditional idea or the current prejudice on the given subject, whatever that may be. Or else it may mean a rational acquiescence in the fact that the bulk of your contemporaries are not yet prepared either to embrace the new idea, or to change their ways of living in conformity to it. In the one case, the compromiser rejects the highest truth, or dissembles his own acceptance of it. In the other, he holds it courageously for his ensign and device, but neither forces nor expects the whole world straightway to follow. The first prolongs the duration of the empire of prejudice, and retards the arrival of improvement. The second does his best to abbreviate the one, and to hasten and make definite the other, yet he does not insist on hurrying changes which, to be effective, would require the active support of numbers of persons not yet ripe for them. It is legitimate compromise to say: – 'I do not expect you to execute this improvement, or to surrender that prejudice, in my time. But at any rate it shall not be my fault if the improvement remains unknown or rejected. There shall be one man at least who has surrendered the prejudice, and who does not hide that fact.' It is illegitimate compromise to say: – 'I cannot persuade you to accept my truth; therefore I will pretend to accept your falsehood.'

That this distinction is as sound on the evolutionary theory of society as on any other is quite evident. It would be odd if the theory which makes progress depend on modification forbade us to attempt to modify. When it is said that the various successive changes in thought and institution present and consummate themselves spontaneously, no one means by spontaneity that they come to pass independently of human effort and volition. On the contrary, this energy of the members of the society is one of the spontaneous elements. It is quite as indispensable as any other of them, if indeed it be not more so. Progress depends upon tendencies and forces in a community. But of these tendencies and forces, the organs and representatives must plainly be found among the men and women of the community, and cannot possibly be found anywhere else. Progress is not automatic, in the sense that if we were all to be cast into a deep slumber for the space of a generation, we should awake to find ourselves in a greatly improved social state. The world only grows better, even in the moderate degree in which it does grow better, because people wish that it should, and take the right steps to make it better. Evolution is not a force, but a process; not a cause, but a law. It explains the source, and marks the immovable limitations, of social energy. But social energy itself can never be superseded either by evolution or by anything else.[†]

The reproach of being impracticable and artificial attaches by rights not to those who insist on resolute, persistent, and uncompromising efforts to remove abuses, but to a very different class – to those, namely, who are credulous enough to suppose that abuses and bad customs and wasteful ways of doing things will remove themselves. This credulity, which is a cloak for indolence or ignorance or stupidity, overlooks the fact that there are bodies of men, more or less numerous, attached by every selfish interest they have to the maintenance of these abusive customs. 'A plan,' says Bentham, 'may be said to be too good to be practicable, where, without adequate inducement in the shape of personal interest, it requires for its accomplishment that some individual or class of individuals shall have made a sacrifice of his or their personal interest to the interest of the whole. When it is on the part of a body of men or a multitude of individuals taken at random that any such sacrifice is reckoned upon, then it is that in speaking of the plan the term *Utopian* may without impropriety be applied.' And this is the very kind of sacrifice which must be anticipated by those who so misunderstand the doctrine of evolution as to believe that the world is improved by some mystic and self-acting social discipline, which dispenses with the necessity of pertinacious attack upon institutions that have outlived their time, and interests that have lost their justification.

We are thus brought to the position – to which, indeed, bare observation of actual occurrences might well bring us, if it were not for the clouding disturbances of selfishness, or of a true philosophy of society wrongly applied – that a society can only pursue its normal course by means of a certain progression of changes, and that these changes can only be initiated by individuals or very small groups of individuals. The progressive tendency can only be a tendency, it can only work its way through the inevitable obstructions around it, by means of persons who are possessed by the special progressive idea. Such ideas do not spring up uncaused and unconditioned in vacant space. They have had a definite origin and ordered antecedents. They are in direct relation with the past. They present themselves to one person or little group of persons rather than to another, because circumstances, or the accident of a superior faculty of penetration, have placed the person or group in the way of such ideas. In matters of social improvement the most common reason why one hits upon a point of progress and not another, is that the one happens to be more directly touched than the other by the unimproved practice. Or he is one of those rare intelligences, active, alert, inventive, which by constitution or training find their chief happiness in thinking in a disciplined and serious manner how things can be better done. In all cases the possession of a new idea, whether practical or speculative, only raises into definite speech what others have needed without being able to make their need articulate. This is the principle on which experience shows us that fame and popularity are distributed. A man does not become celebrated in proportion to his general capacity, but because he does or says something which happened to need doing or saying at the moment.

This brings us directly to our immediate subject. For such a man is the holder of a trust. It is upon him and those who are like him that the advance of a community depends. If he is silent, then repair is checked, and the hurtful elements of worn-out beliefs and waste institutions remain to enfeeble the society, just as the retention of waste products, enfeebles or poisons the body. If in a spirit of modesty which is often genuine, though it is often only a veil for love of ease, he asks why he rather than another should speak, why he before others should refuse compliance and abstain from conformity, the answer is that though the many are ultimately moved, it is always one who is first to leave the old encampment. If the maxim of the compromiser were sound, it ought to be capable of universal application. Nobody has a right to make an apology for himself in this matter, which he will not allow to be valid for others. If one has a right to conceal his true opinions, and to practise equivocal conformities, then all have a right. One plea for exemption is in this case as good as another, and no better. That he has married a wife, that he has bought a yoke of oxen and must prove them, that he has bidden guests to a feast – one excuse lies on the same level as the rest. All are equally worthless as answers to the generous solicitation of enlightened conscience. Suppose, then, that each man on whom in turn the new ideas dawned were to borrow the compromiser's plea and imitate his example. We know what would happen. The exploit in which no one will consent to go first, remains unachieved. You wait until there are persons enough agreeing with you to form an effective party? But how are the members of the band to know one another, if all are to keep their dissent from the old, and their adherence to the new, rigorously private? And how many members constitute the innovating band an effective force! When one-half of the attendants at a church are unbelievers, will that warrant us in ceasing to attend, or shall we tarry until the dissemblers number two-thirds? Conceive the additions which your caution has made to the moral integrity of the community in the meantime. Measure the enormous hindrances that will have been placed in the way of truth and improvement, when the day at last arrives on which you and your two-thirds take heart to say that falsehood and abuse have now reached their final term, and must at length be swept away into the outer darkness. Consider how much more terrible the shock of change will be when it does come, and how much less able will men be to meet it, and to emerge successfully from it.

Perhaps the compromiser shrinks, not because he fears to march alone, but because he thinks that the time has not yet come for the progressive idea which he has made his own, and for whose triumph one day he confidently hopes. This plea may mean two wholly different states of the case. The time has not yet come for what? For making those positive changes in life or institution, which the change in idea must ultimately involve? That is one thing. Or for propagating, elaborating, enforcing the new idea, and strenuously doing all that one can to bring as many people as possible to a state of theory, which will at last permit the requisite change in practice to be made with safety and success? This is another and entirely different thing. The time may not have come for the first of these two courses. The season may not be advanced enough for us to push on to active conquest. But the time has always come, and the season is never unripe, for the announcement of the fruitful idea.

We must go further than that. In so far as it can be done by one man without harming his neighbours, the time has always come for the realisation of an idea. When the change in way of living or in institution is one which requires the assent and co-operation of numbers of people, it may clearly be a matter for question whether men enough are ready to yield assent and co-operation. But the expression of the necessity of the change and the grounds of it, though it may not always be appropriate, can never be premature, and for these reasons. The fact of a new idea having come to one man is a sign that it is in the air. The innovator is as much the son of his generation as the conservative. Heretics have as direct a relation to antecedent conditions as the orthodox. Truth, said Bacon, has been rightly named the daughter of Time.† The new idea does not spring up uncaused and by miracle. If it has come to me, there must be others to whom it has only just missed coming. If I have found my way to the light, there must be others groping after it very close in my neighbourhood. My discovery is their goal. They are prepared to receive the new truth, which they were not prepared to find for themselves. The fact that the mass are not yet ready to receive, any more than to find, is no reason why the possessor of the new truth should run to hide under a bushel the candle which has been lighted for him. If the time has not come for them, at least it has come for him. No man can ever know whether his neighbours are ready for change or not. He has all the following certainties, at least: – that he himself is ready for the change; that he believes it would be a good and beneficent one; that unless some one begins the work of preparation, assuredly there will be no consummation; and that if he declines to take a part in the matter, there can be no reason why every one else in turn should not decline in like manner, and so the work remain for ever unperformed. The compromiser who blinds himself to all these points, and acts just as if the truth were not in him, does for ideas with which he agrees, the very thing which the acute persecutor does for ideas which he dislikes – he extinguishes beginnings and kills the germs.

The consideration on which so many persons rely, that an existing institution, though destined to be replaced by a better, performs useful functions provisionally, is really not to the point. It is an excellent reason why the institution should not be removed or fundamentally modified, until public opinion is ripe for the given piece of improvement. But it is no reason at all why those who are anxious for the improvement, should speak and act just as they would do if they thought the change perfectly needless and undesirable. It is no reason why those who allow the provisional utility of a belief or an institution or a custom of living, should think solely of the utility and forget the equally important element of its provisionalness. For the fact of its being provisional is the very ground why every one who perceives this element, should set himself to act accordingly. It is the ground why he should set himself, in other words, to draw opinion in every way open to him – by speech, by voting, by manner of life and conduct – in the direction of new truth and the better practice. Let us not, because we deem a thing to be useful for the hour, act as if it were to be useful for ever. The people who selfishly seek to enjoy as much comfort and ease as they can in an existing state of things, with the desperate maxim,

'After us, the deluge,' are not any worse than those who cherish present comfort and ease and take the world as it comes, in the fatuous and self-deluding hope, 'After us, the millennium.' Those who make no sacrifice to avert the deluge, and those who make none to hasten their millennium, are on the same moral level. And the former have at least the quality of being no worse than their avowed principle, while the latter nullify their pretended hopes by conformities which are only proper either to profound social contentment, or to profound social despair. Nay, they seem to think that there is some merit in this merely speculative hopefulness. They act as if they supposed that to be very sanguine about the general improvement of mankind, is a virtue that relieves them from taking trouble about any improvement in particular.

If those who defend a given institution are doing their work well, that furnishes the better reason why those who disapprove of it and disbelieve in its enduring efficacy, should do their work well also. Take the Christian churches, for instance. Assume, if you will, that they are serving a variety of useful functions. If that were all, it would be a reason for conforming. But we are speaking of those for whom the matter does not end here. If you are convinced that the dogma is not true; that a steadily increasing number of persons are becoming aware that it is not true; that its efficacy as a basis of spiritual life is being lowered in the same degree as its credibility; that both dogma and church must be slowly replaced by higher forms of faith, if not also by more effective organisations; then, all who hold such views as these have as distinctly a function in the community as the ministers and upholders of the churches, and the zeal of the latter is simply the most monstrously untenable apology that could be invented for dereliction of duty by the former.

If the orthodox to some extent satisfy certain of the necessities of the present, there are other necessities of the future which can only be satisfied by those who now pass for heretical. The plea which we are examining, if it is good for the purpose for which it is urged, would have to be expressed in this way: – The institution is working as perfectly as it can be made to do, or as any other in its place would be likely to do, and therefore I will do nothing by word or deed towards meddling with it. Those who think this, and act accordingly, are the consistent conservatives of the community. If a man takes up any position short of this, his conformity, acquiescence, and inertia at once become inconsistent and culpable. For unless the institution or belief is entirely adequate, it must be the duty of all who have satisfied themselves that it is not so, to recognise its deficiencies, and at least to call attention to them, even if they lack opportunity or capacity to suggest remedies. Now we are dealing with persons who, from the hypothesis, do not admit that this or that factor in an existing social state secures all the advantages which might be secured if instead of that factor there were some other. We are speaking of all the various kinds of dissidents, who think that the current theology, or an established church, or a monarchy, or an oligarchic republic, is a bad thing and a lower form, even at the moment while they attribute provisional merit to it. They can mean nothing by classing each of these as bad things, except that they either bring with them certain serious drawbacks, or exclude certain valuable advantages. The fact that they perform their functions well, such as they are, leaves the fundamental vice or defect of these functions just where it was. If any one really thinks that the current theology involves depraved notions of the supreme impersonation of good, restricts and narrows the intelligence, misdirects the religious imagination, and has become powerless to guide conduct, then how does the circumstance that it happens not to be wholly and unredeemedly bad in its influence, relieve our dissident from all care or anxiety as to the points in which, as we have seen, he does count it inadequate and mischievous? Even if he thinks it does more good than harm – a position which must be very difficult for one who believes the common supernatural conception of it to be entirely false – even then, how is he discharged from the duty of stigmatising the harm which he admits that it does?

Again, take the case of the English monarchy. Grant, if you will, that this institution has a certain function, and that by the present chief magistrate this function is estimably performed. Yet if we are of those who believe that in the stage of civilisation which England has reached in other matters, the monarchy must be either obstructive and injurious, or else merely decorative; and that a merely decorative monarchy tends in divers ways to engender habits of abasement, to nourish lower social ideals, to lessen a high civil self-respect in the community; then it must surely be our duty not to lose any opportunity of pressing these convictions. To do this is not necessarily to act as if one were anxious for the immediate removal of the throne and the crown into the museum of political antiquities. We may have no urgent practical solicitude in this direction, on the intelligible principle that a free people always gets as good a kind of government as it deserves. Our conviction is not, on the present hypothesis, that monarchy ought to be swept away in England, but that monarchy produces certain mischievous consequences to the public spirit of the community. And so what we are bound to do is to take care not to conceal this conviction; to abstain scrupulously from all kinds of action and observance, public or private, which tend ever so remotely to foster the ignoble and degrading elements that exist in a court and spread from it outwards; and to use all the influence we have, however slight it may be, in leading public opinion to a right attitude of contempt and dislike for these ignoble and degrading elements, and the conduct engendered by them. A policy like this does not interfere with the advantages of the monarchy, such as they are asserted to be, and it has the effect of making what are supposed to be its disadvantages as little noxious as possible. The question whether we can get others to agree with us is not relevant. If we were eager for instant overthrow, it would be the most relevant of all questions. But we are in the preliminary stage, the stage for acting on opinion. The fact that others do not yet share our opinions, is the very reason for our action. We can only bring them to agree with us, if it be possible on any terms, by persistency in our principles. This persistency, in all but either very timid or very vulgar natures, always has been and always will be independent of external assent or co-operation. The history of success, as we can never too often repeat to ourselves, is the history of minorities. And what is more, it is for the most part the history of insurrection exactly against what the worldly spirits of the time, whenever it may have been, deemed mere trifles and accidents, with which sensible men should on no account dream of taking the trouble to quarrel.

'Halifax,' says Macaulay, 'was in speculation a strong republican and did not conceal it. He often made hereditary monarchy and aristocracy the subjects of his keen pleasantry, while he was fighting the battles of the court and obtaining for himself step after step in the peerage.' We are perfectly familiar with this type, both in men who have, and men who have not, such brilliant parts as Halifax. Such men profess to nourish high ideals of life, of character, of social institutions. Yet they never think of these ideals, when they are deciding what is practically attainable. One would like to ask them what purpose is served by an ideal, if it is not to make a guide for practice, and a landmark in dealing with the real. A man's loftiest and most ideal notions must be of a singularly ethereal and, shall we not say, senseless kind, if he can never see how to take a single step that may tend in the slightest degree towards making them more real. If an ideal has no point of contact with what exists, it is probably not much more than the vapid outcome of intellectual or spiritual self-indulgence. If it has such a point of contact, then there is sure to be something which a man can do towards the fulfilment of his hopes. He cannot substitute a new national religion for the old, but he can at least do something to prevent people from supposing that the adherents of the old are more numerous than they really are, and something to show them that good ideas are not all exhausted by the ancient forms. He cannot transform a monarchy into a republic, but he can make sure that one citizen at least shall aim at republican virtues, and abstain from the debasing complaisance of the crowd.†

'It is a very great mistake,' said Burke, many years before the French Revolution is alleged, and most unreasonably alleged, to have alienated him from liberalism: 'it is a very great mistake to imagine that mankind follow up practically any speculative principle, either of government or of freedom, as far as it will go in argument and logical illation. All government, indeed every human benefit and enjoyment, every virtue, and every prudent act, is founded on compromise and barter. We balance inconveniences; we give and take; – we remit some rights that we may enjoy others.... Man acts from motives relative to his interests; and not on metaphysical speculations.'[3] These are the words of wisdom and truth, if we can be sure that men will interpret them in all the fulness of their meaning, and not be content to take only that part of the meaning which falls in with the dictates of their own love of ease. In France such words ought to be printed in capitals on the front of every newspaper, and written up in letters of burnished gold over each faction of the Assembly, and on the door of every bureau in the Administration.† In England they need a commentary which shall bring out the very simple truth, that compromise and barter do not mean the undisputed triumph of one set of principles. Nor, on the other hand, do they mean the mutilation of both sets of principles, with a view to producing a *tertium quid* that shall involve the disadvantages of each, without securing the advantages of either. What Burke means is that we ought never to press our ideas up to their remotest logical issues, without reference to the conditions in which we are applying them. In politics we have an art. Success in politics, as in every other art, obviously before all else implies both knowledge of the material with which we have to deal, and also such concession as is necessary to the qualities of the material. Above all, in politics we have an art in which development depends upon small modifications. That is the true side of the conservative theory. To hurry on after logical perfection is

3 *Speech on Conciliation with America.*

to show one's self ignorant of the material of that social structure with which the politician has to deal. To disdain anything short of an organic change in thought or institution is infatuation. To be willing to make such changes too frequently, even when they are possible, is foolhardiness. That fatal French saying about small reforms being the worst enemies of great reforms is, in the sense in which it is commonly used, a formula of social ruin.

On the other hand, let us not forget that there is a sense in which this very saying is profoundly true. A small and temporary improvement may really be the worst enemy of a great and permanent improvement, unless the first is made on the lines and in the direction of the second. And so it may, if it be successfully palmed off upon a society as actually being the second. In such a case as this, and our legislation presents instances of the kind, the small reform, if it be not made with reference to some large progressive principle and with a view to further extension of its scope, makes it all the more difficult to return to the right line and direction when improvement is again demanded. To take an example which is now very familiar to us all. The Education Act of 1870 was of the nature of a small reform. No one pretends that it is anything approaching to a final solution of a complex problem. But the government insisted, whether rightly or wrongly, that their Act was as large a measure as public opinion was at that moment ready to support. At the same time it was clearly agreed among the government and the whole of the party at their backs, that at some time or other, near or remote, if public instruction was to be made genuinely effective, the private, voluntary, or denominational system would have to be replaced by a national system. To prepare for this ultimate replacement was one of the points to be most steadily borne in mind, however slowly and tentatively the process might be conducted. Instead of that, the authors of the Act deliberately introduced provisions for extending and strengthening the very system which will have eventually to be superseded. They thus by their small reform made the future great reform the more difficult of achievement. Assuredly this is not the compromise and barter, the give and take, which Burke intended. What Burke means by compromise, and what every true statesman understands by it, is that it may be most inexpedient to meddle with an institution merely because it does not harmonise with 'argument and logical illation.' This is a very different thing from giving new comfort and strength with one hand, to an institution whose death-warrant you pretend to be signing with the other.

In a different way the second possible evil of a small reform may be equally mischievous – where the small reform is represented as settling the question. The mischief here is not that it takes us out of the progressive course, as in the case we have just been considering, but that it sets men's minds in a posture of contentment, which is not justified by the amount of what has been done, and which makes it all the harder to arouse them to new effort when the inevitable time arrives.

In these ways, then, compromise may mean, not acquiescence in an instalment, on the ground that the time is not ripe to yield us more than an instalment, but either the acceptance of the instalment as final, followed by the virtual abandonment of hope and effort; or else it may mean a mistaken reversal of direction, which augments the distance that has ultimately to be traversed. In either of these senses, the small reform may become the enemy of the great one. But a right conception of political method, based on a rightly interpreted experience of the conditions on which societies unite progress with order, leads the wise conservative to accept the small change, lest a worse thing befall him, and the wise innovator to seize the chance of a small improvement, while incessantly working in the direction of great ones. The important thing is that throughout the process neither of them should lose sight of his ultimate ideal; nor fail to look at the detail from the point of view of the whole; nor allow the near particular to bulk so unduly large as to obscure the general and distant.

If the process seems intolerably slow, we may correct our impatience by looking back upon the past. People seldom realise the enormous period of time which each change in men's ideas requires for its full accomplishment. We speak of these changes with a peremptory kind of definiteness, as if they had covered no more than the space of a few years. Thus we talk of the time of the Reformation, as we might talk of the Reform Bill or the Repeal of the Corn Duties. Yet the Reformation is the name for a movement of the mind of northern Europe, which went on for three centuries. Then if we turn to that still more momentous set of events, the rise and establishment of Christianity, one might suppose from current speech that we could fix that within a space of half a century or so. Yet it was at least four hundred years before all the foundations of that great superstructure of doctrine and organisation were completely laid. Again, to descend to less imposing occurrences, the transition in the Eastern Empire from the old Roman system of national organisation to that other system to which we give the specific name of Byzantine, – this transition, so infinitely less important as it was than either of the two other movements, yet occupied no less than a couple of hundred years. The conditions of speech make it indispensable for us to use definite and compendious names for movements that were both tardy and complex. We are forced to name a long series of events as if they were a single event. But we lose the reality of history, we fail to recognise one of the most striking aspects of human affairs, and above all we miss that most invaluable practical lesson, the lesson of patience, unless we remember that the great changes of history took up long periods of time which, when measured by the little life of a man, are almost colossal, like the vast changes of geology. We know how long it takes before a species of plant or animal disappears in face of a better adapted species. Ideas and customs, beliefs and institutions, have always lingered just as long in face of their successors, and the competition is not less keen nor less prolonged, because it is for one or other inevitably destined to be hopeless. History, like geology, demands the use of the imagination, and in proportion as the exercise of the historic imagination is vigorously performed in thinking of the past, will be the breadth of our conception of the changes which the future has in store for us, as well as of the length of time and the magnitude of effort required for their perfect achievement.[4]

This much, concerning moderation in political practice. No such considerations present themselves in the matters which concern the shaping of our own lives, or the publications of our social opinions. In this region we are not imposing charges upon others, either by law or otherwise. We therefore owe nothing to the prejudices or habits of others. If any one sets serious value upon the point of difference between his own ideal and that which is current, if he thinks that his 'experiment in living' has promise of real worth, and that if more persons could be

---

4 'Toute énormité dans les esprits d'un certain ordre n'est souvent qu'une grande vue prise hors du temps et du lieu, et ne gardant aucun rapport réel avec les objets environnants. Le propre de certaines prunelles ardentes est de franchir du regard les intervalles et de les supprimer. Tantôt c'est une idée qui retarde de plusieurs siècles, et que ces vigoureux esprits se figurent encore présente et vivante; tantôt c'est une idée qui avance, et qu'ils croient incontinent réalisable. M. de Couaën était ainsi; il voyait 1814 dès 1804, et de là une supériorité; mais il jugeait 1814 possible dès 1804 ou 1805, et de là tout un chimérique entassement. – Voilà un point blanc à l'horizon, chacun jurerait que c'est un nuage. "C'est une montagne," dit le voyageur à l'œil d'aigle; mais s'il ajoute: "Nous y arriverons ce soir, dans deux heures;" si, à chaque heure de marche, il crie avec emportement: "Nous y sommes," et le veut démontrer, il choque les voisins avec sa poutre, et donne l'avantage aux yeux moins perçants et plus habitués à la plaine.' – Ste. Beuve's *Volupté*, p. 262.†

induced to imitate it, some portion of mankind would be thus put in possession of a better kind of happiness, then it is selling a birthright for a mess of pottage to abandon hopes so rich and generous, merely in order to avoid the passing and casual penalties of social disapproval. And there is a double evil in this kind of flinching from obedience to the voice of our better selves, whether it takes the form of absolute suppression of what we think and hope, or only of timorous and mutilated presentation. We lose not only the possible advantage of the given change. Besides that, we lose also the certain advantage of maintaining or increasing the amount of conscientiousness in the world. And everybody can perceive the loss incurred in a society where diminution of the latter sort takes place. The advance of the community depends not merely on the improvement and elevation of its moral maxims, but also on the quickening of moral sensibility. The latter work has mostly been effected, when it has been effected on a large scale, by teachers of a certain singular personal quality. They do nothing to improve the theory of conduct, but they have the art of stimulating men to a more enthusiastic willingness to rise in daily practice to the requirements of whatever theory they may accept. The love of virtue, of duty, of holiness, or by whatever name we call this powerful sentiment, exists in the majority of men, where it exists at all, independently of argument. It is a matter of affection, sympathy, association, aspiration. Hence, even while, in quality, sense of duty is a stationary factor, it is constantly changing in quantity. The amount of conscience in different communities, or in the same community at different times, varies infinitely. The immediate cause of the decline of a society in the order of morals is a decline in the quantity of its conscience, a deadening of its moral sensitiveness, and not a depravation of its theoretical ethics. The Greeks became corrupt and enfeebled, not for lack of ethical science, but through the decay in the numbers of those who were actually alive to the reality and force of ethical obligations. Mahometans triumphed over Christians in the East and in Spain – if we may for a moment isolate moral conditions from the rest of the total circumstances – not because their scheme of duty was more elevated or comprehensive, but because their respect for duty was more strenuous and fervid.

The great importance of leaving this priceless element in a community as free, as keen, and as active as possible, is overlooked by the thinkers who uphold coercion against liberty, as a saving social principle. Every act of coercion directed against an opinion or a way of living is in so far calculated to lessen the quantity of conscience in the society where such acts are practised. Of course, where ways of living interfere with the lawful rights of others, where they are not strictly self-regarding in all their details, it is necessary to force the dissidents, however strong may be their conscientious sentiment. The evil of attenuating that sentiment is smaller than the evil of allowing one set of persons to realise their own notions of happiness, at the expense of all the rest of the world. But where these notions can be realised without unlawful interference of that kind, then the forcible hindrance of such realisation is a direct weakening of the force and amount of conscience on which the community may count. There is one memorable historic case to illustrate this. Lewis XIV., in revoking the Edict of Nantes, and the author of the still more cruel law of 1724, not only violently drove out multitudes of the most scrupulous part of the French nation; they virtually offered the most tremendous bribes to those of less stern resolution, to feign conversion to the orthodox faith. This was to treat conscience as a thing of mean value. It was to scatter to the wind with both hands the moral resources of the community. And who can fail to see the strength which would have been given to France in her hour of storm, a hundred years after the revocation of the Edict of Nantes, if her protestant sons, fortified by the training in the habits of individual responsibility which protestantism involves, had only been there to aid?†

This consideration brings us to a new side of the discussion. We may seem to have been unconsciously arguing as strongly in favour of a vigorous social conservatism, as of a self-asserting spirit of social improvement. All that we have been saying may appear to cut both ways. If the innovator should decline to practise silence or reserve, why should the possessor of power be less uncompromising, and why should he not impose silence by force?† If the heretic ought to be uncompromising in expressing his opinions, and in acting upon them, in the fulness of his conviction that they are right, why should not the orthodox be equally uncompromising in his resolution to stamp out the heretical notions and unusual ways of living, in the fulness of his conviction that they are thoroughly wrong? To this question the answer is that the hollow kinds of compromise are as bad in the orthodox as in the heretical. Truth has as much to gain from sincerity and thoroughness in one as in the other. But the issue between the partisans of the two opposed schools turns upon the sense which we design to give to the process of stamping out. Those who cling to the tenets of liberty limit the action of the majority, as of the minority, strictly to persuasion.

Those who dislike liberty, insist that earnestness of conviction justifies either a majority or a minority in using not persuasion only, but force. I do not propose here to enter into the great question which Mr. Mill pressed anew upon the minds of this generation. His arguments are familiar to every reader, and the conclusion at which he arrived is almost taken for a postulate in the present essay.[5] The object of these chapters is to reiterate the importance of self-assertion, tenacity, and positiveness of principle. The partisan of coercion will argue that this thesis is on one side of it a justification of persecution, and other modes of interfering with new opinions and new ways of living by force, and the strong arm of the law, and whatever other energetic means of repression may be at command. If the minority are to be uncompromising alike in seeking and realising what they take for truth, why not the majority? Now this implies two propositions. It is the same as to say, first, that earnestness of conviction is not to be distinguished from a belief in our own infallibility: second, that faith in our infallibility is necessarily bound up with intolerance

Neither of these propositions is true. Let us take them in turn. Earnestness of conviction is perfectly compatible with a sense of liability to error. This has been so excellently put by a former writer that we need not attempt to better his exposition. 'Every one must, of course, think his own opinions right; for if he thought them wrong, they would no longer be his opinions: but there is a wide difference between regarding ourselves as infallible, and being firmly convinced of the truth of our creed. When a man reflects on any particular doctrine, he may be impressed with a thorough conviction of the improbability or even impossibility of its being false: and so he may feel with regard to all his other opinions, when he makes them objects of separate contemplation. And yet when he views them in the aggregate, when he reflects that not a single being on the earth holds collectively the same, when he looks at the past history and present state of mankind, and observes the various creeds of different ages and nations, the peculiar modes of thinking of sects and bodies and individuals, the notions once firmly held, which have been exploded, the prejudices once universally prevalent, which have been removed, and the endless controversies which have distracted those who have made it the business of their

---

[5] It is sometimes convenient to set familiar arguments down once more; so I venture to reprint in a note at the end of the chapter a short exposition of the doctrine of liberty, which I had occasion to make in considering Sir J. F. Stephen's vigorous attack on that doctrine.[†]

lives to arrive at the truth; and when he further dwells on the consideration that many of these, his fellow-creatures, have had a conviction of the justness of their respective sentiments equal to his own, he cannot help the obvious inference, that in his own opinion it is next to impossible that there is not an admixture of error; that there is an infinitely greater probability of his being wrong in some than right in all.'[6]

Of course this is not an account of the actual frame of mind of ordinary men. They never do think of their opinions in the aggregate in comparison with the collective opinions of others, nor ever draw the conclusions which such reflections would suggest. But such a frame of mind is perfectly attainable, and has often been attained, by persons of far lower than first-rate capacity. And if this is so, there is no reason why it should not be held up for the admiration and imitation of all those classes of society which profess to have opinions. It would thus become an established element in the temper of the age. Nor need we fear that the result of this would be any flaccidity of conviction, or lethargy in act. A man would still be penetrated with the rightness of his own opinion on a given issue, and would still do all that he could to make it prevail in practice. But among the things which he would no longer permit himself to do, would be the forcible repression in others of any opinions, however hostile to his own, or of any kind of conduct, however widely it diverged from his own, and provided that it concerned themselves only. This widening of his tolerance would be the natural result of a rational and realised consciousness of his own general fallibility.

Next, even belief in one's own infallibility does not necessarily lead to intolerance. For it may be said that though no man in his senses would claim to be incapable of error, yet in every given case he is quite sure that he is not in error, and therefore this assurance in particular is tantamount by process of cumulation to a sense of infallibility in general. Now even if this were so, it would not of necessity either produce or justify intolerance. The certainty of the truth of your own opinions is independent of any special idea as to the means by which others may best be brought to share them. The question between persuasion and force remains apart – unless, indeed, we may say that in societies where habits of free discussion have once begun to take root, those who are least really sure about their opinions, are often

---

[6] Mr. Samuel Bailey's *Essays on the Formation and Publication of Opinions*, etc., p. 138. (1826.)

most unwilling to trust to persuasion to bring them converts, and most disposed to grasp the rude implements of coercion, whether legal or merely social. The cry, 'Be my brother, or I slay thee,' was the sign of a very weak, though very fiery, faith in the worth of fraternity. He whose faith is most assured, has the best reason for relying on persuasion, and the strongest motive to thrust from him all temptations to use angry force. The substitution of force for persuasion, among its other disadvantages, has this further drawback, from our present point of view, that it lessens the conscience of a society and breeds hypocrisy. You have not converted a man, because you have silenced him. Opinion and force belong to different elements. To think that you are able by social disapproval or other coercive means to crush a man's opinion, is as one who should fire a blunderbuss to put out a star. The acquiescence in current notions which is secured by law or by petulant social disapproval, is as worthless and as essentially hypocritical, as the conversion of an Irish pauper to protestantism by means of soup-tickets, or that of a savage to Christianity by the gift of a string of beads. Here is the radical fallacy of those who urge that people must use promises and threats in order to encourage opinions, thoughts, and feelings which they think good, and to prevent others which they think bad. Promises and threats can influence acts. Opinions and thoughts on morals, politics, and the rest, after they have once grown in a man's mind, can no more be influenced by promises and threats than can my knowledge that snow is white or that ice is cold. You may impose penalties on me by statute for saying that snow is white, or acting as if I thought ice cold, and the penalties may affect my conduct. They will not, because they cannot, modify my beliefs in the matter by a single iota. One result therefore of intolerance is to make hypocrites. On this, as on the rest of the grounds which vindicate the doctrine of liberty, a man who thought himself infallible either in particular or in general, from the Pope of Rome down to the editor of the daily newspaper, might still be inclined to abstain from any form of compulsion. The only reason to the contrary is that a man who is so silly as to think himself incapable of going wrong, is very likely to be too silly to perceive that coercion may be one way of going wrong.

The currency of the notion that earnest sincerity about one's opinions and ideals of conduct is inseparably connected with intolerance, is indirectly due to the predominance of legal or juristic analogies in social discussion. For one thing, the lawyer has to deal mainly with acts, and to deal with them by way of repression. His attention is primarily fixed on the deed, and only secondarily on the mind of the doer. And so a habit of thought is created, which treats opinion as something equally in the sphere of coercion with actions. At the same time it favours coercive ways of affecting opinion. Then, what is still more important, the jurist's conception of society has its root in the relation between sovereign and subject, between lawmaker and those whom law restrains. Exertion of power on one hand, and compliance on the other – this is his type of the conditions of the social union. The fertility and advance of discussion on social issues depends on the substitution of the evolutional for the legal conception. The lawyer's type of proposition is absolute. It is also, for various reasons which need not be given here, inspired by involuntary reference to the lower, rather than to the more highly developed, social states. In the lower states law, penalties, coercion, compulsion, the strong hand, a sternly repressive public opinion, were the conditions on which the community was united and held together. But the line of thought which these analogies suggest, becomes less and less generally appropriate in social discussion, in proportion as the community becomes more complex, more various in resource, more special in its organisation, in a word, more elaborately civilised. The evolutionist's idea of society concedes to law its historic place and its actual part. But then this idea leads directly to a way of looking at society, which makes the replacement of law by liberty a condition of reaching the higher stages of social development.

The doctrine of liberty belongs to the subject of this chapter, because it is only another way of expressing the want of connection between earnestness in realising our opinions, and anything like coercion in their favour. If it were true that aversion from compromise, in carrying out our ideas, implied the rightfulness of using all the means in our power to hinder others from carrying out ideas hostile to them, then we should have been preaching in a spirit unfavourable to the principle of liberty. Our main text has been that men should refuse to sacrifice their opinions and ways of living (in the self-regarding sphere) out of regard to the *status quo*, or the prejudices of others. And this, as a matter of course, excludes the right of forcing or wishing any one else to make such a sacrifice to us. Well, the first foundation-stone for the doctrine of liberty is to be sought in the conception of society as a growing and developing organism. This is its true base, apart from the numerous minor expediencies which may be adduced to complete the structure of the argument. It is fundamentally advantageous that in societies which have reached our degree of complex and intricate organisation, unfettered liberty should be conceded to ideas and, within the self-regarding sphere, to conduct also. The reasons for this are of some such kind as the following. New ideas and new 'experiments in living' would not arise, if there were not a certain inadequateness in existing ideas and ways of living. They may not point to the right mode of meeting inadequateness, but they do point to the existence and consciousness of it. They originate in the social capability of growth. Society can only develope itself on condition that all such novelties (within the limit laid down, for good and valid reasons, at self-regarding conduct) are allowed to present themselves. First, because neither the legislature nor any one else can ever know for certain what novelties will prove of enduring value. Second, because even if we did know for certain that given novelties were pathological growths and not normal developments, and that they never would be of any value, still the repression necessary to extirpate them would involve too serious a risk both of keeping back social growth at some other point, and of giving the direction of that growth an irreparable warp. And let us repeat once more, in proportion as a community grows more complex in its classes, divisions and sub-divisions, more intricate in its productive, commercial, or material arrangements, so does this risk very obviously wax more grave.

In the sense in which we are speaking of it, liberty is not a positive force, any more than the smoothness of a railroad is a positive force.[7] It is a condition. As a force, there is a sense in which it is true to call liberty a negation. As a condition, though it may still be a negation, yet it may be indispensable for the production of certain positive results. The vacuity of an exhausted receiver is not a force, but it is the

---

[7] There is a sense, and a most important sense, in which liberty is a positive force. It is its robust and bracing influence on character, which makes wise men prize freedom and strive for the enlargement of its province. As Mr. Mill expressed this: – 'It is of importance not only what men do, but what manner of men they are that do it.' Milton pointed to the positive effect of liberty on character in the following passage: – 'They are not skilful considerers of human things who imagine to remove sin by removing the matter of sin. Though ye take from a covetous man his treasure, he has yet one jewel left; ye cannot bereave him of his covetousness. Banish all objects of lust, shut up all youth into the severest discipline that can be exercised in any hermitage, ye cannot make them chaste that came not thither so. Suppose we could expel sin by this means; look how much we thus expel of sin, so much we expel of virtue. And were I the chooser, a dram of well-doing should be preferred before many times as much the forcible hindrance of evil-doing. For God sure esteems the growth and completing of one virtuous person, more than the restraint of ten vicious.' †

indispensable condition of certain positive operations. Liberty as a force may be as impotent as its opponents allege. This does not affect its value as a preliminary or accompanying condition. The absence of a strait-waistcoat is a negation; but it is a useful condition for the activity of sane men. No doubt there must be a definite limit to this absence of external interference with conduct, and that limit will be fixed at various points by different thinkers. We are now only urging that it cannot be wisely fixed for the more complex societies by any one who has not grasped this fundamental preconception, that liberty, or the absence of coercion, or the leaving people to think, speak, and act as they please, is in itself a good thing. It is the object of a favourable presumption. The burden of proving it inexpedient always lies, and wholly lies, on those who wish to abridge it by coercion, whether direct or indirect.

One reason why this truth is so reluctantly admitted, is men's irrational want of faith in the self-protective quality of a highly developed and healthy community. The timid compromiser on the one hand, and the advocate of coercive restriction on the other, are equally the victims of a superfluous apprehension. The one fears to use his liberty for the same reason that makes the other fearful of permitting liberty. This common reason is the want of a sensible confidence that, in a free western community, which has reached our stage of development, religious, moral, and social novelties – provided they are tainted by no element of compulsion or interference with the just rights of others – may be trusted to find their own level.[†] Moral and intellectual conditions are not the only motive forces in a community, nor are they even the most decisive. Political and material conditions fix the limits at which speculation can do either good or harm. Let us take an illustration of the impotence of moral ideas to override material circumstances; and we shall venture to place this illustration somewhat fully before the reader.

There is no more important distinction between modern civilised communities and the ancient communities than the fact that the latter rested on Slavery, while the former have abolished it. Hence there can hardly be a more interesting question than this – by what agencies so prodigious a transformation of one of the fundamental conditions of society was brought about. The popular answer is of a very ready kind, and it passes quite satisfactorily. This answer is that the first great step towards free labour, the transformation of personal slavery into serfdom, was the result of the spiritual change which was wrought in men's minds by the teaching of the Church. It is unquestionable that the influence of the Church tended to mitigate the evils of slavery, to humanise the relations between master and slave, between the lord and the serf. But this is a very different thing from the radical transformation of those relations. If we think of society as an organism, we instantly understand that so immense a change as this could not possibly have been effected without the co-operation of the other great parts of the social system, any more than a critical evolution could take place in the nutritive apparatus of an animal, without a change in the whole series of its organs. Thus in order that serfage should be evolved from slavery, and free labour again from serfage, it could not be enough that an alteration should have been wrought in men's ideas as to their common brotherhood, and the connected ideas as to the lawfulness or unlawfulness of certain human relations. There must have been an alteration also of the economic and material conditions. History confirms the expectations which we should thus have been led to entertain. The impotence of spiritual and moral agencies alone in bringing about this great metamorphosis, is shown by such facts as these.[†] For centuries after the new faith had consolidated itself, slavery was regarded without a particle of that deep abhorrence which the possession of man by man excites in us now. In the ninth and tenth centuries the slave trade was the most profitable branch of the commerce that was carried on in the Mediterranean. The historian tells us that, even so late as this, slaves were the principal article of European export to Africa, Syria, and Egypt, in payment for the produce of the East which was brought from those countries. It was the crumbling of the old social system which, by reducing the population, lessening the wealth, and lowering the standard of living among the free masters, tended to extinguish slavery, by diminishing the differences between the masters and their bondsmen. Again, it was certain laws enacted by the Roman government for the benefit of the imperial fisc, which first conferred rights on the slave. The same laws brought the free farmer, whose position was less satisfactory for the purposes of the revenue, down nearer and nearer to a servile condition. Again, in the ninth and tenth centuries, pestilence and famine accelerated the extinction of predial slavery by weakening the numbers of the free population. 'History,' we are told by that thoroughly competent authority,[†] Mr. Finlay, 'affords its testimony that neither the doctrines of Christianity, nor the sentiments of humanity, have ever yet succeeded in extinguishing slavery, where the soil could be cultivated with profit by slave labour. No Christian community of slave-holders has yet voluntarily abolished slavery. In no country where it prevailed, has rural slavery ceased, until the price of productions raised by slave labour has fallen so low as to leave no profit to the slave-owner.'†

The moral of all this is the tolerably obvious truth, that the prosperity of an abstract idea depends as much on the medium into which it is launched, as upon any quality of its own.† Stable societies are amply furnished with force enough to resist all effort in a destructive direction. There is seldom much fear, and in our own country there is hardly any fear at all, of hasty reformers making too much way against the spontaneous conservatism which belongs to a healthy and well-organised community. If dissolvent ideas do make their way, it is because the society was already ripe for dissolution. New ideas, however ardently preached, will dissolve no society which was not already in a condition of profound disorganisation. We may be allowed just to point to two memorable instances, by way of illustration, though a long and elaborate discussion would be needed to bring out their full force. It has often been thought since, as it was thought by timorous reactionaries at the time, that Christianity in various ways sapped the strength of the Roman Empire, and opened the way for the barbarians. In truth, the most careful and competent students know now that the Empire slowly fell to pieces, partly because the political arrangements were vicious and inadequate, but mainly because the fiscal and economic system impoverished and depopulated one district of the vast empire after another. It was the break-up of the Empire that gave the Church its chance; not the Church that broke up the Empire. It is a mistake of the same kind to suppose that the destructive criticism of the French philosophers a hundred years ago was the great operative cause of the catastrophe which befel the old social régime. If Voltaire, Diderot, Rousseau, had never lived, or if their works had all been suppressed as soon as they were printed, their absence would have given no new life to agriculture, would not have stimulated trade, nor replenished the bankrupt fisc, nor incorporated the privileged classes with the bulk of the nation, nor done anything else to repair an organisation of which every single part had become incompetent for its proper function.† It was the material misery and the political despair engendered by the reigning system, which brought willing listeners to the feet of the teachers who framed beneficent governments on the simple principles of reason and the natural law.† And these teachers only busied themselves with abstract politics, because the real situation was desperate. They had no alternative but to evolve social improvements out of their own consciousness. There was not a single sound organ in the body politic, which they could have made the starting-point of a reconstitution of a society on the base of its actual or historic structure. The mischiefs which resulted from their method are patent and undeniable. But the method was made inevitable by the curse of the old régime.[8]

Nor is there any instance in history of mere opinion making a breach in the essential constitution of a community, so long as the political conditions were stable and the economic or nutritive conditions sound. If some absolute monarch were to be seized by a philanthropic resolution to transform the ordering of a society which seemed to be at his disposal, he might possibly, by the perseverance of a lifetime, succeed in throwing the community into permanent confusion. Joseph II. perhaps did as much as a modern sovereign can do in this direction. Yet little came of his efforts, either for good or harm. But a man without the whole political machinery in his power need hardly labour under any apprehension that he may, by the mere force of speculative opinion, involuntarily work a corresponding mischief. If it is true that the most fervent apostles of progress usually do very little of the good on which they congratulate themselves, they ought surely on the same ground to be acquitted of much of the harm for which they are sometimes reviled. In a country of unchecked and abundant discussion, a new idea is not at all likely to make much way against the objection of its novelty, unless it is really commended by some quality of temporary or permanent value. So far therefore as the mere publication of new principles is concerned, and so far also as merely self-regarding action goes, one who has the keenest sense of social responsibility, and is most scrupulously afraid of doing anything to slacken or perturb the process of social growth, may still consistently give to the world whatever ideas he has gravely embraced. He may safely trust, if the society be in a normal condition, to its justice of assimilation and rejection. There are

---

8 There is, I think, nothing in this paragraph really inconsistent with De Tocqueville's well-known and striking chapter, 'Comment les hommes de lettres devinrent les principaux hommes politiques du pays, et des effets qui en résultèrent.' (*Ancien Régime*, iii. i.) Thus Sénac de Meilhan writes in 1795: – 'C'est quand la Révolution a été entamée qu'on a cherché dans Mably, dans Rousseau, des armes pour sustenter le système vers lequel entrainait l'effervescence de quelques esprits hardis. Mais ce ne sont point les auteurs que j'ai cités qui ont enflamme les têtes; M. Necker seul a produit cet effet, et déterminé l'explosion.' ... 'Les écrits de Voltaire ont certainement nui à la religion, et ébranlé la croyance dans un assez grand nombre; mais ils n'ont aucun rapport avec les affaires du gouvernement, et sont plus favorables que contraires à la monarchie. ...' Of Rousseau's *Social Contract:* – 'Ce livre profond et abstrait était peu lu, et entendu de bien peu de gens.' Mably – 'avait peu de vogue.' *Du Gouvernement, etc., en France*, p. 129, etc.[†]

a few individuals for whom newness is a recommendation. But what are these few among the many to whom newness is a stumbling-block? Old ideas may survive merely because they are old. A new one will certainly not, among a considerable body of men in a healthy social state, gain any acceptance worth speaking of, merely because it is new.

The recognition of the self-protecting quality of society is something more than a point of speculative importance. It has a direct practical influence. For it would add to the courage and intrepidity of the men who are most attached to the reigning order of things. If such men could only divest themselves of a futile and nervous apprehension, that things as they are have no root in their essential fitness and harmony, and that order consequently is ever hanging on a trembling and doubtful balance, they would not only gain by the self-respect which would be added to them and the rest of the community, but all discussion would become more robust and real. If they had a larger faith in the stability for which they profess so great an anxiety, they would be more free alike in understanding and temper to deal generously, honestly, and effectively with those whom they count imprudent innovators. There is nothing more amusing or more instructive than to turn to the debates in parliament or the press upon some innovating proposal, after an interval since the proposal was accepted by the legislature. The flaming hopes of its friends, the wild and desperate prophecies of its antagonists, are found to be each as ill-founded as the other. The measure which was to do such vast good according to the one, such portentous evil according to the other, has done only a part of the promised good, and has done none of the threatened evil. The true lesson from this is one of perseverance and thoroughness for the improver, and one of faith in the self-protectiveness of a healthy society for the conservative. The master error of the latter is to suppose that men are moved mainly by their passions rather than their interests, that all their passions are presumably selfish and destructive, and that their own interests can seldom be adequately understood by the persons most directly concerned. How many fallacies are involved in this group of propositions, the reader may well be left to judge for himself.

We have in this chapter considered some of the limitations which are set by the conditions of society on the duty of trying to realise our principles in action. The general conclusion is in perfect harmony with that of the previous chapters. A principle, if it be sound, represents one of the larger expediencies. To abandon that for the sake of some seeming expediency of the hour, is to sacrifice the greater good for the less, on no more creditable ground than that the less is nearer. It is better to wait, and to defer the realisation of our ideas until we can realise them fully, than to defraud the future by truncating them, if truncate them we must, in order to secure a partial triumph for them in the immediate present. It is better to bear the burden of impracticableness, than to stifle conviction and to pare away principle until it becomes mere hollowness and triviality. What is the sense, and what is the morality, of postponing the wider utility to the narrower? Nothing is so sure to impoverish an epoch, to deprive conduct of nobleness, and character of elevation.†

Note to Page 154†

The Doctrine of Liberty

Mr. Mill's memorable plea for social liberty† was little more than an enlargement, though a very important enlargement, of the principles of the still more famous Speech for Liberty of Unlicensed Printing with which Milton ennobled English literature two centuries before. Milton contended for free publication of opinion mainly on these grounds: First, that the opposite system implied the 'grace of infallibility and incorruptibleness' in the licensers. Second, that the prohibition of bold books led to mental indolence and stagnant formalism both in teachers and congregations, producing the 'laziness of a licensing church.' Third, that it 'hinders and retards the importation of our richest merchandise, truth;' for the commission of the licenser enjoins him to let nothing pass which is not vulgarly received already, and 'if it come to prohibiting, there is not aught more likely to be prohibited than truth itself, whose first appearance to our eyes, bleared and dimmed with prejudice and custom, is more unsightly and unplausible than many errors, even as the person is of many a great man slight and contemptible to see to.' Fourth, that freedom is in itself an ingredient of true virtue, and 'they are not skilful considerers of human things who imagine to remove sin by removing the matter of sin; that virtue therefore, which is but a youngling in the contemplation of evil, and knows not the utmost that vice promises to her followers, and rejects it, is but a blank virtue, not a pure; her virtue is but an excremental virtue, which was the reason why our sage and serious poet Spenser, whom I dare be known to think a better teacher than Scotus or Aquinas, describing true temperance under the form of Guion, brings him in with his palmer through the cave of Mammon and the tower of earthly bliss, that he might see and know and yet abstain.'

The four grounds on which Mr. Mill contends for the necessity of freedom in the expression of opinion to the mental wellbeing of mankind, are virtually contained in these. His four grounds are, (1) that the silenced opinion may be true; (2) it may contain a portion of truth, essential to supplement the prevailing opinion; (3) vigorous contesting of opinions that are even wholly true, is the only way of preventing them from sinking to the level of uncomprehended prejudices; (4) without such contesting, the doctrine will lose its vital effect on character and conduct.

But Milton drew the line of liberty at what he calls 'neighbouring differences, or rather indifferences.' The Arminian controversy had loosened the bonds with which the newly liberated churches of the Reformation had made haste to bind themselves again, and weakened that authority of confessions, which had replaced the older but not more intolerant authority of the universal church. Other controversies which raged during the first half of the seventeenth century, – those between catholics and protestants, between prelatists and presbyterians, between socinians and trinitarians, between latitudinarians, puritans, and sacramentalists, – all tended to weaken theological exclusiveness. This slackening, however, was no more than partial. Roger Williams, indeed, the Welsh founder of Rhode Island, preached, as early as 1631, the principles of an unlimited toleration, extending to catholics, Jews, and even infidels. Milton stopped a long way short of this. He did not mean 'tolerated popery and open superstition, which, as it extirpates all religious and civil supremacies, so itself should be extirpate, provided first that all charitable and compassionate means be used to win and regain the weak and the misled: that also which is impious or evil absolutely either against faith or manners no law can possibly permit that intends not to unlaw itself.'

Locke, writing five-and-forty years later, somewhat widened these limitations. His question was not merely whether there should be free expression of opinion, but whether there should furthermore be freedom of worship and of religious union. He answered both questions affirmatively, – not on the semi-sceptical ground of Jeremy Taylor, which is also one of the grounds taken by Mr. Mill, that we cannot be sure that our own opinion is the true one, – but on the strength of his definition of the province of the civil magistrate. Locke held that the magistrate's whole jurisdiction reached only to civil concernments, and that 'all civil power, right, and dominion is bounded to that only care of promoting these things; and that it neither can nor ought in any manner to be extended to the saving of souls. This chiefly because the power of the civil magistrate consists only in outward force, while true and saving religion consists in the inward persuasion of the mind, without which nothing can be acceptable to God, and such is the nature of the understanding that it cannot be compelled to the belief of anything by outward force.... It is only light and evidence that can work a change in men's opinions; and that light can in no manner proceed from corporal sufferings, or any other outward penalties.' 'I may grow rich by an art that I take not delight in; I may be cured of some disease by remedies that I have not faith in; but I cannot be saved by a religion that I distrust and a ritual that I abhor.' (*First Letter concerning Toleration.*) And much more in the same excellent vein. But Locke fixed limits to toleration. 1. No opinions contrary to human society, or to those moral rules which are necessary to the preservation of civil society, are to be tolerated by the magistrate. Thus, to take examples from our own day, a conservative minister would think himself right on this principle in suppressing the Land and Labour League; a catholic minister in dissolving the Education League; and any minister in making mere membership of the Mormon sect a penal offence. 2. No tolerance ought to be extended to 'those who attribute unto the faithful, religious, and orthodox, that is in plain terms unto themselves, any peculiar privilege or power above other mortals, in civil concernments; or who, upon pretence of religion, do challenge any manner of authority over such as are not associated with them in their ecclesiastical communion.' As I have seldom heard of any sect, except the Friends, who did not challenge as much authority as it could possibly get over persons not associated with it, this would amount to a universal proscription of religion; but Locke's principle might at any rate be invoked against Ultramontanism in some circumstances. 3. Those are not at all to be tolerated who deny the being of God. The taking away of God, *though but even in thought*, dissolves all society; and promises, covenants, and oaths, which are the bonds of human society, have no hold on such. Thus the police ought to close Mr. Bradlaugh's Hall of Science, and perhaps on some occasions the Positivist School.

Locke's principles depended on a distinction between civil concernments, which he tries to define, and all other concernments. Warburton's arguments on the alliance between church and state turned on the same point, as did the once-famous Bangorian controversy. This distinction would fit into Mr. Mill's cardinal position, which consists in a distinction between the things that only affect the doer or thinker of them, and the things that affect other persons as well. Locke's attempt to divide civil affairs from affairs of salvation, was satisfactory enough for the comparatively narrow object with which he opened his discussion. Mr. Mill's account of civil affairs is both wider and more definite; naturally so, as he had to maintain the cause of tolerance in a much more complex set of social conditions, and amid a far greater diversity of speculative energy, than any one dreamed of in Locke's time. Mr.

Mill limits the province of the civil magistrate to the repression of acts that directly and immediately injure others than the doer of them. So long as acts, including the expression of opinions, are purely self-regarding, it seems to him expedient in the long run that they should not be interfered with by the magistrate. He goes much further than this. Self-regarding acts should not be interfered with by the magistrate. Not only self-regarding acts, but all opinions whatever, should, moreover, be as little interfered with as possible by public opinion, except in the way of vigorous argumentation and earnest persuasion in a contrary direction; the silent but most impressive solicitation of virtuous example; the wise and careful upbringing of the young, so that when they enter life they may be most nobly fitted to choose the right opinions and obey the right motives.

The consideration by which he supports this rigorous confinement of external interference on the part of government, or the unorganised members of the community whose opinion is called public opinion, to cases of self-protection, are these, some of which have been already stated: –

1. By interfering to suppress opinions or experiments in living, you may resist truths and improvements in a greater or less degree.

2. Constant discussion is the only certain means of preserving the freshness of truth in men's minds, and the vitality of its influence upon their conduct and motives.

3. Individuality is one of the most valuable elements of wellbeing, and you can only be sure of making the most of individuality, if you have an atmosphere of freedom, encouraging free development and expansion.

4. Habitual resort to repressive means of influencing conduct tends more than anything else to discredit and frustrate the better means, such as education, good example, and the like. (*Liberty*, 148.)

The principle which he deduces from these considerations is – 'that the sole end for which mankind are warranted, individually or collectively, in interfering with the liberty of action of any of their number is self-protection; the only purpose for which power can be rightfully exercised over any member of a civilised community, is to prevent harm to others. His own good, either physical or moral, is not a sufficient warrant. He cannot be rightfully compelled to do or forbear because it will make him happier, because in the opinion of others to do so would be wise or even right. These are good reasons for remonstrating with him, or reasoning with him, or persuading him, or entreating him, but not for compelling him, or visiting him with any evil in case he do otherwise. To justify that, the conduct from which it is desired to deter him must be calculated to produce evil to others.' (*Liberty*, 22.)

Two disputable points in the above doctrine are likely at once to reveal themselves to the least critical eye. First, that doctrine would seem to check the free expression of disapproval; one of the most wholesome and indispensable duties which anybody with interest in serious questions has to perform, and the non-performance of which would remove the most proper and natural penalty from frivolous or perverse opinions and obnoxious conduct. Mr. Mill deals with this difficulty as follows: – 'We have a right in various ways to act upon our unfavourable opinion of any one, not to the oppression of his individuality, but in the exercise of ours. We are not bound, for example, to seek his society; we have a right to avoid it (though not to parade the avoidance), for we have a right to choose the society most acceptable to us. We have a right, and it may be our duty, to caution others against him, if we think his example or conversation likely to have a pernicious effect on those with whom he associates. We may give others a preference over him in optional good offices, except those which tend to his improvement. In these various modes a person may suffer very severe penalties at the hands of others for faults which directly concern only himself; but he suffers these penalties only in so far as they are the natural, and as it were the spontaneous, consequences of the faults themselves, not because they are purposely inflicted on him for the sake of punishment.' (*Liberty*, 139.) This appears to be a satisfactory way of meeting the objection. For though the penalties of disapproval may be just the same, whether deliberately inflicted, or naturally and spontaneously falling on the object of such disapproval, yet there is a very intelligible difference between the two processes in their effect on the two parties concerned. A person imbued with Mr. Mill's principle would feel the responsibility of censorship much more seriously; would reflect more carefully and candidly about the conduct or opinion of which he thought ill; would be more on his guard against pharisaic censoriousness, and that desire to be ever judging one another, which Milton well called the stronghold of our hypocrisy. The disapproval of such a person would have an austere colour, a gravity, a self-respecting reserve, which could never belong to an equal degree of disapproval in a person who had started from the officious principle, that if we are sure we are right, it is straightway our business to make the person whom we think wrong smart for his error. And in the same way such disapproval would be much more impressive to the person whom it affected. If it was justified, he would be like a froward child who is always less effectively reformed – if reformable at all – by angry chidings and passionate punishments than by the sight of a cool and austere displeasure which lets him persist in his frowardness if he chooses.

The second weak point in the doctrine lies in the extreme vagueness of the terms, protective and self-regarding. The practical difficulty begins with the definition of these terms. Can any opinion, or any serious part of conduct, be looked upon as truly and exclusively self-regarding? This central ingredient in the discussion seems insufficiently laboured in the essay on Liberty. Yet it is here more than anywhere else that controversy is needed to clear up what is in just as much need of elucidation, whatever view we may take of the inherent virtue of freedom – whether we look on freedom as a mere negation, or as one of the most powerful positive conditions of attaining the highest kind of human excellence.

To some persons the analysis of conduct, on which the whole doctrine of liberty rests, seems metaphysical and arbitrary. They are reluctant to admit there are any self-regarding acts at all. This reluctance implies a perfectly tenable proposition, a proposition which has been maintained by nearly all religious bodies in the world's history in their non-latitudinarian stages. To distinguish the self-regarding from the other parts of conduct, strikes them not only as unscientific, but as morally and socially mischievous. They insist that there is a social as well as a personal element in every human act, though in very different proportions. There is no gain, they contend, and there may be much harm, in trying to mark off actions in which the personal element decisively preponderates, from actions of another sort. Mr. Mill did so distinguish actions, nor was his distinction either metaphysical or arbitrary in its source. As a matter of observation, and for the practical purposes of morality, there are kinds of action whose consequences do not go beyond the doer of them. No doubt, you may say that by engaging in these kinds in any given moment, the doer is neglecting the actions in which the social element preponderates, and therefore even acts that seem purely self-regarding have indirect and negative consequences to the rest of the world. But to allow considerations of this sort to prevent us from using a common-sense classification of acts by the proportion of the personal element in them, is as unreasonable as if we allowed the doctrine of the conservation of physical force, or the evolution of one mode of force into another, to prevent us from classifying the affections of matter independently, as light, heat, motion, and the rest. There is one objection obviously to be made to most of the illustrations which are designed to show the public element in all private conduct. The connection between the act and its influence on others is so remote (using the word in a legal sense), though quite certain, distinct, and traceable, that you can only take the act out of the self-regarding category, by a process which virtually denies the existence of any such category. You must set a limit to this 'indirect and at-a-distance argument,' as Locke called a similar plea, and the setting of this limit is the natural supplement to Mr. Mill's 'simple principle.'

The division between self-regarding acts and others, then, rests on observation of their actual consequences. And why was Mr. Mill so anxious to erect self-regarding acts into a distinct and important class, so important as to be carefully and diligently secured by a special principle of liberty? Because observation of the recorded experience of mankind teaches us, that the recognition of this independent provision is essential to the richest expansion of human faculty. To narrow or to repudiate such a province, and to insist exclusively on the social bearing of each part of conduct, is to limit the play of motives, and to thwart the doctrine that 'mankind obtain a greater sum of happiness when each pursues his own, under the rules and conditions required by the rest, than when each makes the good of the rest his only object.' To narrow or to repudiate such a province is to tighten the power of the majority over the minority, and to augment the authority of whatever sacerdotal or legislative body may represent the majority. Whether the lawmakers be laymen in parliament, or priests of humanity exercising the spiritual power, it matters not.†

We may best estimate the worth and the significance of the doctrine of Liberty by considering the line of thought and observation which led to it. To begin with, it is in Mr. Mill's hands something quite different from the same doctrine as preached by the French revolutionary school; indeed one might even call it reactionary, in respect of the French theory of a hundred years back. It reposes on no principle of abstract right, but, like the rest of its author's opinions, on principles of utility and experience. Dr. Arnold used to divide reformers into two classes, popular and liberal. The first he defined as seekers of liberty, the second as seekers of improvement; the first were the goats, and the second were the sheep. Mr. Mill's doctrine denied the mutual exclusiveness of the two parts of this classification, for it made improvement the end and the test, while it proclaimed liberty to be the means. Every thinker now perceives that the strongest and most durable influences in every western society lead in the direction of democracy, and tend with more or less rapidity to throw the control of social organisation into the hands of numerical majorities. There are many people who believe that if you only make the ruling body big enough, it is sure to be either very wise itself, or very eager to choose wise leaders. Mr. Mill, as any one who is familiar with his writings is well aware, did not hold this opinion. He had no more partiality for mob rule than De Maistre or Goethe or Mr. Carlyle. He saw its evils more clearly than any of these eminent men, because he had a more scientific eye, and because he had had the invaluable training of a political administrator on a large scale, and in a very responsible post. But he did not content himself with seeing these evils, and he wasted no energy in passionate denunciation of them, which he knew must prove futile. Guizot said of De Tocqueville, that he was an aristocrat who accepted his defeat. Mr. Mill was too penetrated by popular sympathies to be an aristocrat in De Tocqueville's sense, but he likewise was full of ideas and hopes which the unchecked or undirected course of democracy would defeat without chance of reparation. This fact he accepted, and from this he started. Mr. Carlyle, and one or two rhetorical imitators, poured malediction on the many-headed populace, and with a rather pitiful impatience insisted that the only hope for men lay in their finding and obeying a strong man, a king, a hero, a dictator. How he was to be found, neither the master nor his still angrier and more impatient mimics could ever tell us.

Now Mr. Mill's doctrine laid down the main condition of finding your hero; namely, that all ways should be left open to him, because no man, nor majority of men, could possibly tell by which of these ways their deliverers were from time to time destined to present themselves. Wits have caricatured all this, by asking us whether by encouraging the tares to grow, you give the wheat a better chance. This is as misleading as such metaphors usually are. The doctrine of liberty rests on a faith drawn from the observation of human progress, that though we know wheat to be serviceable and tares to be worthless, yet there are in the great seed-plot of human nature a thousand rudimentary germs, not wheat and not tares, of whose properties we have not had a fair opportunity of assuring ourselves. If you are too eager to pluck up the tares, you are very likely to pluck up with them these untried possibilities of human excellence, and you are, moreover, very likely to injure the growing wheat as well. The demonstration of this lies in the recorded experience of mankind.

Nor is this all. Mr. Mill's doctrine does not lend the least countenance to the cardinal opinion of some writers in the last century, that the only need of human character and of social institutions is to be let alone. He never said that we were to leave the ground uncultivated, to bring up whatever might chance to grow. On the contrary, the ground was to be cultivated with the utmost care and knowledge, with a view to prevent the growth of tares – but cultivated in a certain manner. You may take the method of the Inquisition, of the more cruel of the Puritans, of De Maistre, of Mr. Carlyle; or you may take Mr. Mill's method of cultivation. According to the doctrine of Liberty, we are to devote ourselves to prevention, as the surest and most wholesome mode of extirpation. Persuade; argue; cherish virtuous example; bring up the young in habits of right opinion and right motive; shape your social arrangements so as to stimulate the best parts of character. By these means you will gain all the advantages that could possibly have come of heroes and legislative dragooning, as well as a great many more which neither heroes nor legislative dragooning could ever have secured.

It is well with men, Mr. Mill said, moreover, in proportion as they respect truth. Now they at once prove and strengthen their respect for truth, by having an open mind to all its possibilities, while at the same time they hold firmly to their own proved convictions, until they hear better evidence to the contrary. There is no anarchy, nor uncertainty, nor paralysing air of provisionalness in such a frame of mind. So far is it from being fatal to loyalty or reverence, that it is an indispensable part of the groundwork of the only loyalty that a wise ruler or teacher would care to inspire – the loyalty springing from a rational conviction that, in a field open to all comers, he is the best man they can find. Only on condition of liberty without limit is the ablest and most helpful of 'heroes' sure to be found; and only on condition of liberty without limit are his followers sure to be worthy of him. You must have authority, and yet must have obedience. The noblest and deepest and most beneficent kind of authority is that which rests on an obedience that is rational and spontaneous.

The same futile impatience which animates the political utterances of Mr. Carlyle and his more weak-voiced imitators, takes another form in men of a different training or temperament. They insist that if the majority has the means of preventing vice by law, it is folly and weakness not to resort to those means. The superficial attractiveness of such a doctrine is obvious. The doctrine of liberty implies a broader and a more patient view. It says: – Even if you could be sure that what you take for vice is so – and the history of persecution shows how careful you should be in this preliminary point – even then it is an undoubted and, indeed, a necessary tendency of this facile repressive legislation, to make those who resort to it neglect the more effective, humane, and durable kinds of preventive legislation. You pass a law (if you can) putting down drunkenness; there is a neatness in such a method very attractive to fervid and impatient natures. Would you not have done better to leave that law unpassed, and apply yourselves sedulously instead to the improvement of the dwellings of the more drunken class, to the provision of amusements that might compete with the ale-house, to the extension and elevation of instruction, and so on? You may say that this should be done, and yet the other should not be left undone; but, as matter of fact and history, the doing of the one has always gone with the neglect of the other, and ascetic law-making in the interests of virtue has never been accompanied either by law-making or any other kinds of activity for making virtue easier or more attractive. It is the recognition how little punishment can do, that leaves men free to see how much social prevention can do. I believe, then, that what seems to the criminal lawyers and passionate philanthropists self-evident, is in truth an illusion, springing from a very shallow kind of impatience, heated in some of them by the addition of a cynical contempt for human nature and the worth of human existence.

If people believe that the book of social or moral knowledge is now completed, that we have turned over the last page and heard the last word, much of the foundation of Mr. Mill's doctrine would disappear. But those who hold this, can hardly have much to congratulate themselves upon. If it were so, and if governments were to accept the principle that the only limits to the enforcement of the moral standard of the majority are the narrow expediencies of each special case, without reference to any deep and comprehensive principle covering all the largest considerations, why, then, the society to which we ought to look with most admiration and envy, is the Eastern Empire during the ninth and tenth centuries, when the Byzantine system of a thorough subordination of the spiritual power had fully consolidated itself![†]

THE END

Editor's Notes

Notes to pp. 51–69

On Compromise] Both the 1874 and deLuxe editions include the following epigraph:

> I have read over a pamphlet which I wrote in 1791 when in my twenty-fifth year, and though my better, at least older, judgment and taste condemn some instances of hasty and erroneous opinions rashly hazarded, much superficial and inaccurate reasoning, – yet at the end of forty years I abide by most of the principles that I then maintained.
> Chief Justice Bushe (1831)

visible to us] The following four paragraphs are omitted in the Edition deLuxe.

great democratic experiment] The Grant administration (1869–77) had been rocked by a series of scandals involving insider trading, congressional fraud and the bribery of cabinet officials.

fits of revolution] The following two paragraphs are not included in the *FR*.

flames of the Commune] 'Mr. Darwin on the Descent of Man', *The Times*, 8 April 1871, p. 5.

respect for one's own] This paragraph is deleted in the Edition deLuxe.

late sovereign of France] Louis Napoleon (1808–73), elected president of the French Republic in 1848, but made himself emperor following a *coup d'état* in 1851.

take it for true?] References to the 'last century' and 'now' in the two previous sentences were unchanged between 1874 and 1921, while similar time-sensitive words were elsewhere modified.

independent opinion] The taxes, duties and restrictions on publishing, imposed from 1712, were gradually reduced and repealed between 1833 and 1861. See J. Wiener, *The War of the Unstamped* (Ithaca: 1969).

part of ourselves] In the *FR* the final four sentences are replaced with: 'Of the evil elements themselves we shall incidentally see more in future pages.'

these religious systems] For an elaboration of this statement in relation to the 'modern politics' of the 1870s, see J. P. Parry, *Democracy and Religion: Gladstone and the Liberal Party: 1867–1875* (Cambridge: 1986).

Œuv.] *iii.481* The final paragraph is not found in the FR, and is here slightly modified from its original version in the 1874 edition.

temporarily undisturbed] Text in the FR, from here to the end of the following paragraph, simply reads: 'That there is such a confusion is shown by the force that is so frequently attributed to the various pleas for error, which I shall now shortly set forth as a means of refreshing our faith.'

Morley expanded his discussion in response to the 'truly remarkable sentence' – 'that religion may be morally useful without being intellectually sustainable' – which he found in Mill's posthumously published *Three Essays on Religion* (1874). Morley previously had dealt with this sentence in his review, 'Mr. Mill's Three Essays on Religion', *Fortnightly Review* 97 (January 1875), p. 112; also in *Nineteeth Century Essays*, 199.

after the new] This paragraph and note are not included in the FR. It is largely drawn, as he indicates in his note, from his 1875 review 'Mr. Mill's Three Essays on Religion'. However, see pp. 160–1, which, though not attributed to Mill, is drawn from the same passage.

Système de la Nature, *i. xiii*] By Paul Heinrich Dietrich, Baron d'Holbach. This footnote is not included in the FR.

practice of the Church] Francis Bacon, 'On Superstition', in *Essays, Civil and Moral*.

avowedly put away] 'Those' reads 'M. Renan' in the FR.

history is a pis-aller] In the Edition deLuxe this becomes: 'Whether it be true or not that history is a *pis aller*'.

hinders social progress] 'Human progress' in the FR.

to the Heathen] I Corinthians 9: 20–1.

the Unknown God] Acts 17: 22–3.

The coarsest and most revolting shape] This becomes 'the boldest shape' in the Edition deLuxe.

is in the other] The final four sentences of this paragraph are not included in the FR.

live laborious days] Milton, 'Lycidas'.

essentially political] Here, Morley echoes Bagehot. See *The English Constitution*, 2nd edn (London: 1872), pp. 46–7.

the great Taskmaster's eye] Milton: 'On his being arrived at the age of twenty-three.' The line actually reads: 'As ever in my great Task-master's eye.'

dreaming spires] Matthew Arnold, 'The Scholar Gypsy'.

dishing Whigs] On Lord Derby's infamous statement, see W. Jones, *Lord Derby and Victorian Conservatism* (Athens, GA: 1956), p. 319.

lest it should not pay] The final two sentences in this paragraph are omitted in the Edition deLuxe.

emotional comfort first] The first two sentences of this paragraph are not included in the *FR*.

most potent of our weapons] The final three sentences of this paragraph are not included in the *FR*.

Religious Conformity] The Edition deLuxe includes the following epigraph:

> 'Lascia dir le gent:
> Sta come torre ferma, che non crolla
> Giammai la cima per soffiar dei venti.
>
> Let the people talk as they will:
> stand thou a solid tower, unshaken,
> firm, against all storms that rage around its height. –
>
> Purg. v. 13'

excessive petulance] Note is not included in the *FR*.

Formation of Opinion, §7] Note is not included in the *FR*.

Christianity is assailed] In the *FR*, 'a high ecclesiastical authority' reads 'one of the Archbishops'.

Catholicism plus Science] The *FR* and 1874 editions include the following note: 'See Dr. Congreve's volume of *Essays, Political, Social, and Religious*, just published (Longmans), p. 265.'

pilgrims on the earth] Hebrews 11: 13.

Sermon on Subjects of the Day, *p. 205*] Note is not included in the *FR* or 1874 editions.

a Judæis ad Judæos apud Judæos] From the Jews to the Jews about the Jews.

to be full of sorrow] Keats, 'Ode to a Nightingale'.

reality of new faith] Note is not included in the *FR*.

lives in the next street] Note is not included in the *FR*.

a thousand stars] Christopher Marlowe, *Doctor Faustus*. Original reads 'clad in' for 'clothed with'.

ye cannot overthrow it] See Acts 5: 25–40.

largest human interests] This paragraph is omitted from the Edition deLuxe.

an infidel haruspex] Final clause is omitted from the Edition deLuxe.

intellectual quality and temper] This sentence is omitted from the Edition deLuxe.

to a nullity] This note first appeared in an alternate form in the 1874 edition.

nor men either] This sentence is omitted from the Edition deLuxe.

judgments being sound] The two sentences of this paragraph are omitted from the Edition deLuxe.

it is good] The previous three sentences are omitted from the Edition deLuxe.

ground of his hypocrisy] This sentence is omitted from the Edition deLuxe.

it lacked unction] In the Edition deLuxe this sentence is expanded to read: 'The congregation in the old French story were untouched by an eloquent sermon preached by the Devil in a friar's disguise. The friar was annoyed at his friend's unsparing attack on the Evil One and all his works. "Bless you," cried the preacher, "that sort of sermon will do me no harm; *it had no unction*".'

V. v. 126] Note is not included in the *FR* or 1874 editions.

as best they can] In the Edition deLuxe, the first five sentences of this paragraph are omitted and replaced with the following:

> In 1879 Dr. Ludwig Haller published a German version of *On Compromise* under the slightly unmusical title *Überzeugungstreue* (Carl Ruempler, Hannover, 1879). Dr. Haller does not agree with the author in the above passage, and points out that, in his opinion, married people cannot live together in harmony, while their convictions and conclusions differ so widely. He has it that the more characters mature, the more keenly the difference will be felt, and that 'it is not enough that both parties should mean well'.

See pp. 228–9, herein.

notions of others] Note is not included in the *FR*. In the 1874 edition, 'orthodox ways' in the first sentence reads 'ways of superstition'.

barbarism and degradation] The final three sentences in this paragraph are omitted from the Edition deLuxe.

Autobiography, *ii. 442*] Note is not included in the *FR* or 1874 editions.

truth-speaking and wholeness] The previous three paragraphs are not included in the *FR*.

gross and obscuring mists] In the Edition deLuxe this paragraph reads: 'Those who think conformity, in the matters of which we have been speaking, harmless and unimportant, must do so either from indifference or else from despair. It is difficult to convince any one who is possessed by either one or other of these two evil spirits. Men who have once accepted them, do not easily relinquish philosophies that relieve their professors from disagreeable obligations of courage and endeavour. To the indifferent one can say nothing. To those who despair of human improvement or the spread of light in the face of the huge mass of rough prejudice, we can only urge that the enormous weight and the firm hold of baseless prejudice and false commonplace are the very reasons which make it so important that those who are not of the night nor of the darkness, should the more strenuously insist on living their own lives. To those, finally, who do not despair, but think that the new faith will come so slowly that it is not worth while for the poor mortal of a day to make himself a martyr, we must suggest that the new faith when it comes will be of little worth, unless it has been shaped by generations of fearless men, and unless it finds in those who are to receive it a fearless temper. Our plea is not for a life of perverse disputings or busy proselytising, but only that we should learn to look at one another with a clear and steadfast eye, and march forward along the paths we choose with firm step and erect front. The first advance towards either the renovation of one faith or the growth of another, must be the abandonment of those habits of insincere conformity and compliance that have filled our distracted area with gross and obscuring mists.'

The Realisation of Opinion] The Edition deLuxe includes the following epigraph: 'I am a great enemy of indifference, a great friend of indulgence. – Turgot'

neighbour to all the rest] The *FR* adds 'from the "infant mewling and puking in the nurses arms," down to "second childeshness and mere oblivion".'

or by anything else] In the *FR*, the final sentence reads: 'But neither evolution nor anything else, short of a supernatural and incessantly active providence, can supersede social energy.'

the daughter of Time] Francis Bacon, *The Advancement of Learning*. The previous four sentences are not included in the *FR*.

complaisance of the crowd] The previous two paragraphs are omitted from the Edition deLuxe.

every bureau in the Administration] The Edition deLuxe adds the note: 'If Burke's words, as cited by the author, deserve to be printed everywhere in France in gold, the same might be said of the author's own words, as regards Germany, since the approval given by a very large part of the nation to the so-called Kulturkampf Laws, which are antiliberal and show a sad decline in our political development, is almost exclusively due to the negation of the truth contained in these words. – Dr. Ludwig Haller, in German version of *On Compromise* (*Überzeugungstreue*, Hannover, 1879).'

Ste. Beuve's Volupté, *p. 262*] This note was first included in the 1877 edition.

been there to aid] The previous five sentences are not included in the *FR*.

silence by force] The previous three sentences are not included in the *FR*.

attack on that doctrine] Note is not included in the *FR*; a close variant was added in the 1874 edition.

restraint of ten vicious] Note is not included in the *FR*.

to find their own level] The remainder of this paragraph and the following paragraph are not included in the *FR*.

such facts as these] This sentence is not included in the Edition deLuxe.

that thoroughly competent authority] These four words are omitted from the Edition deLuxe.

profit to the slave-owner] Morley first used this quotation from Finlay in his 'Mr. Mill's Three Essays on Religion', in *Nineteenth-Century Essays*, ed. P. Stansky, p. 190.

quality of its own] This sentence is not included in the *FR*.

for its proper function] The remainder of this paragraph is not included in the *FR*.

the natural law] The remainder of this paragraph is not included in the Edition deLuxe.

en France, p. 129, etc.] This note is included only in the 1877 edition.

character of elevation] The final two sentences are omitted from the Edition deLuxe. The *FR* adds: 'And this reference to the narrower utility of a matter is the essence of compromise.'

Note to page 154] Included as Chapter VI in the Edition deLuxe. Represents about one third of Morley's 'Mr. Mill's Doctrine of Liberty', first published in *Fortnightly Review* 80 (August 1873): 234–56; also in *Nineteenth Century Essays*, 111–38.

plea for social liberty] The Edition deLuxe begins: 'Mill associated his memorable plea for liberty with writers in various tongues and ages, and he owned further that his leading thought was one that mankind have probably at no time since the beginning of civilization been entirely without. It is, however, no bad thing when we are able to confederate a powerful line of thought in one century with a name of power in another. His essay. ....'

it matters not] The previous two paragraphs are not included in the *FR*.

had fully consolidated itself] The Edition deLuxe concludes with the following paragraph:

> People with right minds will not let themselves be discouraged by the qualifications in a passage of Diderot's: 'Yes, my dear breathern in criticism, take my word for it, our judgments are too much of a single piece; we should learn to bring more freedom into them. We ought to inspire ourselves with more of that clearest result of all the lessons of life, that everything even among the greatest of all the sons of men is incomplete, mixed, relative; everything is possible in the way of contradictions and limits; every virtue neighbours elements of uncongenial alloy, all heroism may hide points of bitterness; all genius has its days of shortened vision.' Diderot was the most energetic and least despondent writer of a hopeful age, and, all these reminders of his notwithstanding, it is the great guiding, moving, and positive names in thought, feeling, character, and act, that people of right minds will ardently seek and prize.

Mr. Swinburne's New Poems: Poems and Ballads*

(*Saturday Review*, 4 August, 1866)

It is mere waste of time, and shows a curiously mistaken conception of human character, to blame an artist of any kind for working a certain set of subjects rather than at some other set which the critic may happen to prefer. An artist, at all events an artist of such power and individuality as Mr. Swinburne, works as his character compels him. If the character of his genius drives him pretty exclusively in the direction of libidinous song, we may be very worry, but it is of no use to advise him and to preach to him. What comes of discoursing to a fiery tropical flower of the pleasant fragrance of the rose or the fruitfulness of the fig-tree? Mr. Swinburne is much too stoutly bent on taking his own course to pay any attention to critical monitions as to the duty of the poet, or any warnings of the worse than barrenness of the field in which he has chosen to labour. He is so firmly and avowedly fixed in an attitude of revolt against the current notions of decency and dignity and social duty that to beg of him to become a little more decent, to fly a little less persistently and gleefully to the animal side of human nature, is simply to beg him to be something different from Mr. Swinburne. It is a kind of protest which his whole position makes it impossible for him to receive with anything but laughter and contempt. A rebel of his calibre is not to be brought to a better mind by solemn little sermons on the loyalty which a man owes to virtue. His warmest prayer to the gods is that they should

> Come down and redeem us from virtue

His warmest hope for men is that they should change

> The lilies and languors of virtue
> For the raptures and roses of vice.

---

* Poems and Ballads. By Algernon Charles Swinburne. London: E. Moxon & Co. 1866.

It is of no use, therefore, to scold Mr. Swinburne for grovelling down among the nameless shameless abominations which inspire him with such frenzied delight. They excite his imagination to its most vigorous efforts, they seem to him the themes most proper for poetic treatment, and they suggest ideas which, in his opinion, it is highly to be wished that English men and women should brood upon and make their own. He finds that these fleshly things are his strong part, so he sticks to them. Is it wonderful that he should? And at all events he deserves credit for the audacious courage with which he has revealed to the world a mind all aflame with the feverish carnality of a schoolboy over the dirtiest passage in Lemprière. It is not every poet who would ask us all to go hear him tuning his lyre in a stye. It is not everybody who could care to let the world know that he found the most delicious food for poetic reflection in the practices of the great island of the Ægean, in the habits of Messalina, of Faustina, of Pasiphaë. Yet these make up Mr. Swinburne's version of the dreams of fair women, and he would scorn to throw any veil over pictures which kindle, as these do, all the fires of his imagination in their intensest heat and glow. It is not merely 'the noble, the nude, the antique' which he strives to reproduce. If he were a rebel against the fat-headed Philistines and poor-blooded Puritans who insist that all poetry should be such as may be wisely placed in the hands of girls of eighteen, and is fit for the use of Sunday schools, he would have all wise and enlarged readers on his side. But there is an enormous difference between an attempt to revivify among us the grand old pagan conceptions of joy, and an attempt to glorify all the bestial delights that the subtleness of Greek depravity was able to contrive. It is a good thing to vindicate passion, and the strong and large and rightful pleasures of sense, against the narrow and inhuman tyranny of shrivelled anchorites. It is a very bad and silly thing to try to set up the pleasures of sense in the seat of the reason they have dethroned. And no language is too strong to condemn the mixed vileness and childishness of depicting the spurious passion of a putrescent imagination, the unnamed lusts of sated wantons, as if they were the crown of character and their enjoyment the great glory of human life. The only comfort about the present volume is that such a piece as 'Anactoria' will be unintelligible to a great many people, and so will the fevered folly of 'Hermaphroditus', as well as much else that is nameless and abominable. Perhaps if Mr. Swinburne can a second and a third time find a respectable publisher willing to issue a volume of the same stamp, crammed with pieces which many a professional vendor of filthy prints might blush to see if he only knew what they meant,

English readers will gradually acquire a truly delightful familiarity with these unspeakable foulnesses; and a lover will be able to present to his mistress a copy of Mr. Swinburne's latest versus with a happy confidence that she will have no difficulty in seeing the point of every allusion to Sappho or the pleasing Hermaphroditus, or the embodiment of anything else that is loathsome and horrible. It will be very charming to hear a drawingroom discussion on such verses as these for example:–

> Stray breaths of Sapphic song that blew
>   Through Mitylene
> Shook the fierce quivering blood in you
>   By night, Faustine.
>
> The shameless nameless love that makes
>   Hell's iron gin
> Shut on you like a trap that breaks
>   The soul, Faustine.
>
> And when your veins were void and dead,
>   What ghosts unclean
> Swarmed round the straitened barren bed
>   That hid Faustine?
>
> What sterile growths of sexless root
>   Or epicene?
> What flower of kisses without fruit
>   Of love, Faustine?

We should be sorry to be guilty of anything so offensive to Mr. Swinburne as we are quite sure an appeal to the morality of all the wisest and best men would be. The passionate votary of the goddess whom he hails as 'Daughter of Death and Priapus' has got too high for this. But it may be presumed that common sense is not too insulting a standard by which to measure the worth and place of his new volume. Starting from this sufficiently modest point, we may ask him whether there is really nothing in women worth singing about except 'quivering flanks' and 'splendid supple thighs', 'hot sweet throats' and 'hotter hands than fire', and their blood as 'hot wan wine of love'? Is purity to be expunged from the catalogue of desirable qualities? Does a poet show respect to his own genius by gloating, as Mr. Swinburne does, page after page and poem after poem, upon a single subject, and that subject kept steadily in a single light? Are we to believe that having exhausted hot lustfulness, and wearied the reader with a luscious and nauseating iteration of the same fervid scenes and fervid ideas, he has got to the end of his tether? Has he nothing more to say, no further poetic task but to go on again and again about

> The white wealth of thy body made whiter
>   By the blushes of amorous blows,
> And seamed with sharp lips and fierce fingers,
>   And branded by kisses that bruise.

And to invite new Félises to

> Kiss me once hard, as though a flame
>   Lay on my lips and made them fire.

Mr. Swinburne's most fanatical admirers must long for something newer than a thousand times repeated talk of

> Stinging lips wherein the hot sweet brine
> That Love was born of burns and foams like wine.

And

> Hands that sting like fire,

And of all those women,

> ... Swift and white,
>   And subtly warm and half perverse,
> And sweet like sharp soft fruit to bite,
>   And like a snake's love lithe and fierce.

This stinging and biting, all these 'lithe lascivious regrets,' all this talk of snakes and fire, of blood and wine and brine, of perfumes and poisons and ashes, grows sickly and oppressive on the senses. Every picture is hot and garish with this excess of flaming violent colour. Consider the following two stanzas:—

> From boy's pierced throat and girl's pierced bosom
> Drips, reddening round the blood-red blossom,

> The slow delicious bright soft blood,
> Bathing the spices and the pyre,
> Bathing the flowers and fallen fire,
> Bathing the blossom by the bud.
>
> Roses whose lips the flame has deadened
> Drink till the lapping leaves are reddened
> And warm wet inner petals weep;
> The flower whereof sick sleep gets leisure,
> Barren of balm and purple pleasure,
> Fumes with no native steam of sleep.

Or these, from the verses to Dolores, so admirable for their sustained power and their music, if hateful on other grounds –

> Cold eyelids that hide like a jewel
> Hard eyes that grow soft for an hour;
> The heavy white limbs and the cruel
> Red mouth like a venomous flower;
> When these are gone by with their glories
> What shall rest of thee then, what remain,
> O mystic and sombre Dolores,
> Our Lady of Pain?
>
> * * *
>
> By the ravenous teeth that have smitten
> Through the kisses that blossom and bud,
> By the lips intertwisted and bitten
> Till the foam has a savour of blood,
> By the pulse as it rises and falters,
> By the hands as they slacken and strain,
> I adjure thee, respond from thine altars,
> Our Lady of Pain.
>
> * * *
>
> Thy skin changes country and colour,
> And shrivels or swells to a snake's.
> Let it brighten and bloat and grow duller,
> We know it, the flames and the flakes,
> Red brands on it smitten and bitten,
> Round skies where a star is a stain,

And the leaves with thy litanies written,
   Our Lady of Pain.

* * *

Where are they, Cotytto or Venus,
   Astarte or Ashtaroth, where?
Do their hands as we touch come between us?
   Is the breath of them hot in thy hair?
From their lips have thy lips taken fever,
   With the blood of their bodies grown red?

It was too rashly said, when *Atalanta in Calydon* appeared, that Mr. Swinburne had drunk deep at the springs of Greek poetry, and had profoundly conceived and assimilated the divine spirit of Greek art. *Chastelard* was enough to show that this had been very premature. But the new volume shows with still greater plainness how far removed Mr. Swinburne's tone of mind is from that of the Greek poets. Their most remarkable distinction is their scrupulous moderation and sobriety in colour. Mr. Swinburne riots in the profusion of colour of the most garish and heated kind. He is like a composer who should fill his orchestra with trumpets, or a painter who should exclude every colour but a blaring red, and a green as of sour fruit. There are not twenty stanzas in the whole book which have the faintest tincture of soberness. We are in the midst of fire and serpents, wine and ashes, blood and foam, and a hundred lurid horrors. Unsparing use of the most violent colours and the most intoxicated ideas and images is Mr. Swinburne's prime characteristic. Fascinated as everybody must be by the music of his verse, it is doubtful whether part of the effect may not be traced to something like a trick of words and letters, to which he resorts in season and out of season with a persistency that any sense of artistic moderation must have stayed. The Greek poets in their most impetuous moods never allowed themselves to be carried on by the swing of words, instead of by the steady, though buoyant, flow of thoughts. Mr. Swinburne's hunting of letters, his hunting of the same word, to death is ceaseless. We shall have occasion by and by to quote a long passage in which several lines will be found to illustrate this. Then, again, there is something of a trick in such turns as these:—

Came flushed from the full-flushed wave.
Grows dim in thine ears and deep as the deep dim soul of a star.
White rose of the rose-white water, a silver splendour and flame.

There are few pages in the volume where we do not find conceits of this stamp doing duty for thoughts. The Greeks did not wholly disdain them, but they never allowed them to count for more than they were worth. Let anybody who compares Mr. Swinburne to the Greeks read his ode to 'Our Lady of Pain', and then read the well known scene in the *Antigone* between Antigone and the Chorus, beginning *zowc avizars puxav*, or any of the famous choruses in the *Agamemnon*, or an ode of Pindar. In the height of all their passion there is an infinite soberness of which Mr. Swinburne has not a conception. Yet, in spite of all its atrocities, the present volume gives new examples of Mr. Swinburne's forcible and vigorous imagination. The 'Hymn to Proserpine' on the proclamation of the Christian faith in Rome, full as it is of much that many persons may dislike, contains passages of rare vigour:–

> All delicate days and pleasant, all spirits and sorrows are cast
> Far out with foam of the present that sweeps to the surf of the past:
> When beyond the extreme sea-wall, and between the remove sea-gates,
> Waste water washes, and tall ships founder, and deep death waits:
> Where, mighty with deepening sides, clad about with the seas as with wings,
> And impelled to invisible tides, and fulfilled of unspeakable things,
> White-eyed and poisonous-finned, shark-toothed and serpentine curled,
> Rolls under the whitening wind of the future the wave of the world.
> The depths stand naked in sunder behind it, the storms flee away;
> In the hollow before it the thunder is taken and snared as a prey;
> In its sides is the north-wind bound; and its salt of all men's tears;
> With light of ruin, and sound of changes and pulse of years:
> With travail of day after day, and with trouble of hour upon hour;
> And bitter as blood is the spray; and the crests are as fangs that devour;
> And its vapour and storm of its steam as the sighing of spirits to be;
> And its noise as the noise in a dream; and its depth as the roots of the sea:
> And the height of its head as the utmost stars of the air:
> And the ends of the earth at the might thereof tremble, and time is made bare.

The variety and rapidity and sustention, the revelling in power, are not more remarkable here than in many other passages, though even here it is not variety and rapidity of thought. The anapæst to which Mr. Swinburne so habitually resorts is the only foot that suffices for his never-staying impetuosity. In the 'Song in Time of Revolution' he employs it appropriately, and with a sweeping force of the elements:–

> The heart of the rulers is sick, and the high priest covers his head!
> For this is the song of the quick that is heard in the ears of the dead.
> The poor and the halt and the blind are keen and mighty and fleet:
> Like the noise of the blowing of wind is the sound of the noise of their feet.

There are, too, sweet and picturesque lines scattered in the midst of this red fire which the poet tosses to and fro about his verses. Most of the poems, in his wearisomely iterated phrase, are meant 'to sting the senses like wine,' but to some stray pictures one may apply his own exquisite phrases on certain of Victor Hugo's songs, which, he says,

> Fell more soft than dew or snow by night,
> Or wailed as in some flooded cave
> Sobs the strong broken spirit of a wave.

For instance, there is a perfect delicacy and beauty in four lines of the hendecasyllabics – a metre that is familiar in the Latin line often found on docks and sundials, *Horae nam pereunt et imputantur*:–

> When low light was upon the windy reaches,
> Where the flower of foam was blown, a lily
> Dropt among the sonorous fruitless furrows
> And green fields of the sea that make no pasture.

Nothing can be more simple and exquisite than

> For the glass of the years is brittle wherein we gaze for a span.

Or than this:–

> In deep wet ways by grey old gardens
> Fed with sharp spring the sweet fruit hardens;
>   They know not what fruits wane or grow;
> Red summer burns to the utmost ember;
> They know not, neither can remember,
>   The old years and flowers they used to know.

Or again:–

> With stars and sea-winds for her raiment
>   Night sinks on the sea.

Up to a certain point, one of the deepest and most really poetical pieces is that called the 'Sundew'. A couple of verses may be quoted to illustrate the graver side of the poet's mind:–

> The deep scent of the heather burns
> About it; breathless though it be,
> Bow down and worship; more than we
> Is the least flower whose life returns,
> Least weed renascent in the sea.

* * *

> You call it sundew: how it grows,
> If with its colour it have breath,
> If life taste sweet to it, if death
> Pain its soft petal, no man knows:
> Man has no right or sense that saith.

There is no finer effect of poetry than to recall to the minds of men the bounds that have been set to the scope of their sight and sense, to inspire their imaginations with a vivid consciousness of the size and the wonders and the strange remote companionship of the world of force and growth and form outside of man. '*Qui se considérera de la sorte*,' said Pascal, '*s'effraiera, sans doute, de se voir comme suspendu dans la masse que la nature lui a donnée entre ces deux abimes de l'infini et du néant.*' And there are two ways in which a man can treat this affright that seizes his fellows as they catch interrupted glimpses of their position. He can transfigure their baseness of fear into true poetic awe, which shall underlie their lives as a lasting record of solemn rapture. Or else he can jeer and mock at them, like an unclean fiery imp from the pit. Mr. Swinburne does not at all events treat the lot of mankind in the former spirit. In his best mood, he can only brood over 'the exceeding weight of God's intolerable scorn, not to be borne;' he can only ask of us, 'O fools and blind, what seek ye there high up in the air,' or 'Will ye beat always at the Gate, Ye fools of fate.' If he is not in his best mood he is in his worst – a mood of schoolboy lustfulness. The bottomless pit encompasses us on one side, and stews and bagnios on the other. He is either the vindictive and scornful apostle of a crushing iron-shod despair, or else he is the libidinous laureate of a pack of satyrs. Not all the fervour of his imagination, the beauty of his melody, the splendour of many phrases and pictures, can blind us to the absence of judgment and reason, the reckless contempt for anything like a balance, and the audacious counterfeiting of strong and noble passion by mad intoxicated sensuality. The lurid clouds of lust or of fiery despair and defiance never lift to let us see the pure and peaceful and bounteous kindly aspects of the great landscape of human life. Of enlarged *meditation*, the note of the highest poetry, there is not a trace, and there are too many signs that Mr. Swinburne is without any faculty in that direction. Never have such bountifulness of imagination, such mastery of the music of verse, been yoked with such thinness of contemplation and such poverty of genuinely impassioned thought.

Appendix I

[Anon.], *The Athenaeum*, 17 October 1874, pp. 505–6.

On Compromise. By John Morley, M. A. (Chapman & Hall.)

'ON COMPROMISE' is a series of five vigorous essays which originally appeared in the congenial pages of the *Fortnightly Review*, and the object of which is, according to the author, 'to consider, in a short and direct way, some of the limits that are set by sound reason to the practice of the various arts of accommodation, economy, management, conformity, or compromise.' Those who are at all familiar either with Mr. John Morley himself, or with the spirit of that school of thought to which he belongs, and of which the *Fortnightly Review* – still so called, although it appears once a month, like any other magazine – is the representative, will easily be able to anticipate the tone in which he deals with what he considers to be the moral defects of the age. His complaint, in effect, is that the majority of men – with the exception, of course, of the more immediate representatives and followers of Auguste Comte – are indifferent to truth, and amenable only to the lower and baser considerations of expediency; that they do not worship truth as they ought; that they do not seek after her with that passionate longing which she ought to inspire; that they take no real trouble to form correct ideas, and to satisfy themselves as to the soundness of their ultimate formulæ; that even where they have formed beliefs of this kind, they are cautious not to express them; and, finally, that they never make a sufficient effort to reduce their beliefs to practice. To put the matter in its most concrete form, it is, according to Mr. Morley, one of the first duties which a man owes to himself and to humanity – (it is fair to state that the illustration is our own) – to satisfy himself whether he does or does not believe in the existence of a God. Suppose him, after long meditation, to arrive at the opinions which were recently so frankly enunciated by Mr. Winwood Reade, and to satisfy himself that the belief in a God is a blind and unreasoning superstition. It then becomes his duty to proclaim to everybody that this is his view of the matter, and to lose no opportunity of impressing it upon his relations, upon his friends, and, as far as he can, upon the general public. And, lastly, it is his clear duty upon all occasions of public action, to sternly refuse his countenance to any political act by which the existence of a God is even tacitly and indirectly affirmed, as, for example, the prayers with which the sitting of the House of Commons is opened, or an oath upon the Bible in a court of law, or the endowment of a new Bishopric. In short, the one man in all England who best realizes Mr. Morley's ideal of staunch, hearty, earnest, uncompromising devotion to truth, is Mr. Charles Bradlaugh; and nothing, we suspect, would please Mr. Morley so much as to see us a nation of Bradlaughs. We may be doing the learned and able editor of the *Fortnightly Review* an injustice, but we are honestly stating what we believe to be the net result of his essay.

The book positively bristles with epigrams. There is nothing hazy or misty about Mr. Morley. He knows what he means to say, and he says it. Such phrases as 'the natural sloth and the indigenous intellectual haziness of ordinary men,' – 'a deliberate connivance at a plan for the propagation of error,' – 'an idea that error somehow in certain stages, where there is enough of it, actually does good like vaccination,' – 'the new *disciplina arcani*, which means the dissimulation of truth with a view to the perpetuation of error,' are perpetually cropping up, and when Mr. Morley concludes a fierce attack upon infidels who conceal their infidelity from their wives by reminding us that 'it is a poor saying, that the world is to become void of spiritual sincerity, because Xanthippe has a turn for respectable theology,' we see how erroneous is the ordinary conception that Positivists, like Scotchmen, have no sense of humour. Here and there, indeed, are passages which are really finely written. Most of us probably agree with Mr. Morley that a beneficed clergyman who, being at heart an atheist, yet goes on preaching his weekly sermon, celebrating his weekly service, and drawing his quarterly stipend, is a miserable kind of creature. But Mr. Morley denounces such faint-hearted Blougrams with all the energy of an Isaiah: –

'Let thus much have been said as to those who deliberately and knowingly sell their intellectual birthright for a mess of pottage, making a brazen compromise with what they hold despicable, lest they should have to win their bread honourably. Men need expend no declamatory indignation upon them. They have a hell of their own; words can add no bitterness to it. It is no light thing to have secured a livelihood on condition of going through life masked and gagged. To be compelled, week after week, and year after year, to recite the symbols of ancient faith and lift up his voice in the echoes of old hopes, with the blighting thought in his soul that the faith is a lie, and the hope no more than the folly of the crowd; to read hundreds of times in a twelvemonth with solemn unction as the inspired word of the Supreme what to him are meaningless as the Abracadabras of the conjuror in a booth; to go on to the end of his days administering to simple folk holy rites of commemoration and solace, when he has in his mind at each phrase what dupes are these simple folk and how wearisomely counterfeit their rites: and to know through all that this is really to be the one business of his prostituted life, that so dreary and hateful a piece of play-acting will make the desperate retrospect of his last hours – here is of a truth the very βδέλγμα της ἐρημωσως, the abomination of desolation of the human spirit indeed.'

Or, again: –

'The man of the world despises Catholics for taking their religious opinions on trust and being the slaves of tradition. As if he had himself formed his own most important opinions either in religion or anything else. He laughs at them for their superstitious awe of the Church. As if his own inward awe of the majority were one whit less of a superstition. He mocks their deference for the past. As if his own absorbing deference to the present were one tittle better bottomed or a jot more respectable. The modern emancipation will profit us very little, if the *status quo* is to be fastened round our necks with the despotic authority of a heavenly dispensation, and if in the stead of ancient Scriptures we are to accept the plenary inspiration of majorities.'

It is, of course, impossible to argue with a man whose first principles are diametrically opposed to your own; and, for this reason, it is impossible for us to properly criticize Mr. Morley's essay. As a *tour de force*, – as a piece of clever monthly journalism, – it is as good a thing, in its way, as Mr. Fitzjames Stephens's 'Liberty, Equality, and Fraternity.' But when we come to the positive duty of making up our minds one way or the other, we find ourselves unable to agree with Mr. Morley either in his premisses or in his conclusions. When Positivism first grew rampant at Oxford, – where, like Tractarianism, Ritualism, Hegelianism, Æstheticism, and every other kind of creed, it has not been without its day, – it was said of a certain well-known Don who had thoroughly accepted the new Gospel, that if you did not cut the round of beef upon positivist principles he considered you a scoundrel, and told you as much, and we need, perhaps, hardly be reminded how Grote used to consider any disposition to believe in the intuitional system of philosophy, and to reject the latest discoveries of Mr. Bain, as a grave moral defect. Prof. Jowett, in his Introduction to his Plato, after pointing out how much and on how many matters he disagrees with Grote, adds, if we rightly remember the words, 'But I must not "lay hands on my father Parmenides," who will, I hope, forgive me for differing from him on these points.' Of this spirit Mr. Morley seems to us to have no notion. The intolerance of the school of philosophy to which he belongs runs through every sentence that he writes. To our thinking, if an atheist accepts an invitation to a country-house belonging to old-fashioned country people, it is his duty on Sunday morning to go to church. This may be a failing on our part, and Mr. Morley will, no doubt, put it down to 'natural sloth, and indigenous intellectual haziness.' His notion clearly is that a man ought, under such circumstances, to say to his host, 'I shall not go to church with you and your family, and I shall not do so because I am an atheist, and hold your religion to be an abominable and degrading superstition.' If Mr. Morley's principles are worth anything, such an answer is the only one that a man with a proper sense of moral responsibility ought to be able to give under the circumstances. To our mind, the arrogance and vulgarity of it entirely obscure the slight moral worth that otherwise attaches to its frankness. Mr. Tennyson is not, perhaps, a great philosopher, or even an original thinker, but he has somewhere addressed those

> who after toil and storm
>   May seem to have reached a purer air
>   Whose faith has centre everywhere,
> Nor cares to fix itself to form;

and he advises such –

> Leave thou thy sister when she prays,
>   Her early heaven, her happy views;
>   Nor thou with shadowed hint confuse
> A life that leads melodious days.

> Her faith through form is pure as thine,
>   Her hands are quicker unto good:

> Oh, sacred be the flesh and blood
> To which she links a truth divine!

To do Mr. Morley justice, he makes a single exception to his rules, and holds that it is bad taste in a young Comtist who has a country parson for his father to obtrude his peculiar views upon his sire under the paternal rooftree. But in the case of a sister, or a wife, or a daughter, his stern sense of duty allows of no such faint-heartedness.

His position is the more extraordinary when we come to consider what his intellectual creed really is. 'Moral principles,' he tells us, 'when they are true, are at bottom only registered generalizations from experience. They record certain uniformities of antecedence and consequence in the region of human conduct.' Now it is a little difficult to see why a man who holds this uncompromising theory of the empirical character of moral truth should be so eaten up with zeal in its behalf. *Magna est veritas et prævalebit* can be interpreted in two ways. If a man believes of a given proposition that it not only *is*, but also *must be* true – as a good Mohammedan believes of the Koran – it then becomes clearly his duty, not only to profess it openly, but, if necessary, to force it upon other people. But a truth which is, after all, *ex hypothesi*, a merely approximate generalization, is hardly a matter to be warm about, and a man may well be forgiven if he is willing to agree to a compromise about it. The fact is, that on most of the questions on which men accept a compromise it is very difficult for any one who is not either a Positivist on the one hand, or an Ultramontane on the other, to come to any finally definite conclusion. Mr. Morley mentions as one of the problems on which a man ought to make up his mind decisively, either one way or the other, the representation of minorities. The question is precisely one of those which a Comtist would be able to solve in a minute by a reference to certain infallible first principles. An ordinary man, on the contrary, will, in all probability, frankly confess that the matter is one on which he has, for the present at any rate, no positive opinion. He is aware, of course, that abstract justice requires that minorities should be represented, but, on the other hand, it would clearly be unwise to put a mischievous power into hands that would almost certainly abuse it.

Fiat justitia ruat cœlum is an admirable motto, but, for all that, it is a good deal better that the sky should stand. Life, indeed, would be not only intolerable, but simply impossible, if everybody who had a conviction of any kind were to carry it out into actual practice as consistently as Good Templars do their teetotalism. In a word, Mr.

Morley either means nothing at all, or else he means a great deal too much, and the difficulties which beset his position are nowhere more charmingly illustrated than when, after considering how far it is a duty for an atheist to openly express his opinions, he decides that the one exception to the general rule is in the case of his parents, whose scruples he is bound to treat with a filial respect. Most people would probably claim an equal measure of respect for grandparents, and, indeed, for old age generally. This Mr. Morley would, of course, consider weak-kneed. Why, however, he draws the line at parents, and not somewhere else, we confess ourselves unable to discover.

Appendix II

W. H. Mallock, 'Mr. John Morley and progressive radicalism', *Quarterly Review* 168 (January–April 1889), pp. 249–80.

ART. IX. – *Mr. John Morley's Collected Writings:* – Voltaire, Rousseau, Diderot, Critical Miscellanies, Compromise, and Burke. 10 vols. London, 1886–8.

We have frequently, in this Review, when discussing political questions, made passing reference to the views of Mr. John Morley; and there are perhaps few persons of equal eminence, whose authority we have treated with scantier respect or admiration. We have, however, before now urged, that the views of public men demand and deserve attention, in proportion, not to their intrinsic worth and reasonableness, but to the practical influence which they exercise, or the forces which they represent. On this last ground alone, if on no other, Mr. Morley takes an exceedingly high place amongst those, to whom attention of the most careful kind is due. If there are few politicians who less deserve to be followed, there are few whose opinions it will be more instructive to examine.

We will make our meaning a little more precise. We have spoken of men who exercise practical influence: but it is not his influence which makes Mr. Morley important, neither influence as a thinker nor influence as a politician. We do not believe that, in either character, he has any personal following that numerically is worth speaking about. His importance is due to the fact, not that he wields forces, but that he represents forces, and that he represents them in a way more complete and clear than any other public man in England. That party which, to describe it by the term most acceptable to all of its various sections, we may in a technical sense call the 'Party of Progress,' no doubt possesses and is inspired by a large number of philosophers; but Mr. Morley is the only one of this number who has connected himself with practical life, or been in contact with affairs and statesmen. Nor has this contact been accidental. He is not a philosopher who, like Mr. Arthur Balfour, has turned aside from philosophy to devote himself to some urgent national business. There is, in his case, no turning aside whatever. His position in the practical world is the direct consequence and sequel of his position as a thinker, and takes from his position as a thinker whatever meaning it possesses. The Radical party has sought him out and promoted him, not because he was eminent for any practical tact or ability, but because he was eminent as an exponent of the underlying *rationale* of Radicalism. He has none of that mastery of men's most powerful weaknesses which Mr. Gladstone possesses from being himself a colossal embodiment of them: but his works and his life possess what Mr. Gladstone's do not. There is in them a certain oneness of purpose and coherency, which embrace not only the theory of Radical politics, but also the theories philosophical, social, and religious, with which, on the whole, those politics are inseparably allied. He is the Fénelon or the Cardinal Newman of, we will not say the Radical party, but we will say of the Radical movement. He expresses for that movement the reason of the faith that is in it, or at least as much of that faith as has any reason to be expressed; and hence the interest that attaches to the ten handsome volumes, in which his writings have been recently collected and published, and whose general significance we now propose to discuss.

It is well, indeed, to warn the reader that, when we call these volumes interesting, we do not use the word in the sense which it would bear at a circulating library. With certain notable exceptions, of which we shall speak presently, the style, though close and lucid, is of almost unparalleled dryness. But, if we master our distaste for this strangely repellent medium, we shall find in Mr. Morley's writings a lesson that is singularly instructive, and is certainly very different from any that he means to teach us. We shall see the whole inner spirit of modern democratic progress, represented in its best, its completest, and its most conscientious development. We shall see, not only its political creed and aims, but its religious, its moral, and its philosophical creed also, as they appear to a man who has devoted every effort to bringing them into some consistent and practical whole, and who does not flinch from letting the world know, what many of his party have not the courage to confess, and what still more have not the capacity clearly and consistently to realize. We shall see this, and something else besides. We shall not only see the man as the representative and exponent of a system, but we shall also see a system as re-acting on and affecting the man. We shall see the man bringing to the system many qualities of a high and unusual nature, unusual integrity, unusual intelligence and culture, unusual fairness, and unusual powers of reasoning: but we shall see that, though these qualities are strong, the system is still stronger; and that with a savage and pitiless force it crushes, distorts, or mutilates, whatever of good is unhappily consecrated to defending it. We shall see that, being immoral and irrational in its postulates, in its temper, and in its aims, it makes its defenders immoral and irrational also; that, by an iron and irresistible movement, it tortures tolerance into intolerance, candour into rancorous hatred, scientific scepticism into the blindest and most abject superstition, and logical consistency into confusion and self-contradiction; we shall see, in fact, the man of clear thought and integrity completely broken on the wheel of the creed he has adopted, writhing and exhibiting himself in intellectual attitudes that are only not ridiculous because they are so profoundly pitiable.

It is a well-known device on the part of critics or orators to overpraise the persons whom they design to attack, so that by raising the pedestals they may secure a more ignominious fall for the statues. In our praise, however, of Mr. Morley, we can honestly acquit ourselves of any such insincerity; and we propose to begin our examination of his volumes, by substantiating, with their aid, our estimate of his natural qualities.

Of the three or four thousand pages of which these volumes consist, considerably more than half are devoted to the studies of men who directly or indirectly assisted in the French Revolution. One volume is given to Voltaire, two to Rousseau, two to Diderot, and separate essays, which equal another volume in bulk, are given to Turgot, to Condorcet, and to Robespierre. Six volumes out of the ten are thus practically accounted for. Of the others, one is given to Burke, one to an Essay on Compromise, a production something in the style of Mill's 'Essay on Liberty'; whilst the remaining two consist of various shorter studies of English writers, regarded mainly as revolutionaries, Byron, J. S. Mill, Miss Martineau, and George Eliot, together with one or two pieces almost entirely literary. Mr. Morley's philosophy is nowhere set forth formally; even in his 'Essay on Compromise' it is applied, rather than stated. It is only to be gathered from constant reference and allusion, from parenthetical paragraphs, or sentences of trenchant correction of others. It is held, as it were, in solution, in a mass of biographical and other criticism, from which, however, by the simple chemistry of attention, it is readily made to form itself into a precipitate....

Well may the reader, who knows Mr. Morley as a politician, be astonished at seeing what are his political convictions as a thinker. If he respects Mr. Morley's intellect as sincerely as we do, he will not be astonished at these convictions in themselves; but if they are really the convictions of intellectual Radicalism, what will astonish him is the extraordinary difference between the theories which intellectual Radicals hold, and the theories which they put forward when they are making 'their appeals to the crowd.'

We are not, however, left by Mr. Morley to study this singular phenomenon, so far as he is concerned, in the region of politics only, or only in the inconsistency between his politics in the study and his politics at the public meeting. The same inconsistency is to be traced in his books themselves, running through them like a flaw in a block of marble, or in a bell, and making every part of his system, from politics to religion, ring cracked and false. This is the point to which we are specially anxious to direct our readers' attention; and therefore we are specially anxious to make our precise meaning clear. Mr. Morley's general philosophy of life is nowhere set forth formally and consecutively in his works, but it is plainly to be gathered from a great variety of passages. It is not original, though it is often stated with originality. Its outlines are perfectly familiar, and we at once recognize it as a definite system which the author has consciously adopted, and to which he has given his faith. But side by side with the passages in which this system is stated, is another series of passages, dealing with various subjects, and incidentally expressing judgments formed by the author's intellect in moments when his consciousness of the system has been in abeyance, and he has ceased to be shackled by it. These judgments form the most curious features in Mr. Morley's writings; for they show him, when not consciously on duty as the defender or exponent of Radicalism, as the most trenchant though unconscious critic it would be possible to imagine, of every main proposition on which his formulated Radicalism depends. In the sphere of religion, in the sphere of psychology, in the sphere of morals, this is the case to the same degree as it is in the sphere of politics. Whilst with one hand he is laboriously rearing his theoretical structure, with the other he is steadily unscrewing the fastenings that held this structure together. He is unintentionally playing the part of Balaam inverted; and when he would fain lift his voice to bless his principles, his natural common sense, like an ironical destiny, constrains the unhappy prophet to curse them altogether.

Let us begin with his treatment of that religion of progress which he supposes is to supplant Christianity. The very basis of this religion consists of an exalted view of the dignity of human nature, as contrasted with the depravity which Christianity imputes to it, of a reverence for this present life as contrasted with the Christian contempt for it, and of a belief that the welfare of our fellows is naturally so dear to us, that our sense of union with them is so close, and that the future of humanity is so sublime, that we shall presently come to feel for our forefathers and for our descendants, an emotion as overpowering, as exalting, and as inspiring, as the Christian love for God.[1] These are Mr. Morley's views when he is speaking of the matter officially; but when he forgets the exigencies of his official theory, and trusts to his own observations and knowledge of life, there is not one of them which he does not contradict with a sombre and savage bitterness. Man, whom, as we have seen, he describes officially as an 'excellent and helpful being,' with 'infinite capacities' for all the fine things imaginable, he elsewhere declares to be tainted in his very nature with 'rapacity, lust, and bloody violence.'[2] Officially, he declares that the 'brotherhood' of excellent and helpful beings will supply, by their praise and blame, both the motives and sanction of morality. Unofficially, he breaks out into the following significant exclamation: 'How pitiful a thing seems the approval or disapproval of these creatures of the conventions of an hour, as one figures the merciless vastness of the universe of matter, sweeping along through viewless space!'[3] And those destinies of mortals which officially he calls sublime, unofficially he compares to the most unreal and unsubstantial of things – to the shadows of trees in water.[4] Priests, who abandoned their profession at the French Revolution, declared that they had hardly been able to say mass, owing to the difficulty they felt in suppressing their laughter. Mr. Morley seems hardly able to recite the creed of Humanity without sighing at every article, as if pierced by the thought that, not it is true, but its contrary. What his theory requires him to say, he says, often with unction, always with emphasis; but the emphasis is bitter, as though he winced at forcing himself to apply it. What completely annihilates his theory, seems wrung from the very depth of his intellect and his experience.

This is not true only of his general estimate of humanity; it is true of every detail of that estimate – of the individual lot, as well as of the collective. Officially he speaks of 'the full and ever-festal life,'[5] open to those who know how to seek it; any disbelief in the dignity of man's life he pushes aside as 'mischievous.'[6] Unofficially he points to the impressiveness of Burke's exclamation – 'What shadows we are, and what shadows we pursue!'[7] He declares that 'misery stalks after us all, and a man's life is left to the sting and smart of irrecoverable things;'[8] whilst as an odd comment on the consolation which the religion of

APPENDIX II

Humanity is to give us, 'the black and horrible grave,' he says, 'is indeed the end of our communion.'[9]

A comment still odder on that same religion is this. One of its principal doctrines is the doctrine of progress. It is only by this doctrine that we can 'justify in the sight of humanity our provisional acquiescence in the present lot of millions;'[10] and it is from 'devout contemplation' of this progress, that our spiritual vitality in our struggles against selfishness and despondency is to be nourished.[11] But when we come to examine Mr. Morley's view of progress more closely, we find him declaring that it is an affair of such incalculable slowness that the widest imaginations can hardly carry us to the times when it shall reach its consummation. 'Myriads of lives,' he says, must intervene, 'and immeasurable geologic periods of time.'[12] 'The smallest step is tardy and difficult;'[13] 'a few steps only have yet been traversed.'[14] More disheartening still, this progress is not only slow, but it is 'an exception,' some races being 'fundamentally' deficient in 'civilizable quality:'[15] whilst, to crown all, Mr. Morley in more than one place admits that history, observation, and personal experience, in many ways and often suggest to us, that progress is altogether an illusion.[16]

But the most crushing exposure of the futility of the doctrine, as a means of exciting in the individual a controlling spiritual devotion, is to be found in Mr. Morley's treatment of what seems quite an alien subject. We refer to the way in which he argues the point, that in human conduct there are certain kinds of actions which are to be classed as self-regarding, and therefore to be left free; and that the very possibility of progress depends on our recognition of this. He is arguing against those who maintain that no actions are self-regarding, but that all have some ulterior social consequence; and his contention is, not that his opponents are wrong in point of theory, but that their theory ignores a distinction which is drawn by common experience. All actions very possibly have some ulterior consequence; but the consequences of some are direct and near, others are 'indirect and at a distance.' Thus, he points out, there may be many acts 'by engaging in which at any given moment the doer is neglecting other acts,' which might be socially beneficial. 'But as a matter of observation,' he says, 'and for purposes of practical morality, there are kinds of action whose consequences do not go beyond the doer of them.... The connection between the act and its influence on others is so minute, ... though quite certain, distinct and traceable.'[17] What an admission is this! Here we have a class of acts, whose influence is distinct and traceable in the very age in which the doer lives, probably on the very individuals whom he knows; but because the influence is remote, it is supposed not to concern him: and yet the whole meaning of his life, the source of his highest endeavours, his restraint in temptation, and his comfort in death, is supposed to rest on his vivid and vital recognition, that his acts have an influence infinitely more remote – an influence, which even if certain, is neither distinct nor traceable – an influence, not on people he knows, not on an age he knows, but on 'myriads of lives' whose character he cannot even conjecture, and on vague 'consummations' which will be accomplished only after 'immeasurable geologic periods of time.' Thus the whole possibility of Radical progress depends on our recognizing a distinction, while Radical religion, the supposed soul of that progress, depends on our enthusiastically denying it.

Let us turn to Mr. Morley's psychology and his moral philosophy; and we find him confusing himself, and confusing his own arguments, in the same disastrous manner. He formally commits himself to the great and important doctrine, that the will is not free, and maintains that we must, having discovered this, reconstruct our ideas of ethical praise and blame, and, if we use the old terms, use them in changed senses. It would be impossible, however, to find any writer who bandies about terms of ethical admiration and opprobrium, in a mood more exactly resembling that of a dissenting Christian. His ostensible belief, is the belief of Holbach, that a man is no more to blame for throwing himself out of a window, than he is for being thrown out.[18] He praises Helvetius for his wisdom in recognizing 'that men are what they must be, that all hatred against them is unjust; that a fool produces follies just as a wild shrub produces sour berries, and that to insult him is to reproach the oak for bearing acorns instead of olives.'[19] And yet epithets such as 'degraded,' 'filthy,' 'unclean,' and 'frivolous,' he applies right and left of him, like a lash. A class of men who do nothing but act on his permission, and exercise their discretion in self-regarding actions, he denounces for 'disloyalty' not to their fellows, but 'to their own intellect.' If he does not insult them, he is careful to tell us that it is only because they are beneath 'declamatory indignation,' that 'they have a hell of their own,' and that they realize 'the abomination of desolation of the human spirit.'[20] If we enquire how Mr. Morley justifies this language, we can find in his books an explicit statement to enlighten us; but if the one is surprising, the other is more surprising still. 'It is better,' says Mr. Morley, 'to awaken in an individual a sense of responsibility for his own character, than to do anything ... to dispose him to lay the blame on Society; Society is after all only a name for other people.'[21] So speaks the follower of Holbach and of Helvetius, as if the doctrine, of which he is the professed exponent, were not precisely the doctrine that he here denies, as if the one point in which he differs, as to the subject in question, from his opponents, were not the belief on his part that the responsibility for a man's character, does lie with other people, and not at all with himself – that his very will is the creature of circumstances which others have created for him.

Strangely enough, however, Mr. Morley does not see this. One would have thought that, in reviewing his works, prior to their republication, this extraordinary discrepancy in reasoning would have been noticed by him, and been removed; but instead of having removed it, he repeats it in a subsequent volume; and he repeats it this time not in a passing sentence, but with a solemn elaboration, and a philosophical flourish of trumpets. He deliberately endeavours in his volume on 'Compromise,' to establish, in spite of his rejection of free-will, that the philosopher is justified in judging what has been, by what might have been. Sir James Stephen, he tells us, has joined issue with him on this point, declaring '"that might have been" lies beyond the limits of sane speculation;' and Mr. Morley undertakes to prove that Sir James Stephen is wrong. A more astounding piece of intellectual blundering and floundering it would be hard to find in the writings of any educated man. Mr. Morley's views shall be given in his own words.

'It is surely,' he says, speaking of Sir James Stephen's statement, 'extending optimism too far to insist on carrying this back right through the ages. To me, the history of mankind is a huge *pis-aller*.... Society has a certain order of progress... but within the only possible order there is always room for all kinds and degrees of invention, improvement, and happy and unhappy accident.... Only certain steps are possible at a time; but it is not inevitable that these potential advances shall all be realized. Does any one suppose that Turgot, for example, was the only man that ever lived who might have done more for society than he was allowed to do?... History assuredly has not moved without relation of cause and effect; it is a record of social growth and its conditions; but it is a record also of interruption, and misadventure, and perturbation.... We accept the past for the same reason that we accept the laws of the Solar System, though as Comte says, we can easily conceive them improved in certain respects; but it is surely mere midsummer madness to think that we have come by the easiest of all imaginable routes to our present point in the march.' – 'Compromise,' pp. 80–82 [85–6].

Had Mr. Morley not himself suggested a word, we should ourselves have been completely at a loss to find one which could fitly characterize this farrago of confusion and nonsense. As it is, we may borrow from his own vocabulary, and call it 'mere midsummer madness.' The fundamental confusion, which underlies the whole of it, comes to the surface in three significant words – the words 'potential,' 'conceivable,' and 'imaginable,' all of which are used by Mr. Morley as if they were synonymous with 'possible.' Mr. Morley says that he accepts the facts of the human past, as he is good enough to accept the laws of the solar system; but all the same, in certain respects, he can easily conceive them improved. But what does this mean? It means, and it can mean only, that he can conjure up some sort of picture of a universe which in certain respects might have been better for man. No doubt Mr. Morley can; but surely he speaks too modestly. Not only he, but we ourselves, or anybody, could conceive of a universe improved not only in certain respects, but in countless respects. Our improvements would include amongst other things such changes in the laws of matter, as would make us all immortal, all young, all beautiful, and all rich – as would, in short, make all of us endlessly and supremely happy. But when we say we can conceive of such changes, we mean only that we can conceive them in the form of some airy image, behind which there is nothing. The least change really made in the solar system, would imply some change in every part of it, and not in it only, but in the entire material universe; and the least of these changes, the most minute, the most infinitesimal, would be as absolutely essential to the result, as the greatest and the most overwhelming. Does Mr. Morley mean that he can conceive the whole of these changes? Evidently he does not. Then what does he mean? He means merely that, having the ordinary gift of imagination, he is able to employ it in a childish form of castle-building. He is able to amuse himself as, if we recollect right, Lazy Harry and Fat Kate amused themselves in the nursery story, when, being absolutely penniless both of them, they began to settle what they would do, if Harry found one dollar and Kate gave him another. But what has a man's capacity for fancies of this kind to do with the possibilities of the solar system? Can its laws be altered now? Plainly they cannot. Was there ever a time when they could have been altered? If so, when? And how did the constitution of matter differ then from its constitution now? When, let us ask Mr. Morley, did the solar system resemble Mr. Gladstone in having three courses open to it, or even two? Whatever course it took, that course must have been determined by some cause pre-existing. To question this for an instant, is to upset the very bases of his philosophy: and when Mr. Morley says that the laws of matter might have been improved, he would be speaking every whit as rationally, every whit as much to the purpose, if he said that an acorn might bring forth a canary-bird.

And now let us turn to man and to human history. Mr. Morley admits, we should rather say, he proclaims, that they stand on the same footing as the laws of the solar system, and that the fiction of free-will, which alone made them seem to differ, has been hounded for ever out of the company of sane beliefs. What can he mean then by saying that 'within the only possible order there is always room for all kinds and degrees of improvement'? Let us ask him the following question: How does he suppose that at any given period, improvement of any kind or degree is to be made? By men and by the men then existing – for example, by a man like Turgot, who Mr. Morley cites as an excellent case in point, of a man who *might have done more than he was allowed to do*. By this Mr. Morley means, that there were certain forces in Turgot, which had to act amongst many antagonistic circumstances, and that, had the circumstances been different, the effect of the forces would have been different. But Mr. Morley forgets the most important fact in the situation, that, if Turgot, his genius, and his acts, were, as Mr. Morley asserts, the necessary results of all that had gone before, the circumstances surrounding Turgot were equally necessary also. The events, which by inexorable sequences culminated in Turgot's wisdom, were inexorably linked with other events, which culminated in the ignorance of those others by whom Turgot's wisdom was thwarted: and if the denier of free-will believes that amongst an infinity of remote causes, and of circumstances collaterally connected, there lurks that possibility of a break in the chain of necessity, which in nearer events he denies with such passionate emphasis, we can only say that this belief is the phantom of a brain grown giddy with the contemplation of a problem it was too feeble to grasp. What might have been may be discussed with meaning by the believer in free-will; but for the denier of it nothing might have been but what has been. The actual has been the only possible; and it may be said with equal truth that this is the best of all possible worlds, and the worst also.

> 'With earth's first clay they did the last man knead,
> And there of the last harvest sowed the seed,
> And the first morning of creation wrote
> What the last dawn of reckoning shall read.'

For the thinker who denies free-will, this is the inevitable conclusion. Let him paint his thoughts an inch thick, to this favour they must come. We need not, however, pursue the subject further. We are not writing to convince our readers of a stupendous truth, but to exhibit the absurdity of Mr. Morley's struggles against it. The history of mankind, he says, is to him "a huge *pis-aller*." He might as well say that the climate of the Pole was a huge *pis-aller*, because he can fancy camellia trees growing on an iceberg, and potatoes and truffles maturing themselves in the ice.

We are loth, however, to leave Mr. Morley with a sneer. Indeed to do so would probably leave in the readers' mind a completely false idea of the whole tenor of our criticism. We regard Mr. Morley's works and conduct as a condemnation and exposure of Radicalism, not because we think ill of Mr. Morley, but because we think well of him. If he were not naturally fair and candid, there would be nothing remarkable in his unfairness. If he were not a person of high intellectual powers, there would be nothing remarkable in his pitiable confusion and contradictions. Our design has been to exhibit not his faults, but the faults of the wretched cause to which he has immolated his faculties; and which in his case, we we have said before, has mangled on the wheel a good man, and not a criminal.

Well might Mr. Morley, could he but realize his condition, exclaim with one of his revolutionary heroes, 'Better to be a poor fisher, than to meddle with the governing of men.' Better for him, at least, to have cultivated letters, which he might have so well adorned, and which might have yielded him a spotless fame, than to illustrate in his own person one of his own most melancholy sayings, that when men diverge into new walks in life, and when thus 'the habit of their lives has been sundered, the most immaculate are capable of antics beyond prevision.'[22]

Notes

1. 'Rousseau,' vol. ii. pp. 278, 279. 'Compromise,' p. 167 [121–2].
2. 'Diderot,' vol. ii. p. 223.
3. 'Compromise,' p. 198 [135].
4. 'Rousseau,' vol. ii. p. 328.
5. Ibid. vol. i. p. 153.
6. 'Miscellanies,' vol. ii. p. 277.
7. 'Burke,' p. 138.

8. 'Rousseau,' vol. i. p. 91.
9. Ibid. p. 220.
10. Ibid. pp. 179, 180.
11. Ibid. vol. ii. p. 278.
12. 'Rousseau,' vol. i. p. 180; and 'Compromise,' p. 235 [151].
13. 'Voltaire,' p. 247.
14. 'Compromise,' p. 70 [81].
15. 'Rousseau,' vol. i. p. 177.
16. See 'Diderot,' vol. i. pp. 191, 348.
17. 'Compromise,' pp. 276, 277 [170, 171].
18. 'Diderot,' vol. ii. p. 179.
19. Ibid. p. 153.
20. 'Compromise,' pp. 90–93 [90–1].
21. 'Diderot,' vol. ii. p. 12.
22. 'Miscellanies,' vol. i. p. 11.

Appendix III

Christopher Kent, *Brains and Numbers: Elitism, Comtism, and Democracy in Mid-Victorian England* (Toronto: University of Toronto Press, 1978), pp. 124-33.

References to *On Compromise* commonly emphasize its rationalist character, for it is a rationalistic tract – manifesto, rather – to be classed with such contemporary works as Mill's *The Subjection of Women* and Leslie Stephen's *Essays on Freethinking and Plainspeaking*. Morley was a religious rationalist who wished also to be a political rationalist, and in *Compromise* he attempted to yoke these together, hoping to bring the bold blacks and whites in which he saw religious questions into the greyer realms of politics. But in its neglected political aspect the book can be regarded as a handbook for the intellectual in politics, and specifically an exercise in self-direction. It is a guide through the difficult frontier between speculation and action. In his book Morley tries to formulate certain principles of general application to the conduct of the intellectual by defining the straight and narrow path between the slough of political quietism on the one hand and the vanities of unprincipled activism on the other.[1]

On Compromise is a unblushingly an elitist manifesto, originally addressed to the enlightened vanguard of *Fortnightly* readers: 'What is important is the mind and attitude, not of the ordinary man, but of those who should be extraordinary ... What are the best men in the country striving for?' The answer was discouraging. Morley saw all about him evidences of a cramped mentality, a low tone in national life. He attributed it partly to a sense of disillusionment over the outcome of the various causes which had been enthusiastically taken up by intellectuals over the previous forty years: parliamentary reform in England, the unification of Italy, emancipation in the United States – all had been achieved, but none had realized the high ideals which had been invested in them. The failures of 1848 had also discredited political theory and speculation, particularly in France where ideals had been perverted by the political immorality of the Second Empire.[2]

Morley detected a deeper reason for the enervating mental climate in the insidious spread of the 'Historical Method' beyond the bounds of scholarship and into everyday life. Virtually everything – physical, intellectual, and moral – was now being regarded from its evolutionary aspect. This tendency inevitably encouraged the suspension of judgment not only on the past but on the present which so clearly partook of the past. 'In the last century men asked of a belief or a story, Is it true? We now ask, How did men come to take it for true?' Thus confusion was growing between explanation and justification; relativity was becoming all-pervasive – every abuse could be shown to have a defensible origin, every error to have been relative to a certain system of belief. The historical method was particularly prone to debasement at the hands of those lacking intellectual discipline into a 'slipshod preference of vague general forms over definite beliefs.' Worse still, it tainted the springs of action by its tendency to discount individual effort in accounting for change.[3]

Such speculative tendencies served only to strengthen a characteristic already endemic in Englishmen – their 'profound distrust of all general principles,' a distrust arising from their habit of regarding 'principle' and 'expediency' as necessarily antithetical. Morley proposed one of his judicious redefinitions to meet this difficulty, suggesting that principles were really nothing more than 'larger expediencies.' He was anxious to tighten his countrymen to the pitch of principle, but equally anxious to show that it was not beyond their range. Morley identified the newspaper press as one of the worst offenders against principle. By making a fetish of public opinion it catered to 'vulgar ways of looking at things and vulgar ways of speaking of them,' stereotyping and endlessly repeating them so as to deaden individual and private opinion. The press was particularly hostile to theory and principle and particularly given to improperly applying the political test, damping down speculation with cant about 'the limits of the practicable in politics.' A grotesque example of this was *The Times*' censuring Darwin for publishing his *Descent of Man* 'while the sky of Paris was red with the flames of the Commune.'[4]

The central theme of *Compromise* is the Comtist problem of the separation of the powers (though Morley nowhere mentions Comte in the book.) *The Times*' reaction to Darwin was a case of the illegitimate application of the political test to non-political matters. If the intellectuals adopted this point of view, rejecting principle and worshipping instead practicality and narrow political expediency, then they were not only usurping the proper function of the politician, whose concern this was, but more importantly they were abandoning their own proper function, that of providing the unadulterated flow of higher ideas necessary to political and social progress. The politician was necessarily absorbed by immediate concerns and heedless of new ideas as yet outside the realm of practicality or public acceptance, but if the intellectuals acquiesced in the 'leaden tyranny of the man of the world' by politicizing their speculations and acting as their own censors, then they were removing the politician even further from the realm of pure ideas. Moreover, since their own ideas would still suffer modification at the hands of politicians regardless of their own politicizing efforts, these ideas would achieve realization, if at all, in an even more debased state than otherwise.[5]

Morley observed that it was indispensable to the social welfare of a nation that 'the divorce between political responsibility and intellectual responsibility ... should not be too complete and universal.' But he suggested that this divorce was in England largely the result of the intellectuals accepting, in public at least, the 'House of Commons view of life,' and thus depriving the populace of contact through them with ideas and the concern for truth. Morley was particularly concerned with question of 'dual doctrine' – whether intellectuals should systematically keep their ideas to themselves and 'openly encourage a doctrine for the less enlightened classes which they do not believe to be true for themselves.' He cited its classical formulation in the bargain offered by Ernest Renan to the Catholic church: 'Do not meddle with what we teach or write, and then we will not dispute the common people with you.' Such a doctrine implies a hermetic ideal of an intellectual élite and an idea of knowledge as a rare and special commodity, to be preserved in its purity from the profane crowd. It also implies that truth can be dangerous in the hands of the uninitiated, as in the case of Hume's suggestion that the right of resistance to a tyrant, although a true doctrine, should be concealed from the populace.[6]

Morley dismissed such doctrines out of hand, for they were founded on a principle which he strenuously denied – that error might have social, political, or psychological utility. He devotes a chapter to demolishing this principle which had just received support from an unexpected quarter with the publication of Mill's posthumous essay on 'The Utility of Religion.' Here, to Morley's dismay, his master had suggested that religion might be 'morally useful' without being intellectually sustainable. The fervour of Morley's denial derived from his conviction of the indivisibility of truth – social, political, and psychological. Morley, the evangelical rationalist, fervently believed truth to be an independent, homogeneous, and eternal entity. He was able to do so because his definition of truth is essentially negative: it is the opposite of error, 'inevitable elements in human growth,' have been cleared away. This negative view of progress, which accounts for his un-Comtist sympathy for Voltaire, is readily apparent from Morley's remarks on the course of history. New ideas tend to be 'dissolvent ideas,' and history is 'for the most part, the history of insurrection.' 'To me at any rate,' Morley revealingly observed, 'the history of mankind is a huge *pis aller*, just as our present society is; a prodigious, wasteful, experiment from which a certain number of results have been extracted.'[7]

Morley rejected the dual doctrine and the utility of error which implied an inherent conflict of interest between the intellectual élite and the populace because he saw the common people essentially as allies of the progressive élite against the privileged whose interests lay in preserving the status quo. Public opinion was the political lever of the intellectuals; therefore the masses who eventually sustained that opinion could not be ignored or sacrificed though there was obviously a great gap between the two groups.

It is this gap that creates difficulties for the intellectual elitist. How it is to be bridged, for bridged it must be, depends on how the élite's purpose is defined. Its two chief purposes are to maintain intellectual order and to ensure intellectual progress. Ultimately the two cannot be wholly reconciled, and the emphasis tends towards one or the other of these poles, one of which is essentially authoritarian, the other libertarian in spirit. Comte tried to reconcile order and progress by authoritatively defining the goal of progress – the positive social order whose integrity was to be maintained by a spiritual élite firmly in charge of the proletariat through their control of education. In this Comte came down decisively on the side of order and authority. It was essentially on this crucial point that Mill parted company with him (as did Morley), for Mill, by rejecting the possibility of authoritative blueprints for the ultimate society (in his own time at least), left progress an open question and committed himself to the free, continuing quest of the intellectual élite. The problem of the English Comtist as a proto-spiritual élite, as we have seen, was that of trying to accommodate themselves to conditions anterior to the realization of the society for which that élite was designed. It was their lot to live at a time when they were not yet fully in command, when 'progress' had not yet reached its destination and had still to be encouraged. The proletariat was on their side – the favourable experiences of the early 1860s had indicated this; Comte had confirmed and explained it. But again there was the dilemma: while the proletariat's support would be passive in the positive stage, rather more active support might be useful before the achievement of that stage to help bring it about, to give progress a push. How was this support to be mobilized without compromising the élite's intellectual authority and the proletariat's political purity? The problem for Mill, on the other hand, in opting for libertarian, undetermined progress, was that he continued to feel the need for some sort of organized authority among the intellectuals who were the sources of progress, to ensure that progress moved forward in an orderly, unimpeded manner, since he was not entirely sanguine about the reliability of the masses as supporters of progress. Hence Mill's attraction to Coleridge's clerisy and Comte's spiritual power as types of intellectual organization.

In defining his intellectual élite as the initiatory force on the side of progress, Morley rejected the traditional authoritarian conception in which the élite might be characterised as occupying the apex of an intellectual pyramid. Opposed to this static structural metaphor was Morley's dynamic temporal metaphor, in which the élite are seen as the leaders of a procession, the vanguard of progress. The idea of progress is essential to Morley's élitism. The common conception of a generation as a separate and homogeneous unit, Morley pointed out, does not conform to actuality; each generation has its leaders and laggards, as well as its vast inert bulk: only a small part of each generation 'can have nerve enough to grasp the banner of a new truth, and endurance enough to bear it along rugged and untrodden ways.' But in *Compromise* he tends to evade the important question of authority. Truth reveals itself to those whose minds are open to recognize it, minds in which, to use Morley's Arnoldian phrase, the 'free play and access of intellectual light' is unobstructed. Morley took it for granted that there would be a consensus among such minds as to what the truth was. His élite did not therefore act as guardians of received truth but as intellectual initiators in a world of change. 'Every age is in some sort an age of transition, but our own is characteristically and cardinally an epoch of transition in the very foundation of belief and conduct,' Morley noted. In turning from Comte back to Mill, he turned away from the question 'transition to what?' and confined his attention primarily to the fact of change itself, change as the condition of progress. Though Morley was a perfectibilist, the fulfilment of perfection could conveniently be projected sufficiently far into the future not to be a substantial issue. There was enough work combatting the obstacles of the present without being too concerned with the final goal, which would come of itself, provided the way was clear.⁸

Although Morley yoked the Millite ideal of a progressive libertarian élite to a Comtist faith in the amenability of the populace to authoritative direction, this faith was not wholly naive. The dual doctrine does in fact slip into *Compromise* in a diluted form as the doctrine of 'reserve'. Without believing in the utility of error amongst the populace, Morley did recognize the necessity, especially in an age of transition, of some sort of system for keeping back or reserving from them incomplete or 'unripe' ideas. A believer in a fairly open intellectual market place, Morley was not, however, a believer in the 'plenary inspiration of majorities' as the sole means of judging ideas. Obviously the initiatory élite had certain duties in the preparation and release of ideas for the consumption of the wider populace, but he believed that these were quite limited. He was therefore anxious to establish clearly for the élite the correct boundaries separating 'wise suspense' from 'unavowed disingenuousness' in forming ideas, 'wise reserve' from 'voluntary dissimulation' in expressing ideas, and 'wise tardiness' from 'indolence and pusillanimity' in trying to realize ideas. In establishing these three apparently clear-cut divisions Morley hoped to overcome the English propensity for politicizing speculation by showing intellectuals that only in the third category, the realization of opinion, could political considerations be legitimately introduced. He was trying to provide a workable formula specifying the proper degree of separation between the powers, intellectual and political, while yet providing for a reasonable linkage between them.⁹

In the first category, the formation of opinion, Morley claimed that there were no grounds whatsoever for withholding ideas at least for the intelligent man (and it is always to be remembered that Morley's strenuous advice is aimed entirely at the élite). It was his 'duty' to progress to have clear ideas, if only provisional ones, upon all the most important questions, and deliberately to prefer these ideas to their opposites. The implication that all opinions have clear opposites is a reminder of Morley's tendency to see opinion in simple terms of truth and error. Progress comes through confrontation of opposites; one must either be a clear liberal or a clear conservative. Morley sternly prods his readers into making up their minds, avoiding 'flaccid' latitudinarianism or 'slovenly' suspension of opinion. 'There are too many giggling epigrams,' he remarks sharply. But instead of analyzing the critical problem of transition from tentative idea to firm opinion, he offers only a hectoring rhetoric.¹⁰

'We see in solution an immense number of notions which people think it quite unnecessary to precipitate in the form of convictions,' Morley remarks. Yet it is one thing to speculate on the possible benefits of an idea and quite another to go further and decide that it is 'true' and therefore socially desirable – this is necessarily to introduce the political element, to consider feasibility and expediency. Morley's artificially compartmentalized model of intellectual progress evades the matter, however. According to his rather crude rationalist psychology, the man of intelligence who brings his intelligence firmly to bear on a question will find the view which commands his assent and belief. And because belief is independent of the will, the rational man will believe rationally (belief in superstition being of course the result of an 'irrational state of mind'). Yet, Morley claimed, a belief can be at the same time both firmly and yet provisionally held. Thus earnestness of conviction is quite compatible with a sense of liability to error; nor does belief in one's own infallibility necessarily entail intolerance.[11]

It might be protested that Morley's intellectual élite is composed of rational supermen, intellectual schizoids who can seize an idea, translate it into personal conviction, expound it vigorously, and yet be ready at all times to recognize its falseness, if necessary, and to yield to a rationally superior opposing view. Morley admitted that this was not 'the actual frame of mind of the ordinary man,' but he believed it attainable even by persons of 'far lower than first-rate capacity.' In fact, the intellectual demands upon the rational man were not as severe as one might think, because Morley believed that rational men would generally agree, since in most cases the choice was a simple one between contradictory ideas – indeed, between true and false. It was also usually a choice between old and new; the old being generally obstructive or erroneous, the new necessarily progressive. 'In *all* cases,' Morley wrote, the possession of a new idea, whether practical or speculative, only raises into definite speech what others have *needed* without being able to make their need articulate [my italics]. Morley believed firmly that truth was the daughter of time.[12]

Just as in the formation of opinion, so in the expression of opinion Morley's confidence in the rationalism of the élite enabled him to deny the necessity of reserve. The only area in which he allowed limits to freedom of speech was, interestingly, in the area of religion, where the possibility of inflicting distress on close relatives made certain allowances permissible; yet he believed that the progress of popular opinion would make even this type of reserve increasingly unnecessary.[13] In the sphere of politics, however, no such allowances were required: 'In politics no one seriously contends that respect for the feelings and prejudices of other people requires us to be silent about our opinions.' Morley could say this because he was confident that 'in every stable society ... incessant discussion of the theoretical bases of the social union is naturally considered worse than idle.' Of course even a republican was perfectly free to declare himself in England (as a few of the more daring radicals were doing in the early 1870s); indeed Morley himself cautiously demonstrated this freedom by directing a few criticisms against the institution of monarchy. It is apparent, however, that he expected no new ideas to be aired in the realm of politics that would be any more disturbing than this, no challenges to the political judgement of the rational man any sterner than this. Such enormous confidence was possible in England in 1874. Ironically, in the realm of political speculation, Morley unconsciously rested his optimism on the on the very politicization of thought in England which suppressed truly subversive political ideas and gave the country its political stability. This was the very 'House of Commons view of life' against which he protested so vigorously elsewhere.[14]

It was in the realization of opinion that Morley admitted the need to allow for the awkward realities of human existence: 'To insist on a whole community being made at once to submit to the reign of new practices and new ideas which have just begun to commend themselves to the most advanced speculative intelligence of the time' – this even if possible would do much to make life impractical and promote the breakdown of society. In his final chapter on the realization of opinion he leaves the realm of the people to speak in a Burkean vein of prejudices and customs which may no longer accord with reality but which must be respected nonetheless for their historicity and for their strong hold on common minds. Not for the masses the cold baths of intellectual rationalism, but rather judicious gradualism. The progressive intellectual élite must always be in advance of the people; the gap between the acceptance of a new idea by the élite and its realization in the lives of the people is inevitable. But at this crucial point Morley's formulation breaks down and he is unable to define the boundary between 'wise tardiness' in the realization of opinion and unwise tardiness. He does not clearly indicate either how to determine when an idea is ready for realization or what the appropriate means of realization are. We have now passed over the uncertain boundary and into the realm of political judgment, where even the hard light of truth flickers. Here the intellectual élite are excluded and the best Morley can offer them is to observe somewhat lamely that time is always ripe at least for the 'expression of the necessity' of realizing a new idea.[15]

It is unfair to hold against Morley his failure to rationalize the process of translation from idea to political reality, since it lay, as he recognized, in the realm of political judgment and beyond the criteria of his élite. New ideas were to be strenuously canvassed by the intellectual until a sufficient public opinion was created to move the politician to take the idea in hand. Apparently the intellectual could do little more. But this was enough, Morley felt, given his happy confidence that the élite had only to convince the people of the necessity of new truths, and not to dissuade them from succumbing to new errors. He was writing for his own time, a time when he believed one of the greatest needs of the nation was a smooth and predictable dialectic of change as an alternative to the confused sequence of recoil, prejudice, and expedient with which his countrymen usually responded to the demands of progress. Discussion of any issue tended to be dismissed as premature and a waste of time until either some unforeseen crisis, or else the normal course of events, presented it forcibly for resolution, at which time the results of inadequate consideration of the issue and insufficient preparation of opinion showed up in a botched or hasty settlement. By recognizing and promoting the normal operation of change instead of wilfully disregarding damming its potential only to be compelled by its pent-up force ultimately to submit willy-nilly with makeshifts, the nation would enjoy the full benefits of the disciplined influence of the national intelligence.

'Nearly every Englishman with any ambition is a parliamentary candidate, actual or potential,' Morley pronounced in *Compromise*. Certainly the dominant political note of his last chapter suggests the direction of his own ambitions, for here he almost impatiently sweeps away the unsolved problem of the political role of the intellectual. If the book begins with rational analysis of the activities and duties of the men of ideas, it ends as a profession of faith. Thus he charges those who are reluctant to allow free play to the expression of opinions with an 'irrational want of faith in the self-protective quality of a highly developed and healthy community'; in using the term 'irrational' he of course begs the question. But he then makes a significant statement on the role of ideas in history which marks a striking shift in the balance of his own views. 'Moral and intellectual conditions are not the only forces in a community, nor are they even the most decisive,' he declares. To illustrate this he cites the history of slavery, and declares that in no case has slavery ever been abolished on purely moral or intellectual grounds while the institution was still economically viable (a view that is still very much open to dispute among historians). Similarly, he contends, it is a mistake to believe that the destructive criticism of the French philosophers was 'the great operative cause of the catastrophe which befel the old regime.' In fact Morley seems to suggest that it would have happened even had Voltaire, Diderot, and Rousseau never lived. Morley no longer seems to be addressing the intellectual élite who form the audience for his first chapters. Now he speaks of 'mere opinion' and stresses the importance of circumstances. Having told the élite that the welfare of society depends upon their forming and expressing clear ideas, he turns to the 'men of the world' to tell them they have nothing to fear from the intellectuals. It is as if Morley is now addressing the House of Commons. His closing remarks, however, are addressed to the élite and form a curious contrast with the strenuous injunctions of the previous chapters: 'It is better to wait and to defer the realization of our ideas until we can realize them fully, than to defraud the future by truncating them, if truncate them we must, in order to secure a partial triumph for them in the immediate present.' Such advice to keep ideas pure at all costs underlines Morley's failure to resolve the dilemma of the two powers. He ultimately acquiesces in the inviolability of Comte's separate spheres. Translated into political terms Morley's advice is 'the better is the enemy of the best' – which leads to the sterile politics of postponement.[16]

Notes

1. J. Morley, *On Compromise* (London: 1886), 4, 2 [53, 52].
2. Ibid., 9–14, 28, 23 [55–7, 62–3, 60].
3. Ibid., 29–32 [63–5].
4. Ibid., 33–5, 6, 144, 16–17 [65–6, 53–4, 112, 58–9].
5. Ibid., 117, 98, 118 [101, 93, 101].
6. Ibid., 109, 117, 44–6, 144 [98, 101, 70–1, 112].
7. Ibid., 83, 258, 226, 80 [86, 161, 147, 85].
8. Ibid., 202–3, 42, 36 [137, 69, 66].
9. Ibid., 118, 4 [101, 52–3].
10. Ibid., 95, 222, 127, 135, 130 [92, 145–6, 105, 108–9, 106–7].
11. Ibid., 151, 243–5 [115, 154–5].
12. Ibid., 244, 217 [155, 143–4].
13. An example of Morley confronting a practical 'case of conscience' is provided by a letter to Huxley, urging him not to publish one of the papers which he had read before the Metaphysical Society on the 'Evidence of the Miracle of the Resurrection' (L. Huxley, *Life of T. H. Huxley* (London

1900), I, 319), on account of its highly controversial nature: 'On the whole, though I am strong for the liberty of prophesying in all its forms and degrees, I think it would be wiser for your own peace and freedom from vexations and interruption to let it alone. The publicity of the club is not so great, after all. It only means a little band of experts and initiated and the discussions, though extremely important, because these experts and initiated are leaders of opinion, still will not reach the ears of the wide general public and above all, will not *face* that noisy, abusive and irrelevant criticism from the press, of which you have had such abundant taste before. It is one thing to discuss such a thing at a semi-private table, and another to throw it down like a gauntlet to the profane crowd' (9 Jan 1876), Huxley Papers, Archives of the Imperial College of Science and Technology, London). To court notoriety was, after all, to endanger one's ability to effectively to influence public opinion. Morley did not offer this advice without much consideration as to the line between caution and cowardice.

14. Ibid, 143–4, 223–4 [111–12, 146–7].
15. Ibid., 201–3, 217 [137, 143–4].
16. Ibid., 126, 254, 257–9, 261–2, 265, 230 [105, 159, 160–1, 162, 163–4, 149].

Appendix IV

Maurice Cowling, *Religion and Public Doctrine in Modern England*, vol. 2: *Assaults* (Cambridge: Cambridge University Press, 1985), pp. 171–6.

When he first appeared as a public figure, Morley admired Cobden and Bright on the one hand, and Huxley, Spencer, Lewes, George Eliot and Mill on the other. During his fifteen years as editor of the *Fortnightly Review* he created a composite position which had mainly tactical affiliations with Nonconformity and aimed to capture, and use, the Liberal party in pursuit of a Comtean revolution.

Morley's mother was a Wesleyan; his father was a doctor of Wesleyan family who attended the parish church as a general practitioner in Blackburn. Morley was at school at Cheltenham and at Lincoln College, Oxford, where, in addition to Mill, Spencer and Comte, he was eventually affected by Darwin. An undistinguished undergraduate career was cut short by a quarrel with his father arising in part from Morley's loss of belief in Christianity and unwillingness to be ordained. After a period of private teaching, he began to earn a living in London as a journalist.

In experiencing a religious crisis in early manhood, Morley followed a pattern that was common in his generation. He was typical in finding in public doctrine a substitute for the religion in which he had been brought up. By the time he arrived in London, journalism had taken the place which might have been taken by ordination.

As a journalist in the 1860s, Morley entertained literary ambitions but regarded journalism and literature as preparations for parliament. We owe the distinction of his political writing to the fact that, though he stood for parliament first when he was thirty, he did not enter parliament until he was forty-five, and passed the intervening years producing a more far-reaching statement of modern Radicalism than he would have produced if he had entered parliament earlier.

In the 1860s Morley's ground was the need to make parliament respond to a 'revived national earnestness'. His argument was that even the most democratic suffrage would be useless unless Whiggery was extirpated and the working classes persuaded to follow Culture's lead in completing the work which the French Revolution had begun.

Morley believed in the Revolution's contemporaneity. He treated it as an 'uprising against the middle ages', as the doom of the class and dynastic system which had preceded it and as an attempt to replace the 'decaying order' of feudalism and Catholicism by a new order which had not yet been established at the point at which he was writing. He assumed that the new order was right and probably irresistible, and he treated Burke's *Reflections* and writings in the 1790s as illegitimate attempts to resist it.

In *Burke* Morley conceded the Terror and recognized that it had been a disaster. But he did not concede Burke's explanation. The Revolution's atrocities had been 'invisible' compared with the atrocities of 'churchmen and kings' and Rousseau could no more be held responsible for the one than Christ could be held responsible for the other. It was the old régime which had failed in sympathy and the Jacobins who represented a movement 'as truly spiritual as that of Catholicism and Calvinism'.

Morley had Comtean doubts about the 'absolutist' conceptions and traces of 'deductive method' that he found in the *philosophes*. But the 'supremacy of the natural order', the application of 'comparative method' to social institutions and the foundation of 'scientific history and political economy' were acclaimed for establishing the 'modern principle' that 'productive industry' was more important than asceticism or war. The Revolution itself in the eighty years since it had begun was credited with effecting what Cobden was to be credited with in the *Life of Cobden* – the translation of the 'revolutionary watchword of the Fraternity of Peoples' into the 'true Conservatism of modern societies'.

This was a doctrine about history, and Morley made numerous pronouncements about historical method, the contribution which Comte and Mill had made to defining it and his contemporaries' failure to pursue it. In practice, however, these pronouncements were theoretical. So far from achieving the sociological history that they specified, Morley's history was a history of thought which assumed simple connections between the history of the intelligentsia and the history of the masses, and, in tracing the linear course of human development, pursued methods that were as literary as they were scientific.

In identifying himself as a man-of-letters, Morley characterized literature's 'loftier masters', like the 'loftier masters' of 'every other channel of ... aesthetic culture', as 'priests' who created 'ideal ... shapes' out of a 'predominant system and philosophy'. This was the sense in which Shakespeare, Milton and Burke had exemplified feudalism, Protestantism and Whiggism, Byron the 'weariness' of the 'revolutionary' in the most conservative country in the world, and *Sartor Resartus* the 'reverence' and 'earnestness' which England had experienced since Byron's death. It was in the shadow of this Pantheon that Morley exemplified that resistance to the 'dogmatic temper' which was to underpin the religion of the future.

In his first public discussion of religion Morley had shown off his Comtean sense of the importance of 'organization' and a 'common spiritual faith and doctrine'. It was through discussion of Comte that he was led into discussion of De Maistre, Bonald and Chateaubriand, and to the conclusion that, though Comteanism was to be the religion of the future, Ultramontanism had been the only serious religion in the past.

Morley was conscious of a contrast between the Comtean assumption that significant religion meant Catholicism and the English assumption that it meant Protestantism, and he drew the Tractarian conclusion that the Comtean assumption was right. In Protestantism he discerned many attractive features. But whatever he may have said after he became an M.P., in the 1870s he was unflattering, dismissing the Protestant view of God, seeing the Reformation as an 'emancipation' rather than 'an engine of spiritual regeneration' and contrasting it to its disadvantage with Bossuet's 'profound view of the nature of social development'. It was because Catholicism had had what Protestantism was alleged never to have had – a comprehensive conception of the social function of belief – that it was Catholicism which the religion of the future would resemble most, and it was because France was a Catholic country that Rousseau and the *philosophes* had been able to effect the most significant mental transformation since the fall of the Roman Empire.

Morley sneered at the 'paraphernalia' of 'dogma and mystery', and at Christianity's failure to make 'brotherhood' universal. He assumed that Christianity had been relevant to an age that was past, had been most relevant to the backwardness of Byzantium and had rendered its greatest service, as Turgot had ironically observed, to natural religion.

Morley disliked 'effeminacy and pedantry' while inserting a feminist element into the loathing of the 'man-of-the-world' which he had borrowed from Newman. He was against the 'mimetic rites' of Tractarianism, the 'romping heroics' of 'muscular Christianity' and the 'monstrous flood of sour cant' which had emerged from Puritanism and Evangelicalism. Latitudinarianism, however, he disliked even more, preferring George Eliot's decision to 'do without opium', denying that 'honest doubt had more faith than all your creeds' and finding in 'rational certainty' a 'narrow' land from which to view the 'vast order' that 'stretched out unknown before it'.

Morley believed that 'good natures' displayed sympathy 'extremely early' and could be led readily to subvert the aristocracy of sex as well as the aristocracy of birth. This was the task of the Religion of Humanity and it indicated the task of the 'modern instructor' – to teach the 'voiceless ... unnumbered millions' to think for themselves about a universe from which the Gods had departed.

Morley assumed that eighteenth-century society had needed a new religion and that Voltaire, Diderot and Rousseau had done more than the Jesuits to provide it. To the question, what relevance had this for England, his answer was given in *On Compromise* and *The Struggle for National Education*.

The Struggle for National Education was a statement of the brittle and mistrustful Radicalism of which Joseph Chamberlain had become leader outside parliament in the educational course of the 1868 parliament. In instancing Forster, Gladstone and the Education Act of 1870 as proof of the Liberal Party's conservatism, it explained why the Church of England needed to be dethroned.

Morley's reasons for wishing to dethrone the Church of England were the reasons he supposed the *philosophes* had had for wishing to dethrone the Church of France – that 'the tendencies of civilization' demanded it, that ecclesiastical predominance in an Erastian régime destroyed freedom while state predominance destroyed spirituality and that refusal to recognize the principle of 'the free church in the free state' obstructed that exercise of responsibility which was characteristic of a modern mentality.

In *The Struggle for National Education*, Morley adopted the Nonconformist as well as the Comtean version of 'the free church in the free state'. There was a tension between the two, however, and he left the impression of using a Nonconformist principle to replace Nonconformity by 'secular integrity'. This was what Morley stood for in the 1870s – the demand to stand up and be counted against Christianity, and his position, as it was explained in *On Compromise*, depended on the assumption that in some respects the Gladstonian Liberal Party was as much its enemy as the Conservative Party and the Church of England.

On Compromise was a work of responsible Radicalism, teaching that conscience should assist at the march which progress would make into the future, while incorporating both the Burkean and the Comtean antipathy to violent revolution. It recognized that conscience needed the interposition of time and the preparation of opinion if it was to be effective, and that a struggle was going on in which Rousseau, the *philosophes*, the Ultramontanes and the Tractarians had been on the right side, and 'men of the world', 'practical men' and the 'political spirit' had been on the wrong side.

The 'political spirit' was an historical phenomenon, a patriotic conception and a term of abuse. Morley associated it with the 'lack of imagination', 'robust ... sense' and mistrust of 'theory' characteristic of the English mind in the past, along with the sluggishness, philistinism and 'accommodation with error' that the English were displaying in the present. He represented it as a mentality which feared 'enquiry', 'economised' with Truth and encouraged the 'enlightened classes' to profess beliefs which they had ceased to believe in because they judged them 'useful' for 'less fortunate people'. The political spirit, indeed, was a threat, and *On Compromise* explained that the 'House of Commons view of life' could 'never be useful', that relations between the enlightened classes and the mass of the people should be conducted without guile and that the only remedy for a religious 'void' was for 'honest and fearless' men to march 'with firm step and erect front' on the way to standing up to be counted.

What those who stood up had to be counted against in *On Compromise* was not only Christian dogma but also the 'triumph of the political method in things spiritual'. In this respect, Morley argued, there were no half-way houses and failure to adopt categorical positions would involve a 'futile' intrusion of Anglican fudging into an area where fudging was inappropriate.

Morley aimed to destroy orthodox Christianity, but claimed for the new religion that he was propagating as close a relationship to Christianity as Christianity had had to Judaism. In drawing parallels with the rôle played by the 'Christianizing Jew' in the development of the 'moral and spiritual truth that lay hidden in the primitive Church', he denied that he was 'reconciling the irreconcileable' or turning the dogmas of the Church into 'good friends' of 'history and criticism'. His point was that patience in dealing with dogma would create a state of mind in which dogma's impossibility would become 'spontaneously visible' and 'even those who held fast to Christianity' would admit that the Christianity of the future would have to do without it.

Morley's religion, as he explained it in the 1870s, was a religion of sincerity. But he was as sensitive as Stephen to the dangers of sincerity, and did his best to allay fears that it might lead to revolution. There was, he wrote, 'no instance in history ... of ... mere opinion making a breach in the essential constitution of a community so long as the political position was stable and the economic and nutritive conditions sound', and it was safe, therefore, he implied, for 'unbelievers and doubters' to 'speak out' since Christianity could perfectly well be replaced while property and dividends were preserved. One passage is typical of many that appeared in Morley's writings in the 1870s.

> What is this smile of the world [he asked in Chapter IV of *On Compromise*] to win which we are bidden to sacrifice our moral manhood; this frown of the world, whose terrors are more awful than the withering up of truth and the slow going out of light within the souls of us? Consider the triviality of life and conversation and purpose, in the bulk of those whose approval is held out for our prize and the mark of our high calling. Measure, if you can, the empire over them of prejudice unadulterated by a single element of rationality, and weigh, if you can, the huge burden of custom, unrelieved by a single leavening particle of fresh thought. Ponder the share which selfishness and love of ease have in the vitality and the maintenance of the opinions that we are forbidden to dispute. Then how pitiful a thing seems the approval or disapproval of these creatures of the conventions of the hour, as one figures the merciless vastness of the universe of matter sweeping us headlong through viewless space; as one hears the wail of misery that is for ever ascending to the deaf gods; as one counts the little tale of the years that separate us from eternal silence. In the light of these things, a man should surely dare to live his small span of life with little heed of the common speech upon him or his life, only caring that his days may be full of reality, and his conversation of truth-speaking and wholeness.

On Compromise was a significant book and Morley a significant thinker who played as important a rôle as Gladstone in keeping Liberalism out of the hands of philistine dissent.

Notes

Modern Characteristicks 1865 pp. 135ff. *England and the Annexation of Mysore* (September 1866) p. 257, *Young England and the Political Future* (April 1867) p. 491, *The Liberal Programme* (September 1867) p. 359, *The Chamber of Mediocrity* (December 1868) *passim*, all in *Fortnightly*

Review. The Struggle for National Education 1873 esp. pp. 2 and 47–113. *France in the Seventeenth Century* in *Fortnightly Review* January 1867 pp. 2 and 9–12. *Edmund Burke* 1867 pp. 227–9, 235, 240–3, 249 and 301. *Rousseau* 1873 vol. i pp. 3–5, 268ff and 313, and vol. ii pp. 198, 206–8, 217, 230–3 and 246–7. *Diderot and the Encyclopaedists* 1878 (1903 edn) vol. i esp. pp. 3–9, 55–6, 72ff, 172ff, 218 and 232. *The Life of Richard Cobden* 1879 (1903 edn) esp. p. 948. *George Eliot's Novels* in *Macmillan's Magazine* 1866 p. 272; see also *The Life of George Eliot* (1885) in *Critical Miscellanies* 1886 pp. 93ff. *Voltaire* 1872 (1909 edn) pp. 8, 12, 41, 69, 218, 247 and 277–80. *On Compromise* 1874 (1903 edn) pp. 8, 19, 21, 37, 40, 45, 56, 110, 114–18, 134, 135, 153–63, 197–8, 200 and 261 [55, 59–60, 67, 68, 75, 98–101, 108–9, 115–20, 135–6, 162]. *Mr Lecky's First Chapter* (1869) pp. 519ff and *Mr Froude on the Science of History* (1867) pp. 226ff both in *Fortnightly Review*. *Condorcet* (1870), pp. 50–1, 77–83 and 109, *Byron* (1870), pp. 254–6 and 276–9, *Some Greek Conceptions of Social Growth* (1871) p. 296, *Carlyle* (1870) pp. 224–39, *Joseph de Maistre* (1868) pp. 115, 185 and 189–93, all in *Critical Miscellanies* 1871. *Macaulay* (1876), pp. 371ff, *Robespierre* (1876) pp. 27ff, *The Death of Mr Mill* (1873), *Mr Mill's Autobiography* (1874) and *Mr Mill on Religion* (1874) pp. 240ff, all in *Critical Miscellanies* 1877. *Auguste Comte* (1876) in *Critical Miscellanies* 1886 pp. 337ff. See also D. A. Hamer, *John Morley* 1968 esp. ch. viii and F. W. Hirst *Early Life and Letters of John Morley* 1927 vol. i pp. 7 and 15–40.

Appendix V

Peter C. Erb, 'Adaptation and *Compromise*: An Examination of Ludwig Haller's *Ueberzeugungstreue*'

In 1879 a German student of law and politics, Ludwig Haller issued what he described on the title page as an 'Authorised German Adaptation' of Morley's *On Compromise*, prefacing his publication with a seventy page discussion of the argument.[1] What immediately strikes the reader of the German work is its title, *Ueberzeugungstreue*, best translated as 'fidelity to conviction' and described by Morley himself with perhaps more than a touch of ironic understatement as a 'slightly unmusical title.'[2] The modern German 'Kompromiss' was available to Haller, although its associations with arbitration and its possible negative connotations may have led him to avoid it.

In any event the publication was not, as Haller makes clear in his preface, a simple 'word for word' translation. The German version, Haller indicates, is an adaption of the original: Passages which have no immediate significance for German readers are omitted or summarised; in those places (they are few, the reader is told) where the German adapter is not in agreement with the English author, the issue is taken up in footnotes or in the introduction. All this is done with Morley's express consent, Haller reiterates.

Haller is also concerned that his German readers not be put off by the foreignness of Morley's argument. It was written 'originally for English readers, that is, for a nation whose greatest philosophers were statesmen and whose greatest statesmen were philosophers.' (vi) The close links between philosophy and practical/public life cannot be taken for granted by a German author, and it is Haller's hope that this matter in particular will be of use to German political as well as institutional life, since they are too often separated in his own country.

How fully Morley reviewed Haller's version is difficult to say, but it is unlikely that he studied it or its introduction closely. In his final edition of *On Compromise* Morley responded to only one of Haller's annotations, that on married people living 'together in harmony while their convictions and conclusions differ ... widely.'[3] The general point of Haller's note is clear to Morley. Haller has insisted that 'it is not enough that both parties [in marriage] should mean well;' any initial division between them will grow over time. But Morley fails to recognise that what Haller is objecting to here is not his interpretation of marriage, but the way in which Morley's reflections on marriage might be analogously used to develop a fuller theory of compromise. Thus, Morley comments:

> But let us at least bargain that [the married partners] shall not erect the maxims of their own weakness into a rule for those who are braver. And do not let the accidental exigencies of a personal mistake be made the foundation of a general doctrine. It is a poor saying, that the world is to become void of spiritual sincerity, because Xanthippe has a turn for respectable theology.

Yet this is exactly Haller's point. The German writer is opposed to the type of social construct Morley puts forward in the original passage precisely because it can 'be made the foundation of a general doctrine.' Morley had stated that '[t]he important thing is not that two people should be inspired by the same convictions, but rather that each of them should hold his or her own convictions in the same worthy spirit.' For Haller so far so good. The problem comes for him in his English colleague's next sentence: 'Harmony of aim, not identity of conclusion is the secret of the sympathetic life.' Like Haller, Morley is concerned that there will be no 'lowering and hypocritical conformity;' he proposes an 'accord,' a 'solicitude of that magnanimous sort ... which is the inevitable and not unfruitful portion of every better nature.' Such words must have struck Haller as promoting a fidelity to conviction which rests on the adage 'Impavidi progrediamur' as meaning 'Forward! for nothing will happen to us' rather than 'Forward in spite of what may happen to us!' (Haller, 'Introduction', lxxvii).

'Fidelity to conviction' in the latter sense is central to Haller's reading of the Morley text. This is clear throughout the adaption of the work and Haller's lengthy introduction on the contemporary situation in Germany, which only now and then attends directly to Morley or the English work itself. Thus, Haller does not allow the nuanced, tentative tones in Morley's 'Realisation of Opinion' chapter to stand. The chapter is the final one of the book (the section on freedom is printed as an appendix) and in German reads: 'On the realisation of one's own conviction.'[4] In the closing paragraph, Morley's words 'A principle, if it be sound, represents one of the larger expediences' become in Haller's

German 'The word "principle" is only another name for a utility perceived in the highest sense,' and the paragraph itself ends with a sentence not in the original English version: 'What sense, what justification would it have, to give up the highest for the lowest, and in place of everything which can steel the character, raise up the soul and ennoble our carriage, to follow freely weak resignation!'[5]

Haller's approach is elsewhere evident in his translation and is pressed throughout his introduction, which offers interesting insights into the fluctuating uses of the terms 'liberal' and 'conservative' in the late nineteenth century. Following a discussion of intellectual and material progress, the debate over differences between ancient and modern points of view, and struggles over the Darwinian hypothesis, Haller continues with a lengthy treatment of the church–state relationship in medieval and early modern times and the role of the Protestant Reformation which the German author does not see as a movement renewing pure doctrine, (xxxi) but as the beginning of an era of personal responsibility (xxxviii).

Thus, Protestantism initiated the uninhibited study of scripture by the individual, and in this called for personal fidelity to conviction, formed according to the model of Jesus of Nazareth. In the face of biblical literalists, the followers of the Reformers found it fitting not to give up the principle of uninhibited biblical study, but to change it by limiting its use for its own preservation (xliii), and allowing a union of church and state to arise once more ('although [it arose in Luther's case, unlike that of the English Church] in part more narrowly and in part without forethought' [xlix]).

The problem of the disestablishment of the church is a major one for Haller, and he develops his argument for fidelity to conviction in light of this. Among contemporary Liberals, he proposes, the separation of church and state is 'the most sensible and proper' of all commonplaces. (lii) Indeed, many have been seeking to find a compromise for some time. (Haller uses the German terms 'Comprimiss', and 'compromitieren' only in this section and at one other point at the close of his introduction). But with the May Laws one is not dealing with compromise but with a rejection of the principles of compromise itself. Such laws reflect the 'despotic inclinations' (xliv) of Liberalism, destructive of all forms of fidelity to conviction. The Kulturkampf is 'not a victory, but a nameless embitterment ... We Germans in 1878 are no longer as earlier, ideologues, for we no longer have any ideas ... We no longer have principles ... We have learned to subordinate our personal convictions to the furtherance of Realpolitik's goals, but we are beginning as a result to become aware of the fear that we no longer have personal convictions' (lvii).

But what is to be done? Is one simply to stand aside and allow the crash to come? The answer, as one might expect, is fidelity to conviction:

> To fidelity of conviction belongs the deed of the world. Fidelity to conviction can establish what is generally considered unestablishable: Genius. Or, more properly said: Genius is, in its innermost essence, fidelity to conviction. Le genié, c'est l'art de persévérer! ... [lxiv] As has already been said fidelity to conviction is not alone the signature of fanaticism, but also of a clear ... archimedean perspective of the world sub specie aeternitatis, reaching out beyond the impressions of the moment.

Therefore

> Let every individual in his or her position, above all else, so act for self, that every world from which we have undertaken our journey, be firmly and unshakably bound to the truth and to faith so that it might be served to form the good in intellectual and material circumstances, even at the cost of certain foreseen evils.

In the face of such a situation, Morley's work, Haller insists, offers many valuable suggestions. One needs to place faith in the author's words and then do the best one can. 'Above all one must recognise that in this book there is no specific conviction or system regarding convictions (as finally correct and truly taught), and [xlv] that our task is not to take up this or that conviction, but only to be faithful to the convictions which one has.'

Such a standpoint brings with it inevitable problems, not the least of which, as Haller recognises, is the lack of any possibility of compromise.

> It is the standpoint of Après moi le déluge, but it is a standpoint with a consequence; [67] ... This standpoint is the Beatus possidens of what is true and actually conservative, but which nevertheless does not give way to systematisation and universalisation except in so far as such universalisation is done
>
> > according to the simplest Plan
> > which each one takes, so far he may,
> > and which is held by he who can ...

To be conservative means to hold. One can only be conservative *in actuality*. Anyone who speaks of conservative principles is no longer conservative. The concept of a principle contains general application within itself. When one expresses a principle, one stands aside from an individual egoistic standpoint and takes up an impartial one. The conservative principle can only be stated as follows: Each person should hold what he has ... Hobbes' *Leviathan* is the only attempt worth naming which endeavoured to bring actual conservativism into a system (lxvii).

But Hobbes' attempt has only resulted in individuals wondering whether he really meant it or not.

All other so-called conservative systems rest either openly or hiddenly upon theocratic bases, that is they proceed from a false principle that their standpoint requires a basis in law and for this they call upon what they would not in other situations be able to justify, namely God's order and a proposition unassailable by the human mind (lxviii).

The belief in freedom was then not that of slaves. Brutus and Cassius in their defense of freedom were not liberals. Conservatives defend the status quo, 'the historical Right' (lxix). Liberals work from principles, and understand these as 'impartial' (lxx).

But which route is one to follow? Haller has no doubt but that Morley's pages will be of value in answering the question. The English writer's argument is opposed to those 'freedom-oriented' individuals who direct attention only to freedom and justice in the theoretical form and deny it in practice. These are they who are 'in every way despotically minded vulgar Liberals' (lxxiv). This group is matched by a second – 'those who go forth in the armaments of their system in support of the theocratic principle' supporting 'infallibility and intolerance'.

In the introduction to his work, the author [Morley] describes the present institutional order as one which in its highest form is imperfect and in need of reform. He indicates that it is built on a foundation of error and superstition which can only be preserved by a universal hypocrisy and cowardly dissimulation. He then goes on to require the firm support of one's own intentions and a rejection of hypocrisy and expresses the confident conviction that such are the necessary requirement and at the same time the surest means for overcoming evil and superstition ... The principle which lies at the base of the whole work is that not everything is ordered and a great deal lies in disorder. And thus follows his comment that 'every healthy institution protects itself by and through itself.' On the basis of this, the author asserts that he is writing 'to strengthen the resolution of those supporters of the status quo who struggle in the battle for the practical life and to free them from the eternal dread and concern that the whole construct would collapse in a single night.'

But two questions must be asked at this point: First, 'Is it our responsibility to strengthen the courage of those who support the status quo?' [lxxvi] Secondly, 'Can we honourably strengthen that courage by pointing to the health of the institution after we have made it clear that this institution is throughout unhealthy?' ... If we strengthen [the former] do we not then weaken that which we have preached as the one thing which can meet the need: courage and inflexible fidelity to conviction?

As indicated earlier in this appendix, Haller's answer to the question is to quote the adage 'Impavidi progrediamur' as meaning 'Forward in spite of what may happen to us!' (lxxvii) What remains is fidelity to conviction and this is to be held as the single 'principle' proposed in Morley's treatise which Haller has adapted for German use, a principle of particular importance, Haller believes, in the debate over the teaching of evolutionary theory in the schools, although in this case what must be recognised is not the maintenance of a conviction concerning the evolutionary hypothesis itself, but of the underlying question concerning the relationship between the roles of church and state in the educational process. It is after a detailed review of this debate that Haller draws his introduction to an unMorley-like conclusion:

> For the person who is certain of the future, every battle is welcome and the indolent cessation of hostility before victory is a burden. It is not a fortunate mark of truth that our opponents bound together as they are saw that it was necessary at the very beginning of the battle to offer an involuntary respect to their enemies, to the philosophical thoughts, and to make the 'principles of the existing institutional order' over against police protection, more or less a philosophical concept ... so as to establish the discussion of these principles and their justification properly as the order of the day from which they could not be removed.

And thus, desired or undesired, willing or unwilling, Friend and

Enemy together agree 'that for our race the battle over the present state of being ennobles itself in the battle over truth' (lxxxvi).

Wilfrid Laurier University
Waterloo, Ont.

Notes

1 *Ueberzeugungstreue. Autorisierte deutsche Bearbeitung des Essay 'On Compromise' von John Morley mit Einleitung und Anmerkungen von Dr. Ludwig Haller* (Hannover; Carl Rümpler, 1879). The preface to the piece is dated at Schloss Bürglen, the Black Forest, Baden, August 22, 1878.
2 John Viscount Morley, *On Compromise* (London: Watts, 1933), 111; cf. herein, pp. 130, 178.
3 Ibid.
4 *Ueberzeugungstreue*, 136–172.
5 Ibid., 172.

Appendix VI

Morley's Epigrams

On personal worth:
'A lofty sense of personal worth is one of the surest elements of greatness. That the lion should love to masquerade in the ass's skin is not modesty and reserve, but imbecility and degradation' (*On Compromise*, 56).

On the consequences of putting 'social convenience in the first place, and respect for truth in the second':
'One is conjured to respect the beliefs of others, but forbidden to claim the same respect for one's own' (*On Compromise*, 59).

On the political ethic:
'Thoroughness is a mistake, and nailing your flag to the mast a bit of delusive heroics. Think wholly of to-day, and not at all of to-morrow. Beware of the high and hold fast to the safe. Dismiss conviction, and study general consensus. No zeal, no faith, no intellectual trenchancy, but as much low-minded geniality and trivial complaisance as you please' (*On Compromise*, 60).

On the historical method:
'Character is considered less with reference to its absolute qualities than as an interesting scene strewn with scattered rudiments, survivals, inherited predispositions . . . In the last century men asked of a belief or a story, Is it true? We now ask, How did men come to take it for true?' (*On Compromise*, 64).

On newspapers:
'Then there is the newspaper press, that huge engine for keeping discussion on a low level, and making the political test final . . . for a newspaper must live, and to live it must please, and its conductors suppose, perhaps not altogether rightly, that it can only please by being very cheerful towards prejudices, very chilly to general theories, loftily disdainful to the men of a principle. Their one cry to an advocate of

improvement is some sagacious silliness about recognising the limits of the practicable in politics, and seeing the necessity of adapting theories to facts. As if the fact of taking a broader and wiser view than the common crowd disqualifies a man from knowing what the view of the common crowd happens to be, and from estimating it at the proper value for practical purposes' (*On Compromise*, 65).

On prosperity and religion:
'We have been, in spite of momentary declensions, on a flood tide of high profits and a roaring trade, and there is nothing like a roaring trade for engendering latitudinarians . . . Are we to suppose that it is firm persuasion of the greater scripturalness of episcopacy that turns the second generation of dissenting manufacturers in our busy Lancashire into churchmen?' (*On Compromise*, 66).

On self-interest in the preservation of error:
'This interest was not deliberately sinister or malignant. It may be more correctly as well as more charitably explained by that infirmity of human nature, which makes us very ready to believe what it is on other grounds convenient to us to believe' (*On Compromise*, 84).

On ministers of the church who 'no longer place their highest faith in powers above and beyond men':
'If he is clever enough to see through the vulgar and their beliefs, he is tolerably sure to be clever enough from time to time and in his better moments to see through himself. He begins to suspect himself of being an impostor' (*On Compromise*, 90).

On the English political spirit:
'. . . nearly every Englishman with any ambition is a parliamentary candidate, actual or potential . . . ' (*On Compromise*, 105).

On contemporary tolerance and openness of mind:
'Indolence and timidity have united to popularise among us a flaccid latitudinarianism, which thinks itself a benign tolerance for the opinions of others. It is in truth only a pretentious form of being without settled opinion of our own, and without any desire to settle them' (*On Compromise*, 105).

'Before, however, we congratulate ourselves too warmly on this, let us be quite sure that we are not mistaking for tolerance what is really nothing more creditable than indifference' (*On Compromise*, 105).

On hard reasoning:
'There is always hope of a man so long as he dwells in the region of the direct categorical proposition and the unambiguous term; so long

as he does not deny the rightly drawn conclusion after accepting the major and minor premisses. This may seem a scanty virtue and very easy grace. Yet experience shows it to be too hard of attainment for those who tamper with disinterestedness of conviction, for the sake of luxuriating in the softness of spiritual transport without interruption from a syllogism' (*On Compromise*, 111).

'The beliefs of an ordinary man are a complex structure of very subtle materials, all compacted into a whole, not by logic, but by lack of logic; not by syllogism or sorites, but by the vague' (*On Compromise*, 120).

On hypocrisy:
'As it is, we all of us know men who deliberately reject the entire Christian system, and still think it compatible with uprightness to summon their whole establishments round them at morning and evening, and on their knees to offer up elaborately formulated prayers, which have just as much meaning to them as the entrails of the sacrificial victim had to an infidel haruspex' (*On Compromise*, 123).

On freethinking:
'The prate of new-born scepticism may be as tiresome and as odious as the cant of grey orthodoxy' (*On Compromise*, 128).

'If a man systematically intrudes disrespectful and unwelcome criticism upon a woman who retains the ancient belief, he is only showing that freethinker may be no more than bigot differently writ' (*On Compromise*, 128).

'It is certainly not less possible to disbelieve religiously than to believe religiously' (*On Compromise*, 129).

On those who practise hypocritical conformity:
'A considerable proportion of people, men no less than women, are born invertebrate, and they must get on as they best can. But let us at least bargain that they shall not erect the maxims of their own feebleness into a rule for those who are braver and of stronger principle than themselves' (*On Compromise*, 130).

On fame:
'A man does not become celebrated in proportion to his general capacity, but because he does or says something which happened to need doing or saying at the moment' (*On Compromise*, 142).

On coercion:
'You have not converted a man because you have silenced him . . . To think that you are able by social disapproval or other coercive means

to crush a man's opinion, is as one who should fire a blunderbuss to put out a star' (*On Compromise*, 156).

On Algernon Swinburne:

'And at all events he deserves credit for the audacious courage with which he has revealed to the world a mind all aflame with the feverish carnality of a schoolboy over the dirtiest passage in Lemprière. It is not every poet who would ask us all to go hear him tuning his lyre in a stye' ('Mr. Swinburne's New Poems', 183).

'It is a good thing to vindicate passion, and the strong and large and rightful pleasures of sense, against the narrow and inhuman tyranny of shrivelled anchorites. It is a very bad and silly thing to try to set up the pleasures of sense in the seat of the reason they have dethroned' ('Mr. Swinburne's New Poems', 183).

'And no language is too strong to condemn the mixed vileness and childishness of depicting the spurious passion of a putrescent imagination, the unnamed lusts of sated wantons, as if they were the crown of character and their enjoyment the great glory of human life' ('Mr. Swinburne's New Poems', 183).

'He is either the vindictive and scornful apostle of a crushing iron-shod despair, or else he is the libidinous laureate of a pack of satyrs' ('Mr. Swinburne's New Poems', 191).

Index

Ideas can best be traced through Morley's extended Table of Contents, pp. 47–50, herein.

aestheticism 194
Africa 160
Agamemnon 188
Aids to Faith 108
Alexander, Edward 32 n.
Ambrose 109
Antigone 188
Aquinas, Thomas 166
Arminian controversy 166
Arnold, Matthew 6, 9, 19, 29 n., 34 n., 100, 177 n., 214
Arnold, Thomas 29 n., 171
Asquith, H. H. 16
Atalanta in Calydon 187
Athenaeum 19, 192
Atkins, J. B. 28 n.
Austria 57
Autobiography (Mill) 70

Bacon, Francis 55, 84, 143–4
Bagehot, Walter 20, 64, 176 n.
Bailey, Samuel 114, 154–5
Bain, Alexander 195
Balaam 201
Balfour, Arthur 198–9
Bangorian controversy 167
Beardsley, Aubrey 7
Beesly, Edward Spenser 27
Bentham, Jeremy 141
Bible 101, 113, 118, 121, 122, 132, 178 n., 193
Bonald, Louis Gabriel de 223
Bossuet, Jacques 223
Boyle, Edmund 36
Bradlaugh, Charles 167, 193
Brett, Maurice 29
Bright, John 221

Brutus 232
Burke, Edmund 14, 16, 25, 148, 149, 180 n., 200, 202–3, 217, 222, 224
Bushe, Charles Kendal 175 n.
Bute, John Stuart, 3rd Earl of 89–90
Byron, Lord 200, 222–3
Byzantine Empire 150, 174, 223

Cairnes, J. E. 126 n.
Calvinism 130, 222
Campbell-Bannerman, Henry 10
Carlyle, Thomas 19, 172, 173, 223
Cassius 232
catholicism *see* Roman Catholicism
Chamberlain, Austen 31 n.
Chamberlain, Joseph 6, 7, 8, 13, 20, 27, 30 n.
Chapman and Hall, publishers 19, 40
characters 78, 102–3, 131, 235–8
Chastelard 187
Chateaubriand, François René de 223
Cheltenham 221
Christian Evidence Society 108
Churchill, Winston 16
Cobden, Richard 221, 222
Cockshut, A. O. J. 14
Coleridge, Samuel Taylor 214
Collini, Stefan 16, 33 n.
Comte, Auguste 16, 37, 86, 192, 213, 214, 219, 222
Comtism 18, 22, 25, 116, 211, 215, 221, 223, 224
Condorcet, Marquis de 75–6 n., 79, 200
Congreve, Richard 116, 177 n.

Contemporary Review 21
Conservatism 103
Cook, John Douglas 2, 8
Corn Duties 150
Council of Trent 84
Courtney, Janet 27–8 n.
Courtney, W. L. 27–8 n.
Covenanters 99
Cowling, Maurice 16, 221
Culture and Anarchy 9

Dante, Alighieri 177 n.
Darwin, Charles 58, 211, 221, 230
Davenport-Hines, Richard 13
Demosthenes 97
Derby, Edward George Stanley, 14th Earl of 177 n.
Descartes, René 134
Descent of Man 230
Dicey, Albert Venn 28 n.
Diderot, Denis 100, 161, 181 n., 200, 219, 224
Dilke, Charles 7
Disraeli, Benjamin 20, 31 n.
Doctor Faustus 177 n.
Duns Scotus, John 165

Early Life and Letters of John Morley 36
Edict of Nantes 153
Education Act (1870) 149, 224
education of children 130–3
Education League 167
educational reform 94, 149
Egypt 160
Eliot, George 33 n. 200, 221, 223
Ellis, Havelock 7
Eminent Victorians 4–5
'English Men of Letters' series 8, 20
Esher, William Baliol Brett, 1st Vicount 29 n.
Essays Critical and Historical 68
Essays on the Formation and Publication of Opinions 154–5
Essays on Free-Thinking and Plain-Speaking 118 n., 210
Essays, Political, Social, and Religious 177 n.

Etudes d'Histoire Religieuse 72
Evangelicalism 223
'Evidence of the Miracle of the Resurrection' 219 n.
evolution 106, 233

Faustina 183–4
Fénelon, François de Salignac de La Mothe 199
Finlay, George 160–1, 180 n.
First Letter concerning Toleration 167
First Principles 139 n.
Forster, William 7, 224
Fortnightly Review 2, 3, 6–7, 14, 17–20, 30 n. 35, 40, 45, 192, 193, 210
France 54–5, 58, 60–2, 71, 76, 96, 97, 100, 178 n., 210, 211
free speech 113–14
French Revolution *see* revolution
Freud, Sigmund 5
Friends 167
Froude, James Anthony 8

Gaskell, Elizabeth 133
Germany 54–5, 97, 99, 180 n., 228–33
Gladstone, William Ewart 5, 8, 11, 13, 25, 26, 27, 28 n., 30 n., 31 n., 199, 206, 224, 226
Gladstone Diaries 5
Goethe, Johann Wolfgang von 70, 172
Goschen, George Joachim 28 n.
Gosse, Edmund 6
Grammar of Assent 107
Grant, Ulysses S. 175 n.
Greeks 97, 152, 183, 187–8
Grote, George 195
Guion 165
Guizot, François 172

Halifax, George Savile, Marquis of 147
Hall of Science 167
Haller, Ludwig 178 n., 228–34
Hamer, D. A. 9, 12, 16, 24 n.

INDEX

Harrison, Frederic 8, 9, 13, 17, 18, 19, 26, 27, 33 n.
Hegelianism 194
Helvetius, Claude 204
Hermaphroditus 183–4
Herodotus 132
historic(al) method 63–5, 79, 210, 235
Hirst, Francis 2, 35, 36
Hobbes, Thomas 232
Holbach, Paul Dietrich 204
homosexuality 12, 32 n., 183–4
Hooligans 28 n.
House of Commons 101, 193, 212, 217, 218
Hugo, Victor 189
Hume, David 22, 89–90, 112–13, 212
Hungary 56–7
Huxley, Thomas Henry 219 n., 221

Iliad 132
India 20
individual responsibility 1, 26, 68, 192
Inquisition 173
Ireland 146
Irish disestablishment 93
Irish Home Rule 10, 11
Isaiah 193
Italy 56–7

Jacobins 222
James, Henry 8
Jeremiah 23
Jessop, Augustus 28 n.
Jesuits 224
Jesus 24, 222, 230
Jews 26, 82, 88, 97, 116, 166, 225
Joseph II 162
Jowett, Benjamin 195
Judaism *see* Jews

Keats, John 177 n.
Kent, Christopher 16, 210
Kimberley, John Wodehouse, 1st Earl of 27
Kitson-Clark, George 3

Koran 196
Kulturkampf 180 n., 230

Lancashire 66, 236
Land and Labour League 167
Latitudinarianism 66, 105–7, 166, 215, 223, 236
Lecky, W. H. 37
Lemprière, John 183, 238
Leviathan 230
Lewes, George Henry 221
Liberal Party 10–11, 224
Liberalism 104–5
liberty 87, 153–61, 165–74
Liberty, Equality, Fraternity 17–18, 85, 194
Literary Gazette 2
Lincoln College, Oxford 221
Lloyd George, David 7
Locke, John 166–7, 171
Louis Napoleon *see* Napoleon III
Louis XIV 153
Louis XV 97–8
Lowe, Robert 27
Luther, Martin 134
Lytton, First Earl of 26

Mably, Gabriel Bonnet de 162 n.
Macaulay, Thomas Babbington 147
MacColl, Malcolm 11
Machiavelli, Niccolo 93
Macmillan, Alexander 12, 30 n.
Macmillan, publishers 6, 12, 19, 36, 40, 41
Macmillan's Magazine 3, 6
Maistre, Joseph Marie de 119, 172, 173
Mallock, W. H. 3, 21, 198
Marlowe, Christopher 178 n.
marriage 123–30
Marsais, Chesneau du 76 n.
Martineau, Harriet 134 n., 200
Massingham, H. W. 23
Matthew, H. C. G. 5
Maxse, Frederick Augustus 26, 28 n.
May Laws 230
Meilhan, Sénac de 162 n.
Meredith, George 6, 19, 28 n., 34 n.

Messalina 183
Metaphysical Society 219 n.
Mill, John Stuart 2, 8, 16–20, 37, 61, 70, 83, 100, 154, 158 n., 165–74, 176 n., 181 n., 200, 210, 212–15, 221, 222
Milton, John 94, 100, 158 n., 165, 166, 169, 176 n., 177 n., 222
Moody, Dwight L. 26
Morison, Cotter 6, 8
Morgan, John 14, 21
Morley, Grace (sister) 36
Morley, John
  as biographer 3–5, 10, 200, 222
  destruction of papers 12
  early life and education of 2, 9, 14, 221
  elevated to the House of Lords 10
  élitism of 3, 26, 65, 129–30, 210, 213–17, 219, 222–3
  epigrams of 1–2, 8, 21, 193, 235–8
  as establishment figure 1
  as journalist and editor 2–8, 26–7, 194, 221
  on marriage 124–30
  marriage of 2, 11–12
  personality of 11–15
  as politician 9–11, 31 n., 198–200
  as radical 1, 7–9, 15, 26–7, 199, 217, 221
  relations with
    Chamberlain 7–8, 13
    Dilke 7–8
    Gladstone 24, 31 n.
    Harrison 13
  religious views of 1, 22–4, 26, 113, 121, 135–6, 201–4, 221, 223, 225
  sexuality of 12, 32 n.
  on Truth 1, 25, 42, 90, 111–14, 135, 143–4, 159
  writing style 14–15, 17–21, 199–200
  writings of
    Burke 14, 21, 28 n., 198
    Critical Miscellanies 21, 198
    Cromwell 21
    Diderot 20, 198
    'Liberal Party and its Leaders' 7
    Life of Cobden 222
    Life of Gladstone 4–5, 10
    'Mr. Mill's Doctrine of Liberty' 19, 181 n.
    'Mr. Mill's Three Essays on Religion' 20, 176 n., 180 n.
    'New Ideas' 2
    On Compromise 1–2, 4, 9, 14–26, 36, 40–1, 192–8, 200, 202, 203–5, 208, 210–19, 224–6, 228–9
    Recollections 23, 41 n.
    Struggle for National Education 224
    Walpole 21
Morley, Rose Mary Ayling, Lady 2, 11–12
Mormons 167
'muscular Christianity' 223
Muslims (Mahometans, Mohammedans) 152, 196

Napoleon III 62, 175 n.
Natural History of Enthusiasm 94
Near East 20
Necker, Jacques 162 n.
Newman, John Henry 67–8, 100, 107–8, 116–17 n., 199, 223
New Testament 117 n.
newspapers 65, 211, 235–6
Nineteenth Century 3
nonconformity 66, 224
North and South 133

'Ode to a Nightingale' 177 n.
Old Testament 117 n.
On Liberty 17, 154, 168–9, 200
Oxford 8, 100, 221
Oxford movement 100–1

Pall Mall Gazette 6, 7, 9, 17
Paris commune 58, 211
parliamentary reform 56–7
Pascal, Blaise 106–7, 128, 134, 190
Pasiphae 183
Pater, Walter 6
Pattison, Mark 6

Paul 29 n., 88, 116
Pericles 97
Philistines 183
Plato 195
Poems and Ballads 30 n., 182–91
Poland 56
politics 54–60, 93–4, 96–8, 109, 112, 151
Positivism 10, 193, 196; *see also* Comtism
prelatists 166
presbyterians 166
Priapus 184
The Prince 93
Protestantism 166, 222, 223; *see also* Reformation
Purgatorio 177 n.
Puritans 99, 166, 173, 183, 223

Quakers *see* Friends
Quarterly Review 8, 198

Radical Party 199, 201, 204
Raymond, E. T. 11
Reade, Winwood 192
Reflections on the Revolution in France 222
Reform Bill (1832) 150
Reformation 150, 166, 223, 230
Réforme Intellectuelle et Morale de la France 71
Religion of Humanity 224
'Religion of Inhumanity' 17
Renan, Ernest 71–2, 76, 176 n., 212
republicanism 112, 217
revolutions
    French 61, 148, 171, 200, 202, 219, 221–2
    of 1848 60–1, 210
ritualism 194
Robert Elsmere 29 n.
Robespierre, Maximilien 200
Roman Catholicism 101, 116, 124, 130, 156, 166, 167, 188, 194, 196, 212, 222–3, 225
Roman Empire 150, 160, 161, 188, 223
Roman Republic 96–7

Rousseau, Jean Jacques 19, 78, 110, 128 n., 161, 162 n., 200, 219, 222, 223, 224, 225

sacramentalists 166
Sainte-Beuve, Charles Augustin 151 n.
Salisbury, Lord 11
Sankey, Ira 26
Sappho 184
Sartor Resartus 223
Saturday Review 2, 182
Scotland 99, 193
Scotus *see* Duns Scotus
Shakespeare, William 222
Shaw, George Bernard 7, 30 n.
slavery 56–8, 134–5 n., 159–61, 232
Smith, Elder, & Co. 17
Smith, Goldwin 8, 11
Social Contract 162 n.
socialists 61
socinians 166
Spain 54, 152
Spencer, Herbert 138–9, 221
Spender, J. A. 3, 15
Spenser, Edmund 165
Spinosa, Baruch 134
State Church 67–9, 146
Stead, W. T. 24, 32 n.
Stephen, James Fitzjames 17–18, 85, 154 n., 194, 205, 225
Stephen, Leslie 6, 8, 31 n., 37, 118 n., 210
Strachey, Lytton 4–5, 23, 30 n.
Strachey, St Loe 15
Study of Sociology 138 n.
Subjection of Women 210
Swinburne, Algernon 26, 30 n., 182–91, 238
Symonds, J. A. 8
Syria 160
System of Logic 61

Talmud 82
Taylor, Isaac 94
Taylor, Jeremy 166
Tennyson, Alfred 195
theology 53–4, 109–10, 130, 146

Thompson, A. F. 36
Three Essays on Religion 83, 176 n.
The Times 58
Times Literary Supplement 21
Tocqueville, Alexis de 162 n., 172
Tolstoy, Leo 24
Tract i 100
Tractarianism 100–1, 194, 223, 225
trinitarians 166
Turgot, Anne Robert Jacques 86, 179 n., 200, 207, 223
Turks 261

Uberzeugungstreue 178 n., 180 n., 228–34
Ultramontanism 167, 196, 223, 225
United States of America 54–8, 66, 134–5 n.

'The Utility of Religion' 212

Voltaire 19, 115, 161, 162 n., 200, 219, 224

Warburton, William Bishop 167
Ward, Mrs Humphrey 29 n.
Watts, publishers 41
Webb, Beatrice 33 n.
Whigs 104, 221, 222
Wilde, Oscar 7
Williams, Roger 166
Wilson, Harold 16
woman question 135 n.

Xanthippe 130, 193, 229
Xenophon 89